BUOYANT PASSAGES

THE STORY OF MY FAMILY, MY LIFE AS AN IDENTICAL TWIN, AND MY ESCAPES INTO THE CANADIAN WILDERNESS

DANIEL J. DEMERS

◆ FriesenPress

One Printers Way
Altona, MB R0G 0B0
Canada

www.friesenpress.com

Researching hundreds of years of family history and linking it to historical facts and events can result in some errors and omissions. The story of my life and the escapes I have taken are from my own recall, with help from my wife Linda, my brother Steve, my parents, friends, and some family members. I accept that others might remember some of the details differently, but have tried to be factual and respectful to all individuals who are mentioned. I welcome the opportunity to correct any mistakes in later editions.

Author Photo: Linda Demers
Interior Photos by Author and Linda Demers, except for:
1. Daniel and Steve Demers children photos by Martine Demers
2. Daniel Demers fishing by Gilbert Sabourin
3. Linda Demers at the Oakville Pier by Ron Van Zutphen
4. Daniel and Linda Demers at Hawkesbury home by Lisa Gyokery
5. Daniel Demers at Canoe Lake by Philippe Demers
6. Family photo in Old Quebec City by José Andres Guerra
Some photo sources are unknown.

ISBN
978-1-03-918629-3 (Hardcover)
978-1-03-918628-6 (Paperback)
978-1-03-918630-9 (eBook)

1. BIOGRAPHY & AUTOBIOGRAPHY, PERSONAL MEMOIRS

Distributed to the trade by The Ingram Book Company

TABLE OF CONTENTS

PREFACE

There have been countless times when others have called me Steve (my identical twin brother's name) and started conversations without the slightest clue I wasn't him. Every time this happened, I had seconds to decide whether to have some fun with it or state the facts. The latter would result in responses that usually went something like: "What? But you look so much alike" or "Oh, I'm sorry" or "I don't understand. What is your name?"

There have also been hilarious moments when some have said: "Twins? That can't be" or "Are you also brothers?" or "Does that mean there are two of you?"

It is like the shock of seeing an identical twin leaves their minds muddled. Steve has had many similar encounters. When either of us chose not to divulge, it was usually because we knew it would be a short conversation or part of a simple greeting. Our agreement was to be nice and not put each other at risk of insulting a professional colleague or acquaintance. Once such interactions ended, they were usually followed by a quick call or a text to let the other know that someone had just "seen" him! It was great twin fun. If the mix-up involved a family member or a friend of a friend, we usually let it ride for a while. Innocent laughs.

It's fair to expect such reactions given that most don't interact with identical twins on a frequent basis, if at all. As a shy skinny francophone boy living on the south shore of Montréal, I became desensitized to the frequent declarations from others when they saw us together, such as, "I can't believe how much you look alike."

As I grew older, this same phenomenon continued, albeit less frequently when Steve and I lived in different cities. For me, it is one of the attributes that makes up who I am, like being bilingual. Everyone has particular things about their backgrounds, preferences, talents, or customs that define their uniqueness. It is the multitude of these personal attributes that make this world so amazing, complex, diverse, and full of continuous discovery.

Living in Canada all my life as a "pure laine" Canadian does not make me particularly special. It pales in comparison to the millions who have relocated around the globe, learned foreign languages, experienced war, adapted to new cultures, transformed their careers, and embraced different climates. Their lives are diverse, strong, and full of courage. I recognize the difference in scale and don't pretend that my story is at all comparable. Despite this, my family history, language, and dual francophone and anglophone culture has influenced how I have grown and evolved in this magnificently open country.

I first set out to write this book as a short story about my ancestors: how they arrived in Canada, focused on their community, and established an honest hardworking lifestyle. My goal was to capture our humble family history in a formal way for posterity. To my surprise (and pleasure) I greatly enjoyed the writing process. Soon these groupings of words, themes, and paragraphs evolved into something more. What started as a story about my family is now accompanied by the chronicles of my life so far, along with tales of simple escapes into Canada's wilderness.

Throughout the writing process, I discovered that our simple beginnings mirror what countless others have experienced for centuries and still do today—starting with nothing, relocating in search of a better life, overcoming challenges, taking risks, having some luck, and never quitting. Most importantly, it gave me great optimism about the future: how we will continue to evolve, how we will adapt in new ways, and how good will triumph (even as darkness continues to lurk, as it always has). Everyone has a role to play. Don't look beside or behind you; turn your eyes ahead, and take a positive step forward.

Central-Eastern Canada

MANITOBA

ONTARIO

Radisson

Chisasibi

Otter Rapids

Griswold

Cochrane

Sudbury

Espanola

Eugenia Lake

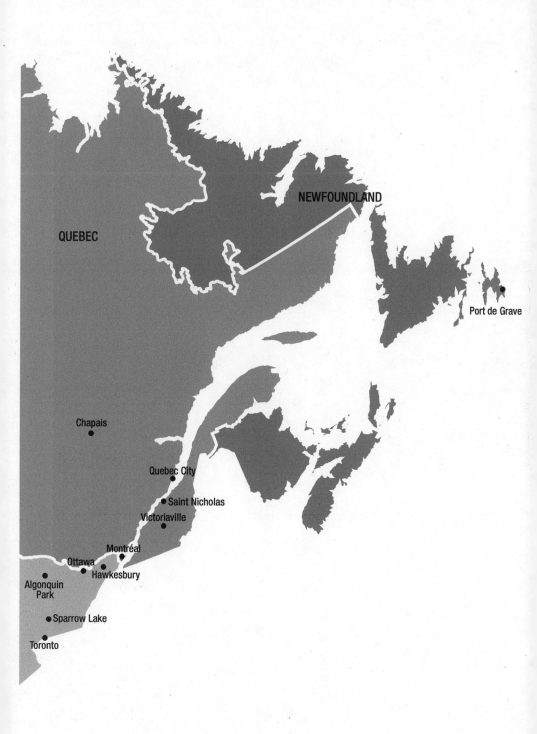

NEWFOUNDLAND

QUEBEC

Port de Grave

Chapais

Quebec City

Saint Nicholas

Victoriaville

Montréal

Ottawa

Hawkesbury

Algonquin
Park

Sparrow Lake

Toronto

BOOK 1

ACROSS THE WATER AND ALONG THE ROADS

"Hard work will not kill you."
Jean Hinse

PROLOGUE 1

My father did not wake early on that beautiful June morning. It was a place he knew well, full of history and character with a constant fresh gentle breeze either from the mountains or the tidal waters. When he was a child, this was a region of mostly religious significance for him as he travelled the nearby routes on regular pilgrimages from his small town in southeastern Quebec to the place of wonder called the Basilica of Sainte-Anne-de-Beaupré. The iconic church is nestled between the almighty St. Lawrence River to the south and the foothills of the Laurentian Mountains to the north. It is where families, visitors, and devout Catholics from throughout North America come seeking miracles to cure the sick and the disabled. To this day the two pillars near the entrance are filled with racks of crutches, canes, braces, and other objects left behind by pilgrims who report having been healed at the basilica. Its significance was why the long road trip, which would take a full day, was always tolerated without complaint. The roads and lanes that snaked between towns and villages were mainly rough pavement or gravel, which never allowed for speed. This was back in the 1950s, and it was a noisy, uncomfortable ride as my father's three sisters were huddled with him in the back of the large Cadillac that his father drove with such care and pride. Today, those days of adventure with his parents and sisters are only memories, but they helped shape the man he has become, a generous and loving husband, father, and grandfather, just like his father and grandfather before him.

In his early years, dad only visited in the summer. He never experienced that part of the country in the winter, as the weather was too brutal and unpredictable. Everything was essentially frozen, and the area's beauty did not really come to life until the ice on the St. Lawrence started to break up due to the strong tides and the warm spring sunshine. It was also a time when that old city did not yet have a renewed sense of significance for tourists and travellers, with many of the iconic buildings and parks known today mostly nondescript and rundown. The citizens were starting to discover warmer places in the United States and the Caribbean for winter escape, leaving the frigid temperature and heavy snow behind.

Now this city, one of the oldest in North America, holds an endless trove of beauty, heritage, and treasures from the past and present. Quebec City is the only fortified metropolis remaining in North America north of Mexico. It is the site of battles and prosperous trading with the Indigenous people, and it is also the site where many families living throughout Canada first settled hundreds of years ago. Rich with diverse backgrounds, cultures, and languages, it was a melting pot of inclusion that would rival today's biggest urban communities.

So, after a good breakfast and a morning coffee (he only has one each day), dad and mom, his wife of over fifty years, began their late-morning walk into Basse-Ville to, once again, marvel at the historical architecture. The Quartier Petit Champlain is renowned for its charm, quaint boutiques, and restaurants. It provided the happy couple with an incredible atmosphere as they celebrated their wedding anniversary. The bright sun was at a perfect angle early that day, giving La Rue du Petit-Champlain warmth and clarity and bringing it fully to life during the weekend of La Fete de la Saint-Jean-Baptiste. This unique holiday, full of traditional music and concerts, is celebrated in Quebec and by many French citizens across Canada and the United States. Once used as a day to signal to others the passionate dreams of Quebec separatists, it has evolved into a more neutral celebration for all.

As they manoeuvred from boutique to boutique and navigated the small crowds, dad read a plaque on an old stone wall of one of the older homes. He has always been an avid history buff, so it is not uncommon for him to stop at a sign that tells a story. But on that special morning, he noticed that this plaque was different. It had a date of 1689 and was titled "Maison Jean-Demers." He read every detail, then stepped back and looked up at the home.

"This is where my ancestor lived!" he exclaimed.

CHAPTER 1
HERE TO STAY

From bottom-left clockwise: Rose Roberge (great-great-grandmother), Emile Demers (great-grandfather), Alphonse Demers (great-great-uncle), and Thomas Demers (great-great-grandfather), circa 1915.

A small wooden boat floated on the waves along the south shore of the English Channel (La Manche). Anchored close to the small fishing town of Mers in the north of France, the boat was always in motion on the tidal waters. It was an area where farmers came to trade their goods and exchange stories during the warmer summer months. Manual labour was the norm for most families who had chosen to live in that cooler area of a large country, which offers near tropical weather in the south on the Mediterranean Sea. They were all trying to make a living and feed their children in a country that was moving from feudalism to an established centralized state under the reign of the Sun King, Louis XIV. France was about to embark on the longest reign in history, lasting from 1643 to 1715, which would solidify an absolute monarch.

Jean was from Mers. The small town is a neighbour to the larger city just south on the coast, Dieppe, which, centuries later, became a shattering location to so many Canadians during World War II. He was not wealthy, nor was his family linked to the influential and the powerful. No special arrangements or connections provided security or the predictability of a prosperous future. His purpose was modest: to work hard and to keep his friends and family safe. Unbeknown to him, his journey would create a cycle that would result in some of his descendants returning to his home shores to fight to the death for freedom.

With the founding of New France in 1608 by Samuel de Champlain, development and population growth was taking hold in the early parts of the seventeenth century, albeit with much hard work, multiple deaths, and challenges to survival during the wicked winter months. Settlements southwest of Quebec City were expanding and becoming permanent cities. Fort Ville-Marie (Montréal) was the most prominent area, its location providing easy access to the Ottawa River and the Great Lakes. It had direct access to the St. Lawrence, a more temperate climate than Quebec City, and direct links to the soaring beaver fur trade, which made it attractive to new arrivals from France. The new country required strong, willing individuals to work the land and expand the population to ensure prosperity and also to provide protection from enemies. The French king and his lieutenants were supportive and ensured proper funding was available for those who would take the risk and relocate across the Atlantic. Incentives had been offered and recruitment had taken place since 1608, but the level of activity was increasing with every decade. The survival of New France also depended on loyal citizens who would counter the English presence, which was a real threat.

Back on the north shore of France, Jean had developed a relationship with a sixteen-year-old girl named Jeanne Vedie who was also from the Dieppe area. He was only nineteen at the time, but in those days, maturity came early, with most people having their prime years of work in their twenties and thirties. Together they answered the recruitment request to Ville-Marie and made the treacherous voyage to New France. Surviving cramped spaces, limited food supply, scurvy, and an overall disease-ridden voyage, they arrived in the city that is now known as Montréal on November 16, 1653. Quickly establishing themselves during an exceptionally cold and difficult first winter, they did not look back as they settled into their new life together. Their marriage took place on November 9, 1654, one year after their arrival. Jean wanted to ensure that he and Jeanne would be stable before starting a family, so their first of twelve children, a girl, was born almost five years later in Montréal on October 21, 1659. Marguerite was soon followed by Jean Jr., born on July 6, 1661. Once Jean Jr. was no longer a newborn the couple decided to relocate to Quebec City, the capital. From 1663 to 1681, Jeanne gave birth to ten more children.

With a large family, Jean began to plan for the future, putting his entrepreneurial skills and positive spirit to good use. Having homes in Sillery and other neighbourhoods in Quebec City since his arrival in 1662, he undertook in 1689 the building of a home with help of professional masons Le Rouge, Regnault, and Charpentier. Built with extraordinary quality and engineering, it still stands today on La Rue du Petit-Champlain as an integral symbol of that charming city's history. The plaque with the inscription "Maison Jean-Demers" is affixed with pride for all descendants to appreciate. This is why my father, Claude A. Demers, felt great elation on that bright sunny morning in June 2014 when he read the following words:

> Jean Demers, from Dieppe, started the
> construction of this home in 1689.
> The masons Le Rouge, Regnault et
> Charpentier worked on the building.
> The home was inhabited by
> the Demers family until 1764.
> The structure of the home resisted the bombardments

of the English Fleet in 1759. The roofs' timber structure
dates back to 1764. The house still holds four original
fireplaces and ancient ceilings of coordinated beams.
Jean Demers and his spouse Jeanne Vedie
are the ancestors of numerous
Demers in the region of Quebec.

The Historical Monuments Commission
classified the home in 1966.
Mr. Paul-Arthur Demers donated
this plaque in 1989.
Quebec.

***

The Demers family name is well known and common in the province of Quebec, just like Smith or Johnson in other parts of Canada and in the United States. Restaurants, hotels, parking lots, stores, funeral homes, and even a famous hockey coach carry the name. Jacques Demers was the head coach of the legendary Montréal Canadiens hockey club when they won their twenty-fourth Stanley Cup in 1993 on the back of Patrick Roy's majestic goaltending. Their triumph was unexpected, and it gave Demers and Roy an iconic status for the rest of their lives (for Habs fans at least!). Although there is no known relation to my Great-Grandfather Emile Demers' direct ancestral line, the name was put into the spotlight, and since 1993 a common question to anyone bearing the Demers name outside of Quebec is, "Are you related to Coach Jacques Demers?" I have been asked that question hundreds of times over the last three decades. Just for fun, sometimes I reply with, "Yes, he's my dad."

Like many other last names during that time, the name was created for people immigrating to New France. Since Jean was from the town of Mers in France (just outside Dieppe), he became Jean "Demers": Jean who is "from" the town of "Mers" (de-Mers). Records indicate that he was the only individual from that small town in France to make the transatlantic journey during that time. Therefore, he and his wife, Jeanne Vedie, are the first and dominant lineage for numerous Demers descendants in North America. Recently, my nephew, Philippe, did a DNA ancestry test, and the results confirmed the link to Jean and Jeanne.

***

The bombardments were imminent. Jean had heard about the recent battles to the south, and rumours were proving true about the motivated mindset of the English general, Sir William Phips. The battle to come worried him greatly since his newly built home was located near the water below the protection of the fortifications at the top of the cliff where Frontenac (the governor general of New France) was continuously adding reinforcements in anticipation of future battles to save the young capital of New France from being conquered. Jean and his neighbours did have a natural advantage since the waters near Basse-Ville where their homes stood were shallow, which limited the ability of large ships to approach. To reach shore, smaller vessels were required, which would be easier targets for the two French artillery units near the river. Nonetheless, it was frightening to have a first line of defence so close to their homes. It could mean the loss of their recent investments and possibly require them to relocate to higher land or even away from the capital. Worse, their lives would be forever changed (if not lost) if the English succeeded in their attack.

General Phips was well aware of the restrictions and disadvantages that the geography offered him. Therefore, he elected to approach farther north on the river near Beauport to establish a ground attack. His troops would be supported by thirty-four warships, which would bombard the Haute and Basse-Ville from afar. Some fifteen hundred cannonballs were fired during the third week of October 1690. Fortunately for the locals, their general was courageous. When Phips sent one of his officers ashore to demand the fort's surrender, Phips was likely taken aback by the response he received from Frontenac. The bold and fearless Frontenac famously replied, "No, I have no reply to make to your general other than from the mouths of my cannons and muskets."

From then on the fight was brief, with the English land attack and the cannonball barrage failing to create the damage that Phips would have hoped for. The counterattack from Frontenac (as he had warned) was much more effective and critically damaged many of the English ships. Having arrived on October 16th, the English general retrenched on the twenty-fourth. Following a quick prisoner exchange, he sailed away with his pride and confidence badly bruised. The return to New England (US) was just as disastrous, leaving four of his large vessels shipwrecked and killing hundreds.

Jean had experienced a vicious battle for the first time and survived with his family intact. As winter arrived in the frigid capital, he used the next few weeks to prepare for the difficult months ahead. He continued to participate in trade and construction while being an active member of the growing Basse-Ville area. The home he built became a haven for him and his wife as they supported their extended family. Feeling a sense of relief now that the battle with the English was behind them, he relished what the next few years would bring during more peaceful times. Unfortunately, his wishes did not hold true, as the next generations endured an even more severe bombardment by the English.

***

With twelve children, Jean and Jeanne made a substantial step to ensuring that the Demers family name was well represented in New France. Jean Jr., who had relocated to Quebec City as a young boy with his parents, stayed in the family home in Basse-Ville, where his son, Louis Joseph, was born in 1703. The expanding region of Quebec City provided opportunities for families to establish farms and use the lands nearby for development. Louis Joseph relocated away from Basse-Ville and moved southwest and across the river to Saint Nicholas. The area was twenty-five kilometres away from his parents but provided rich farming and timber lands along with more protection from the howling winds and vicious snowstorms that pounded Basse-Ville each winter. It was a time when investment and infrastructure took hold with the fortification of Quebec City by the king of France and the beginning of the construction of the Chemin du Roy between Montréal and Quebec City. Louis married Thérèse Gagnon on February 11, 1730, and she gave birth to Louis Jr. just one year later, on April 1, 1731. Subsequent generations of my ancestors called Saint Nicholas home for close to a hundred and fifty years.

Like most people during that time, farming was a way of life for the Demers. Large families supported each other through good and bad times, the latter of which were frequent during the eighteenth century in North America and Europe. Conflict dominated the North American landscape. The uncertainty of the outcomes and the surprise attacks meant short periods of peace with an uncertain future. The French and the British battled constantly on both sides of the Atlantic in addition to engaging in difficult wars with Canada's Indigenous peoples. The most historically important siege of Quebec City started in 1751. It led to British General James Wolfe's victory over the French troops led by the Marquis de Montcalm in 1759 on the now historic Plains of Abraham. This was followed on the last day of 1775 by an attack on Quebec City by George Washington's forces. The Americans were attempting to defeat the British forces as part of the Revolutionary War, but they lost their first major battle on a cold snowy day. Colonel Montgomery was killed, Colonel Arnold was wounded, and future Vice-President Aaron Burr escaped in complete embarrassment. Interestingly, the attack was devised by Washington with support from John Adams, who saw the mainly New Englander troops from his home state depleted during the military operation. It was a crushing moment for Washington and Adams.

During those arduous years the Demers continued to live a simple life, trying to survive the violence and provide for their growing families. Each generation produced many children, which included members of my direct ancestral line. This included the birth of Basile in 1769, Frederic in 1792, and my Great-Great-Great-Grandfather Honoré on January 3, 1816, the first direct ancestor that I have a picture of. He raised his family with the same values, convictions, and qualities as his ancestors. The Demers family that I know and love today began to take shape during that time.

Honoré was also a farmer in Saint Nicholas. He married Ester Bergeron on January 14, 1840. She gave birth to six children from 1840 to 1856, including Thomas in 1851, but she died at age thirty-five on April 20, 1856, just two days after the birth of her sixth child, Joseph-Philias. Her death was devastating and put a significant strain on Honoré and his young children. At age forty-three, he began a second marriage on March 1, 1859, with Adeline Rémillard, who was eighteen years younger than him. They added another eight children to the family from 1860 to 1875 for a staggering total of fourteen. This is the biggest number of children for any one of my Demers ancestors, followed closely by his son, Thomas, who had thirteen children.

Maybe it was the staggering number of kids in the house or his adventurous spirit, but at age seventeen, my great-great grandfather Thomas took the monumental step of moving from his established family roots in Saint

Nicholas. As a young man, he arrived in Victoriaville in 1868. He was not the first Demers to establish roots there, seeing as an extended family member named Julien had arrived a few years earlier. His new home was a small, secluded town about one hundred kilometres southwest of Saint Nicholas with under one thousand residents, who were mainly involved in farming. Victoriaville had begun to establish itself and had recently, in 1861, been named in honour of Queen Victoria, the reigning monarch at that time. The new town had also been made popular in 1854 by the erection of a train station by the Grand Trunk Railway. Since the town was essentially halfway between Montréal and Quebec City, it was ideally located.

Unknown to the farming community of the region, which came to be known as Arthabaska County in the nineteenth century, they were surrounded by lands ideal for high-quality maple syrup production. Along with the eastern townships to the south, the type of maple trees, the soil, the temperature, and the grade is now recognized as the best in the world for the production of maple syrup. It's so good that Quebec is now the world leader in supplying the product around the planet. I always have a good supply in my fridge! Victoriaville also went on to become an important location for the manufacturing of furniture, milk products (Lactancia), and, of course, hockey sticks. Legends of hockey like Bobby Orr used the equipment branded with the name of the city in which they were produced to score hundreds of goals. It helped make the city better known in the twentieth century. I recall as a kid walking by the hockey stick manufacturing plant, which was located just a few streets away from my grandparents' house.

My grandfather, J. Raymond Demers, knew his grandfather, Thomas, very well. He was a young boy when Thomas lived with them prior to Thomas's passing in 1931, and they shared much love and affection. My grandfather wrote the following about Thomas in his 1957 Demers coat of arms book:

> A few years after his arrival in Victoriaville he married. For the first time to Alvina Gagnon but was widowed in 1892. He remarried to Rose Roberge in 1894, and my father Emile was born the next year in Victoriaville.
>
> My grandfather was always a farmer. He raised his family in Victoriaville and worked hard at soil clearing and cultivation

until his retirement in 1921. From that year until his death in 1931, he lived a calm life in the home of my father. My grandmother preceded his tomb by seven years.

I knew both my grandfather and grandmother. He loved me with all his heart.

***

Well established in Victoriaville by the late 1800s, the Demers family continued to grow. Thomas and Rose had Emile in 1895, and he was raised with solid values of respect, discipline, and religion. Deciding to stay permanently in Victoriaville, they participated with other Demers family members in the community and were active in the business sector. As an adult, Emile was also involved in politics and civic planning for the expanding town of Victoriaville. Unlike his father, Emile selected the path of business entrepreneurship, and he shifted completely away from farming and hard labour. Instead, he became a barber—along with some serious sidelines! This included becoming a pioneer in the labour union movement during the 1930s. At a time of poor working conditions and a sputtering economy, he held the position of president of the Union of Barbers and worked closely with the Union of Shoemakers. Although they did not last long, both unions are known to be the first organized union groups in Victoriaville. His values of fairness and equality were beginning to form and would impact his approach to business for the remainder of his life.

His work as a barber provided a stable income for his family of eight while ensuring that he had some time for investments in land and real estate. At the time, vacant land was being sold around the core area of town, and he had the vision to acquire as much as he could. Some years later as developers were looking to build commercial and residential infrastructure for the growing city, he sold it off. The wealth he accumulated was much more than any barber could have imagined at the time. His success enabled him to help his sons start their own businesses or get involved in work that would allow them to support their families and keep the Demers name prominent in the community. Emile was an honest man and demanded the same from his children, which was not always easy as business endeavours grew more complex, involving partners who sometimes tried to round corners. During all these years, his wife, Evelina Beauchesne, was a devoted mother, a good Catholic, and like Emile, extremely honest and devout. She was born in 1897 and raised on her family farm until she relocated to Victoriaville for marriage.

My Grandfather Raymond was born on July 11, 1920. The first of eight children, his brothers and sisters, Robert, Richard, Jean-Marc (the tall one!), Monique, Guy, Suzanne, and Pierrette were born from 1922 to 1941. There were always young children in the house during his youth. Growing up, I knew all my great-uncles and aunts, and they were marvellous. They were always happy to see my dad (whom they loved dearly as the oldest of the next generation) and were quick to tell stories or reminisce about earlier times when they were like brothers and sisters (with my dad being so close in age with many of them). The Demers great-uncle I knew best and revered was Guy. As the youngest boy, he took on the family barber business from his father, Emile, when he retired. Guy was just like his father behind the barber chair, involved in multiple conversations at once and providing opinions on any and all topics, which was much more fun than just cutting hair! I got to experience this first-hand on many occasions since he would cut my hair during every visit we made to Victoriaville. It was like a ritual for me to be at his barbershop with my dad and brother on Saturday morning before 10:00 a.m. to get our hair cut and share in the current gossip. Never needing an appointment, we would just arrive to the raised arms, big smile, and loud welcome from M'Oncle Guy: "Les jumeaux! Comment va, mon Claude?"

I recall the barber shop having two or three chairs, but he ran a solo operation as a true sole proprietor. We would take turns, with dad always going last (and giving us a few dimes and quarters to get a Pepsi or a 7 Up from the old vending machine at the back of the shop). We loved walking around, discovering all things "barbershop." There was constant conversation filled with laughter and joy. My brother and I adored those mornings with dad and were lucky enough to experience them dozens of times from the time we were young kids to when we were teenagers. And to our amazement, it was free! This is because when my Great-Grandfather Emile transferred the barbershop business to Guy, part of the deal was that none of his children or descendants would ever pay for a haircut. Family mattered.

CHAPTER 2
THE GIFT OF LIMITLESS LOVE

Grandparents Réjeanne and Raymond Demers
on their wedding day, May 20, 1944.

The wedding hall went quiet as my Grandfather Raymond Demers stretched his old legs and stood. He was wearing a beautiful blue suit and tie and a bright white shirt with a white boutonniere on the left lapel. A hush settled over the room as chairs shifted and heads turned to ensure a clear view. This was unexpected. At almost eighty years of age, not many believed that the eldest would join the celebration in this way. But Raymond Demers was a man of music. He grew up with music in the house and at the church. There were no radio and television during his youth, so music was a big part of family parties and social gatherings. He was multitalented, able to sing; played the violin, piano, and guitar; and could handle pretty much any instrument he put his hands on. I recall when I was a young boy how he would sit at the piano in his living room with his neck turned slightly to the left as he sang at the top of his lungs while pounding the keys with precise timing and tone. His eyes would be fixed on my brother and me as he embedded the magic of music in us.

Therefore, it was not such a surprise to me when he stood up at my wedding and answered the request that Linda and I had made to "sing a little something" for us to kiss during dinner. He began lightly, then transformed a classic French love song into a full-on concert. Tears flowed, and huge smiles filled the room (I still get goosebumps as I write this twenty-four years later) as we witnessed the power of song. The crowd cheered, and everyone stood to applaud the oldest man in the room for giving us this gift. Linda and I got up and wove between the guests to give him a massive hug. He had just given us another highlight on that special day. We also kissed my grandmother, who was proud that her husband's showmanship was still alive and well. As we walked back to the head table, one of the boys in our wedding party (probably my brother or our emcee, Rémi) shouted, "Now who has the courage to follow that performance?" My grandfather had set the bar high!

***

Born at the start of the 1920s, my grandfather and his family enjoyed some of the growth of that roaring decade. His father, Emile, was deeply involved in the economic, political, and religious aspects of the growing city of Victoriaville. As the eldest son, my grandfather witnessed how his father made positive business deals and collaborated with his partners. This ignited the entrepreneurial spirit in my grandfather. He would not work for others or allow a corporation to control him. Raymond Demers never had a boss. He emulated his father and looked for opportunities to make money. He started to focus on buying and operating businesses, the first being a furniture store in Plessisville (a little blue-collar farming village only twenty-five kilometres northeast of his hometown of Victoriaville). Funnily enough, my mother's aunts worked at his store, something only discovered much later when my parents met in the 1960s. This was during the post-WWII era in Quebec. Industrialization was underway, and the development of Canada was powered by a wave of immigration and a high birth rate. Real estate was burgeoning, and Raymond jumped right in. He opened his own real-estate firm called Immeubles Trans-Québec, which focused on commercial properties like hotels, farms, furniture stores, and other revenue-generating businesses. Success followed, and at one point he had thirty-four office locations in the province of Quebec. He even dabbled in car racing with other business partners and was involved in the creation of one of the province's first circular racetracks. He was never a race car driver, nor did he do any physical labour as the owner of all those businesses. That would have meant taking off his suit, which he never did unless it was a very warm summer day. Then his tie (and maybe his jacket) would be removed. I even recall him wearing his tie after dinner when he watched TV!

He had a specific routine at home and at work from morning to night. I remember how he would get ready in the morning, but never before 8:00 a.m. He would emerge from his room fully dressed and would enter the kitchen to shave, have a quick breakfast, and listen to the local radio station. For some reason, he shaved with an electric razor while standing in the kitchen using a little mirror that hung inside one of the cupboard doors. With four kids crowding the house's only bathroom, it was probably the only spot he could find, though he never changed his habit after they left the house. The final step was a good dose of Aqua Velva After Shave.

I have vivid memories of my grandmother in her bathrobe making us breakfast (fried eggs with lots of butter) while my grandfather was in his suit getting ready to jump into his Cadillac and take care of business. Before leaving he would kiss Réjeanne, wish us a good morning, and then leave through the back door to the kitchen without ever saying where he was going or what he would be handling that morning as an entrepreneur. He returned like clockwork at noon for a full lunch every day.

***

The sun was hot as my grandfather walked down the gravel road behind the cottage. Several large trees along the laneway provided good shade and cooled the warm July air. The sounds of power boats in the distance and kids screaming made him content but also quite weary as he grew older. The financial and patriarchal responsibilities of a large, growing extended family made him feel as if he were losing control, losing his influence, and losing his ability to provide plenty for all. The 1960s had brought a new era to business, and the new generation did not handle affairs in the same way that he had been accustomed to for decades before. The new captains of industry did not value the established rules of professional engagement and business practices of the previous two decades. New families, business leaders, and politicians had immersed themselves in the community, and the Demers name was melting into the masses. He no longer enjoyed the clout and power that his father had wielded. This transition led my grandfather to make deals that were less lucrative and sometimes even unprofitable. But his adaptability never wavered, and he secured a stable income by focusing on work and projects that were more in his control and less risky. It was during this period, in 1962, that a surprise real-estate acquisition occurred when he made a deal with a business acquaintance to swap a lakefront cottage for a small business that my grandfather owned in the nearby rural village.

The cottage was new to the Demers family and a great joy for the four kids. They brought many friends and eventually spouses and partners and grandkids. Between organizing the meals and keeping the place clean, my grandmother didn't have much free time, but she loved it. The activities for the younger ones were mainly in the water and on the sandy shore, with many hours spent pulling waterskiers around the lake. My Aunt Louise was renowned for never letting go of the rope and forcing my father, who was driving the boat, to take another spin around the lake. The place was very busy during the summer, and it was also expensive to run. However, my grandparents had a rule for the cottage that none of the guests or adult children would pay for anything while visiting, a great generosity passed down from my great-grandfather. That was now playing into my grandfather's weariness during his walks at the back of his property, which were regularly interrupted by trips to town to fill up the boat's gasoline tanks. Lac Elgin is a little-known kidney-shaped body of water about seventy-five kilometres southeast of Victoriaville in the heart of the Estrie region and less than a hundred kilometres from the state of Maine. The lake was mainly used by religious groups and local parishes for summer camps and retreats in the mid-twentieth century, with a few private cottages scattered on the western shore. The old Demers family cottage is located only steps away from the renowned Camp Claret, both of which still stand today. The camp continues to operate. It had the same camp director from its inception until his death in 2020. Le Père Carmel Lerma was well known in Quebec, and my grandparents, father, and his siblings knew the famous founder very well when they were neighbours. In those years, we were all allowed to visit the camp and pet the animals there. More importantly, we were given priority to buy the freshly made donuts each Sunday morning. Those little balls of dough were tiny pleasures that melted in our mouths. The Demers cottage gave my parents and their siblings such joy that they carried on the tradition by purchasing their own properties on the same lake for their children to enjoy. My Aunt Louise still has a cottage on Lac Elgin, along with my cousins Karine and Jean-Sebastien.

My grandfather sold the family cottage in 1973. It had become too much to handle, and it wasn't big enough to accommodate the expanding number of grandchildren. My mother and grandmother spent the last week of ownership there during that summer with my brother and me. My mom recalls that the weather was exceptional for late August, and to this day she says it was one of the best weeks of her life, shared with a woman she adored. I was only four years old when we left the Demers cottage for the last time, but I know that cottage helped me develop a lifelong love and passion for escape.

***

We drove in silence through the small lanes of the sacred place. As we entered the area of the prominent tombstones, my grandfather began to call out names and tell my brother and me the stories of the men and women who lay beneath the black-and-grey stones. The Sainte-Victoire Cemetery is located just on the outskirts of Victoriaville. The Catholic church has had to find new land for their dying faithful since the congregation continues to be quite large, and the downtown cemetery has run out of room next to the Sainte-Victoire Church building. Once he closed his real-estate business and became semi-retired, one of my grandfather's jobs was serving as the cemetery's general manager. He took on that role with pride and dedication, the same way he approached his role as choir director for the same church. His many years in charge of the choir made him a pillar in the congregation and a natural choice to assume that most important duty.

As soon as the car stopped, my brother and I jumped out, full of curiosity as grandpapa walked with us toward the dark brown hole. Part of his daily ritual was to inspect the caretaker's work to ensure the plots were ready for the latest departed souls. He would tell us who would rest in the plot, outline some of their history, and explain in detail how the caretaker prepared the space depending on who (if anyone) was already there or who would join in the future. Luckily, the one on that day was a simple "first timer." I could only imagine the creepy feeling when the hole already had a tenant!

I recall a similar visit during the winter (it must have been when we were there for the Christmas holidays) when the ground had started to freeze, and grandpapa showed us how a jackhammer was required to break through the frost and ice. He also shared that sometimes, in the depth of winter when cold gripped the community for weeks, they would have to wait for warmer weather before they could dig the graves, temporarily storing the caskets in an unheated shed. Now there's a story for mystery writers!

The passion, time, and care he took to ensure that everything was well prepared and professional for the grieving families stuck with me. His example was clear: if you do something, no matter how small, do it well. My grandfather held that position for more than a decade, during which he purchased a nice plot with a modest tombstone for his family. He rests there today with my grandmother.

Semi-retirement for Raymond Demers continued into his early seventies. He and my Grandmother Réjeanne went into full-time grandparent mode, which was supplemented by regular card games on weekend nights with friends and, of course, going to church. With eight grandkids and all four of their adult children in successful marriages, it was a good life. Along with the pleasures of spoiling the grandkids (and loving each of us dearly), my grandfather added to the cemetery job the volunteer role of president of the Victoriaville Old Age Club. He also did tax returns for dozens of individuals (first at H&R Block and then at his home office) and continued to lead the church choir. One pleasure that never faded was driving around in his car each day visiting friends, family, and business acquaintances, all while also acting as chauffeur for my grandmother, who did not drive. My brother and I indulged with him as much as we could during our visits, sitting in the car and stopping at multiple locations as he "paraded" his twin grandsons with exuberant pride, saying,

"Voiçi mes petits-fils jumeaux! Daniel et Steve." We loved it.

As I entered my late teenage years, road trips to see our grandparents became less frequent. They continued their routines at home and were active members of the senior community in Victoriaville. Only when his health started to decline did he begin to reduce his workload and ease into full retirement. The catalyst for the slowdown was a massive heart attack, which he suffered with no warning signs.

Throughout his adult years, his car was his lifeline, allowing him to do all the things he enjoyed and visit all the places, family, and friends that had shaped his life in Victoriaville. Unfortunately, a few years after the heart attack, his hearing grew weaker, and his eyesight began to falter, which resulted in a few small car accidents. It was only a matter of time. I clearly remember my aunts Louise and Ginette telling my dad during one of our visits that it was becoming unavoidable that grandpapa would have to relinquish his driver's licence soon and against his will. It was like they were talking about amputating his legs. I was shaken.

By the time he could no longer drive, my grandparents had sold the family house of over forty years and relocated to a nice seniors' home in the city's downtown area. Letting go of the family home paled in comparison to not being able to drive. My proud, happy, strong, and generous grandfather had lost half of himself. He no longer had a reason to have a good breakfast in the morning, put on his suit, shave, and tune into the local radio station. Now he relied solely on the piano (located just outside their apartment door in the reception hall) to bring him joy. The great-grandchildren never knew the change that occurred in him that the rest of us experienced during that time. They were too young to witness the deterioration in his overall abilities since they were still amazed at his piano skills and his singing when they visited him. He always sat up straight in the middle of the piano bench, his head turned slightly to the left toward the children, and let them have it! My grandparents adored this next generation of their beloved family, and they took great comfort in knowing that we were all happy and prospering. I told them during every visit that it was because of them that we had good family values. After many difficult months and a last year that did not bring him very much pleasure, his piano was silenced on September 20, 2006.

***

My Grandmother Demers raised her arms and squealed as we opened the back door of the house leading into the kitchen. Her welcome was always radiant. We felt like we were the only thing that mattered, and we felt love and warmth like no other. That was my Grandmother Demers at every visit during my youth. Making her happy and getting big kisses on both cheeks was worth the long hours in the car travelling down Highway 20 or the 401 (or both) to Victoriaville. I never witnessed her being negative or complaining. I'm sure she had some difficult days and sometimes felt down, but I never saw it. She was always positive, enthusiastic, hardworking, and loving. Along with her younger daughters, Ginette, Louise, and Micheline, she loved my dad dearly as her eldest and only son, and I think she is a big reason for his unwavering positivity and the qualities they share. She was always there, present, engaged, and giving people her full attention.

Raising four children while having a travelling entrepreneurial husband was more than demanding in those days (and still is!). As a devout Catholic, she never missed Mass, and she ensured all the kids were present and dressed to perfection when attending church services or formal events. When my grandmother left the house, she was like the queen, meticulously dressed in fine jewellery, a clean dress, and a fur hat in the winter. The housework was never ending, but she always found time for friends, church, and cherished games of cards on Saturday nights with her sister, Cecile, and her husband Joe. My grandparents loved playing cards. This weekly ritual was never missed, and it was loud! I recall trying to go to sleep with no hope until long after midnight. My brother and I would sneak through the house and hide as we watched them drink, eat, and laugh. The highlight was when my grandfather would pound the table with his knuckles as he laid down the winning hand. That was gaming!

My grandmother's work ethic and tenacity were no coincidence. She was born in 1917 in the little town of Saint-Albert de Warwick, a short horse ride from Victoriaville. Her father, Paul Baril, and mother, Odelie Pinard, were raised on farms and worked constantly. They married in 1909 and had eight children, who joined another eight children that Paul had fathered before with Dame Rheault. The Baril ancestors had resided in the same area of Quebec since the 1600s when Jean Baril had immigrated from France. While my grandmother's father started out as a farmer, he also ventured into construction and became a contractor focused on schools, bridges, and other types of integral infrastructure. Like many successful business owners in those days, he also participated in politics, becoming the mayor of the two small communities of Saint-Albert and Sainte-Rose de Poularies (located in the Abitibi region deep in northwestern Quebec). Odelie was a devout Catholic and a generous mother. She accepted life's challenges without complaint, always ready to serve and provide help to others, an attitude that was tested many times in their business ventures and during one important relocation during WWI. When the war started, Paul had no plans to leave his successful career, but extended recruitment efforts by the military forced his hand. He decided it was better to take the offer of free land in northern Quebec (which the government wanted to develop) than to risk his sons going to war. Paul was determined to make it big and provide a solid financial return by building bridges and other infrastructure in the remote lands of Abitibi. I can only imagine the cold, tough environment that he and his colleagues endured as they established a new community where summer lasted just a few weeks. More impressive is the courage and resilience that my great-grandmother must have had to care for over a dozen kids (and counting).

Unfortunately, challenges and setbacks prevented the business from succeeding over the long-term. They returned to Saint-Albert, never to leave again. My great-grandfather kept working as his oldest children started to leave home. He remained relevant and successful through the Great Depression. However, he died prematurely in 1935 when he fell from the roof of a project that his company was building. Odelie never remarried, living as a widow until the ripe old age of ninety-six. She lived upstairs in the home of my Aunt Cecile for decades. Her life was simple as she attended church and stayed close to all family members. I was only five years of age when she died, but I remember visiting her with my parents. We would walk up the small wooden staircase from the main floor of the big house after dropping off our coats and boots on the main level where my great-aunt lived. My great-grandmother would not get up when we arrived, preferring to stay in her rocking chair, looking stoic and dressed in black. She wore nothing but black after her husband's passing decades earlier. We would speak quietly, my brother and I sitting still for the entire visit. It was not the place where we were allowed to walk around and "discover" like our grandparents allowed us to do in their homes without supervision. I was actually a little terrified during those visits, which is probably why I remember it so well. She was a force to be reckoned with and was respected by all for her courage, her devout approach to life, and, of course, her longevity.

My Grandmother Demers had an infinite well of love for her family. The raised arms and warm embraces whenever we visited never stopped. I was in my early forties when I had my last visit with her. My dad had told me that she was not doing well, had stopped eating most foods, and was no longer interested in talking with others in the seniors' home. Even my aunts Louise and Ginette, who had taken turns visiting my grandparents every day for decades (they are saints), were worried. Well into her nineties, she had been without grandpapa for almost a decade, and with each passing year she told us how bored she was.

It was a cold and wintery day when we pulled up to the seniors' residence where she had been living for a few years in her little room with a window facing southwest. It had a single bed, a small television, a bathroom, and her famous rocking chair. The walls and the windowsill were packed with pictures of family and a portrait of the treasured Demers cottage, which hung in front of the rocking chair where she sat for hours each day.

This time it was different. I had a sense that Linda and the girls would be much more cautious and emotional when they saw her. Dad had also warned me that she might not even recognize us or talk very much. I was also feeling apprehensive and fragile as the elevator doors opened to her floor. To my surprise, she was not in her room but sitting in a wheelchair in the hallway about ten metres to the left of the elevator. As I approached, she did not see us, but when I stood directly in front of her and said, "Allo, grandmaman, c'est Daniel," her face lit up!

Her eyes stared into mine, and she held up her hand for me to hold. During that incredible visit, she kept looking at all of us and quietly answered our questions, all the while never letting go of our hands.

At the end of our visit, we all gave her our usual kisses on her porcelain cheeks and said our goodbyes. I told her that I loved her very much and thanked her for everything she had given me. We all cried as we exited the residence. She passed away peacefully less than thirty days later.

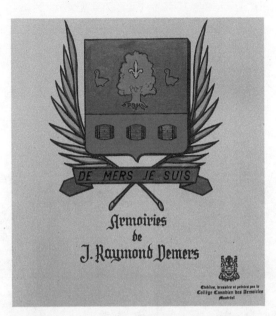

Armoiries
de
J. Raymond Demers

Établies, dressées et peintes par le
Collège Canadien des Armoiries
Montréal

My grandfather had his family coat of arms created in 1957.
The design, colours, and symbols have specific meanings.
Gold – Symbolizes royalty, generosity, and glory.
Oak – In recognition of the name "Beauchesne," which is the maiden name of J. Raymond Demers' mother.
Tree – To acknowledge that we know our family's roots.
Lily Flower – Particular to France, to remember our ancestors and French origins.
Martlet – Two martlets were utilized to designate the Demers name.
Barrels – For the Baril ("Barrel" in English) family, the maiden name of Réjeanne, wife of Raymond Demers.
Green – The colour of wheat, nature, youth, and optimism.
De Mers Je Suis – Affirms the family name and its precise origin, "I come from Mers."

CHAPTER 3
THE FORGOTTEN ONE

My Grandfather Jean Hinse on his one hundredth birthday celebration.
Victoriaville, November 27, 2022.

The rumbling sound of the factory faded as my Grandfather Jean Hinse walked out to a beautiful warm day at the end of his shift early on a Friday afternoon. Each summer he added an hour to his shifts earlier in the week, so he could have a longer weekend. When in his fifties, he finally allowed himself a little time for his new love: golf. Reaching this point in his career was a product of constant, tireless work and dedication to provide for his family. Without a doubt, he was the ultimate example that hard work will not kill anyone. Now in his one hundred and first year, he is living proof!

Grandfather Jean Hinse has been a constant in my life, and knowing that he continues to think of my family and me every day is comforting. He continues to be active and perfectly lucid, takes minimal medications, and has never been challenged with the hardship of a major illness or prolonged stay at a medical facility. It's quite incredible.

Just recently, on my fifty-third birthday, he called me to wish me a happy birthday and asked how Linda and our girls were doing. He brushed off my questions about how he was feeling since it was not interesting to him. He believes this is "bonus time" for his long happy life. When we had a chance to celebrate his ninety-ninth birthday with him and a small group of immediate family members in November 2021, he sat between my brother and me for over two hours and did not stop telling us stories and answering our questions, all while having a glass of champagne and a few slices of good old greasy Quebec pizza—with bacon, of course! As his great-grandchildren looked on from the end of the table during that lunch in Victoriaville, they couldn't help but smile, enchanted by how funny and generous the oldest person they have ever known was acting. My daughter Julia's boyfriend, José, was with us. It was the first time he had met grandpapa, and he couldn't believe the old man's energy. While I write this, Jean is probably enjoying a nice walk around the hallways of his seniors' home looking for someone to talk to—and share a story with.

Grandfather Hinse was born at the start of the 1920s in Plessisville, Quebec, to strict hardworking parents. Discipline was important, along with respect for the church, which made his childhood somewhat regimented. To this day my grandfather shares how stern his mother Blanche was, how he did not like her, and how he still resents her for having inflicted him with a similar "seriousness" early in life. Once he reached an age where he could break free somewhat from their oversight, the Great Depression had arrived, and his father was serious and focused on keeping the family financially sound. As a result, during his youth Jean spent many hours helping at the family restaurant in Plessisville. His father, Joseph, and his mother, Blanche, ran the place with the full involvement of all the kids.

My grandfather's sisters worked pretty much full-time for many years. Their enthusiasm and engaging conversations made the restaurant a bustling gathering place for the community. Over the years it became quite successful, providing the family with a good life, and it even allowed for the luxury of a cottage on the lake next to Saint-Ferdinand, less than twenty kilometres from their hometown. My mother recalls spending many summers and weekends at the large cottage with her cousins when she was a kid. The beautiful two-storey wooden structure was called La Bohème and included plenty of space for all the grandchildren to play and sleep. I recall going to that cottage for a brief visit when I was a teenager. The original building was still standing strong, with its red paint and special roof mouldings giving it a charm that dated back decades. Unfortunately, the water level became problematic in the late 1970s since the lake was linked to a large river that was controlled miles away with no consideration for the cottagers downstream. The cottage stayed in the family when Jos and Blanche passed but was never again a regular destination for my grandfather once he established himself with his family in Victoriaville and the kids got older. Unfortunately, that visit in the early 1980s was my last, and the structure burned to the ground some years later. But it surely contributed to my mother's love for celebrations and family gatherings, which she displayed in full force when she and my dad had their own cottage north of Montréal in Saint-Adolphe-d'Howard years later.

With work being the priority, Jean never attended school beyond the minimum requirement and moved to full-time labour as soon as his father allowed. In his early twenties, he was a big strong man with broad shoulders who always posed in pictures without a smile. He was intense and passionate about the work he did, and did not allow anyone to take advantage of him or his loved ones. His patience was limited and was especially tested when things did not go his way. Although in old age this has completely disappeared, during much of his adult life, he could be stubborn and serious. Fortunately, he met my grandmother early enough in his life for her to counter his moods with her loving, sensible approach to everything. Whenever he got angry, she would come behind and pick up the pieces and make amends with whoever was involved. Another saint! Once Jean and Madeleine Houle married, they soon had my mother, their firstborn, in October 1947. Since my grandfather was working labour jobs, they didn't have enough money to buy a house and establish themselves independently from their parents and other siblings. So, they lived with extended family when my mother was a baby.

My grandfather's first long-term job was with Victoriaville Furniture, located within walking distance of downtown. The company manufactured wooden furniture and employed over three hundred people, which made it one of the largest companies in the growing community. He specialized in mixing paints and stains, which required him to be one of the first people at work each day, so he could prepare everything for the paint shop before production began at 7:00 a.m. His routine was the same for most of his career:

1. Get up at 5:00 a.m.
2. Have breakfast (he always had coffee with a toasted bologna-and-mayonnaise sandwich).
3. Drive, walk, or bike to work.
4. Start working by 6:00 a.m.
5. Take a short lunch break (always at work, never out).
6. Come home by 5:00 p.m.
7. Eat dinner.
8. Go back out for a short shift of work (either in his basement paint shop or at another place of work).
9. Go to bed by 9:00 p.m.
10. Repeat.

His pay was minimal, so there was no extra spending on restaurant lunches, drinks with the boys, or social gatherings. Every paycheque was given to my grandmother, who managed the family's finances. She would give my grandfather a small allowance until his next paycheque. Later in his career, he and my grandmother decided that it would be good to supplement their income by selling homemade sandwiches to the guys who worked with my grandfather. He would take orders each day, and my grandmother and her sister, Annette (who lived with them), would make dozens of sandwiches every night after dinner. The options were egg salad, chicken salad, or minced ham, all on white bread with the option of no crust. This practice went on for years. During our visits, I recall witnessing this nightly ritual with amazement. It was just like a restaurant opera-tion in their kitchen with nothing going to waste. The best part for me was when my grandmother allowed me to operate the manual meat grinder and be part of the production line. I don't know how much money they made, but over several years they must have made thousands of meals, which made my grandfather the most popular guy at work, which he loved.

Once my Uncle Luc and Aunt Marie-Claude were born, it was time for my grandparents to find their own place. With financial help from my Great-Grandfather Jos, they purchased a three-bedroom red-brick bungalow on Rue Boisvert in Victoriaville, the only home they ever owned. It had a big backyard, which allowed my grandmother to grow a large garden each summer. This became a long-term practice for her, and she grew pretty much every vegetable that could grow in that area. It was great to see her walk to the back garden before lunch and dinner and return with tasty vegetables to put into the salad, which she made at every meal. I always thought that my Grandmother Madeleine was ahead of her time in terms of healthy eating and using home-grown products to feed her family. That is probably why my grandfather is still alive. He ate a lot of "grass," as he jokingly called it.

While the new home provided more room for the family and improved their lifestyle, money continued to be tight, so it was time to find ways to add to the cash box. My grandfather worked overtime regularly (which was a necessity for workers in those days before labour unions provided some structure), and he also found part-time work on evenings and weekends, mostly under the table. The most entrepreneurial (and lucrative) idea he had was to start his own paint shop in the basement of his home. Since he was a professional at his craft, why not stain and paint furniture for friends and acquaintances in the comfort of his own home? He started in the 1970s with a few supplies and some buckets of paint as he set to work refinishing, staining, painting, and even modernizing all types of furniture. What started as a small sideline grew into something that took up half the space in the unfinished basement and provided him with immense plea-sure and extra cash well into his retirement years. He even installed an industrial exhaust fan in the basement window to vent the toxic fumes and a full-size air compressor for his paint guns. It was the real deal, and he was very proud of the operation. When we were kids, my brother Steve and I would go down to his paint shop with him to watch and listen as he worked with great care on all kinds of projects. He would tell us about the person who brought the furniture to him (we often got to meet them when they came to deliver or pick up) and what steps were required to complete the job. Apart from lifting a few buckets and maybe moving some furniture, he never let us paint or do the finishing, mostly because it was very specific work that required detailed attention and experience. It made me appreciate that certain trades should only be done by professionals. He never wore a mask, and he washed his hands in paint thinner many times a day. To this day I can't understand how all those toxic chemicals didn't impact his health. He was as strong as a lion.

While half of the basement was taken up by the paint shop, another quarter was occupied by a bedroom and a bathroom (first for my Uncle Luc as a teenager and then as the guest room for my parents when we visited). The remaining space was reserved for the "pool hall." My grandfather never planned to have a play space in the basement, but it came about when his brother, Gaston, offered him a few gems. He owned Victoria Amusements, the local supplier of pool tables, jukeboxes, and pinball machines. On a visit in the late 1970s to his brother's storage space, my great-uncle asked grandpapa which machines he would like. Thinking it would cost him money, he was reluctant to select anything. "You know I can't afford any of this, Gaston," he replied.

Then Gaston told him it was free as part of the family heritage. Not knowing anything about the machines, my grandfather selected a jukebox and bumper pool table. Within a few days they were delivered and installed. The so-called pool hall was not decorated with carpet or painted walls and special lighting. It featured a concrete floor with a light hanging above the pool table. But to us it was like we had been transported to the coolest place in town. During every visit we played pool for hours each day while playing songs on the jukebox non-stop. It was one of the best gifts he ever gave us. What could two young teenage boys enjoy more than listening to loud tunes and competing at a pool table while our grandfather worked in his paint shop only a few feet from us? Whenever he would offer us a Pepsi in the vintage glass bottles, we were elated. It was paradise!

A few years later, a pinball machine was added, to our complete delight. When my grandparents sold their house, my aunt and uncle kept the family treasures in their homes. Then, much later, when we bought our first home in 1999, they offered me the pinball machine, followed a couple of years later by the jukebox and the bumper pool table. The trio had been reunited.

The almost seventy-five-year-old jukebox is especially a treasure. It still has original fortyfive RPM vinyl records from the 1950s to the 1980s, including classics from the Beatles, Barry White, Nazareth, Bing Crosby, Elton John, and a few French acts like Beau Dommage and Joe Dassin. The hardware is also original and continues to handle the selections of songs, which are manually punched into rigid square keys. As the gentlemen who recently completed some maintenance on it shared with me, "It really is quite impressive the level of technical precision of this jukebox, given it was built in the late 1940s."

I'm reminded that it took months, if not years, in those days to design, test, and manufacture such things. In the last decade, I've taken the liberty of replacing a few of the vinyl records, which were damaged, with newer songs, including some rock classics. To my pure joy, I tell its full story to everyone who visits for the first time, and I often get a similar response.

"Wow, look at it. Does this still work?"

"Of course, it works," I reply with pride.

I promised my grandfather that I would keep the jukebox along with his two other pieces and take good care of them. The forty-year-old Bally pinball machine is also in my basement, and it's still working just fine.

***

My Grandmother Madeleine was the quiet one of the two. With my grandfather's active social skills and love for stirring up a conversation with anyone in his vicinity, she did not have the opportunity to own the room. Her passion was loving the children and grandchildren unconditionally and expressing her love with the most well-written notes and letters. She recognized our accomplishments or milestones with touching letters, which were written with exquisite handwriting and expert sentence structure. She took great pride in her writing skills, and the messages I received from her over the years were inspirational. Her other main responsibility was managing the household, including the bank account. She took care of all aspects of their life. I don't recall anything ever being disorganized or poorly planned at their home. And I spent a lot of time with them since we visited many weekends each year in addition to spending vacations there in the summer with my mom when dad stayed home in Montréal (and then Toronto) working long hours. We felt my grandmother's great love for us every time we arrived and departed.

My grandmothers were similar in that way. They adored their grandkids and weren't afraid to show it with powerful hugs and kisses.

When we relocated far from them to Toronto, my Grandma Hinse was devastated. She knew very well that the eight-hour drive meant we would come less often and that she would not see her beloved twin boys as frequently. I didn't realize it at the time as a ten-year-old, but as I got older, I understood the emotional pain she endured every time we left her house to return to Toronto. She always cried as we kissed her goodbye in the kitchen, followed by tearful goodbye waves with my grandfather standing next to her looking out the front window as the car reversed out of the driveway.

"Why is grandmaman so sad?" I asked my mom one day as we left. I don't recall if she answered with any words, but I do remember that my mom also started to cry. My dad stayed quiet with his hands on the steering wheel and his eyes focused on the road as he fought back tears.

As she grew older, my grandmother became a computer and social media star for her age. With the help of my Uncle Luc, she got a computer in the late 1990s with full Internet access and organized herself with all the required tools to stay in touch with the family. She was very wise. As the family grew bigger and she became less mobile, she realized that sharing emails and pictures would be the best way to stay close with everyone she adored. We would get emails from her from time to time telling us about what she was up to and how grandpapa was doing. The pictures started to flow on emails and slideshows from different family members. Linda was great at getting back to her and sharing pictures of our daily life, especially of the girls. While we did not see her as much after she turned seventy-five apart from our annual Christmas visits or other family gatherings (like the annual golf game with grandpapa), it felt like she was present in our lives.

Grandpapa was also very loving. He always wanted to look at the pictures and would spend a lot of time standing behind his wife staring at the screen. Just like when she started to make salads full of fresh vegetables from her garden decades before, now she embraced new technology, once again ahead of her time.

My Grandmaman Madeleine Houle had three siblings: her sister, Annette; her brother, Marcel; and another brother, Maurice, who sadly died at a young age. Born in Victoriaville to a family with very little means, everyone worked. Her father had a long career at the local hardware store and gave everything to support his family. Nevertheless, they depended on their parents and extended family for support and shelter for many years. Already difficult, their lives were made even harder by different serious health issues that impacted her siblings well into adulthood. Although never talked about or acknowledged for decades, traces of alcoholism and mental health illness followed the men in the family throughout their lifetimes. Madeleine was the only sibling who had children.

My mom and her sister, Marie-Claude, had two kids each. My Uncle Luc never had children. Marcel worked in Montréal and was more elusive, so we did not see him often, and he did not visit my grandparents apart from holidays or formal family events.

Annette was a different story. She was like my third grandmother since she lived with my grandparents for decades. "Tante-Tante" was what we called her. She was beyond generous and caring. She worked full-time in the administration office at the Lactantia plant for many years, which provided financial stability, enabled her to help pay for household expenses, and more importantly, spoil her three de facto children and four grandchildren. As I got older, I realized she pretty much bankrolled my parents and all of my uncles and aunts when they were starting out and needed a loan for a large purchase or help with a little extra cash flow. She never charged interest to family members, which was a relief during the 1970s and 1980s when interest rates were high.

When I got my first career job after university, I needed a reliable car (to replace the big old Pontiac Bonneville clunker that would only start when it felt like it), but I only had $200 to my name. When I talked to my parents about it, they suggested I approach Tante-Tante. She was more than happy to help. I think her sideline as the family's financier was one of her great pleasures in life. That was how I got my first new car, a red four-door 1992 Toyota Tercel. And like a good borrower, I paid the loan off before the agreed upon term ended!

***

The locker room was always empty when my grandpapa arrived at the Victoriaville Golf Course before 7:00 a.m. each weekday to put on his golf shoes and prepare for his daily round of eighteen holes. There was no longer a need to book a tee time or make special arrangements with the staff. Since he was the oldest active member of the nicest golf club in the region, the golf pro made sure his treasured member got preferred treatment. His golf bag was placed on the back of a cart since walking the course was no longer an option. The starter was also deliberate in matching my grandfather with either a regular of this early dawn routine or someone that was now labelled as his golf partner. The decades of playing at an older age meant he had to change partners quite a few times, as others would stop playing for health reasons or simply die. He was the survivor.

Grandpapa was never a great player, and in his best years would be labelled as a boggy golfer. As he got older, he depended on fewer and fewer clubs to reach the green and finish off with two putts. He had ten clubs, but he only used three of them: a three-wood, a wedge, and a putter. The three-wood was the main striking weapon he used off the tee and on the fairway, hitting between 120 and 150 yards as straight as an arrow almost every time. I've always been more of a harder hitter with my drive off the tee being the strongest part of my game. The funny thing is, whenever we played together, he pretty much scored the same as me or better. His steady three-wood would get him on the green in three shots max while I mostly stumbled with my irons while trying to reach the green. When calling out our scores after each hole, many times I found myself writing down a score higher than his, which made me start to consider whether it was time to switch to a three-wood club (which I actually did for some years without real success). Playing with him was a real pleasure since the score was secondary. It was a time to enjoy the company of others, to encourage his partners after every bad shot, and most importantly, to get out for exercise and fresh air. Like his hardworking life before retirement kept him young and healthy, daily golf for almost thirty years after retirement kept him strong.

He would finish his round at around 11:00 a.m. and return home (by walking or cycling when he lived one kilometre from the course) to a nutritious lunch that grandmaman had prepared for them. His early afternoon nap occurred around 1:00 p.m., followed by anything and everything that a normal life brings: groceries, appointments, visits with friends, reading, and cycling. Since he was the catalyst for the rest of us to take up golf, we all took turns playing with him at the course or inviting him for rounds at other places. My brother and I tried to play at least once each summer as we got older and busy with our careers. My Uncle Luc joined us many times since he lived in Victoriaville, Trois-Rivière, and Quebec City over the years, all of which were only one hour away. Luc was so much fun to have with us. He was our "cool" uncle because he was single, loved music, travelled extensively, and took us out to different places. He also let us drive his very cool 1980s Honda Prelude! Luc was also excellent at telling us his tales of travel and adventures, which took him to different places in the world and far from Victoriaville. Having moved to Ottawa for university, he was the first one who had taken the biggest step away from home, and his passion for discovery and "worldly" matters has never diminished. He was a positive influence early on, making sure that I understood that there was a lot more to life than little "Victo"!

When grandpapa turned ninety, he started to slow down, reducing the number of holes he played each game and also the number of days he played per week to be able to sustain the sport he loved. He would still go out regularly each week, but he played under sixteen holes before wishing his partners a good finish to their round. By then he had pretty much reached the status of legend at the course. During one of the last years we played together, I think he spent more time saying hello and waving to passing carts than he did hitting the ball. Like my other grandfather, he took every opportunity to introduce me (and my brother if he was there) to random people, saying either, "This is my grandson, and he works at a big bank in Toronto" or "These are my twin grandsons, bigshots at the banks." It was his way of having fun. Steve and I were never bigshots, but we would always smile, honoured that we had accomplished something that our grandfather was proud of. What is hilarious is that he had no clue what we actually did at work!

His last game took place at the same golf course where he was a member on August 15, 2015. The entire family decided to make it a special day to celebrate him and recognize his accomplishment of being a golfer into his nineties. Most of us played eighteen holes, and those who did not play joined for lunch and an afternoon on the clubhouse deck. All of his children, their spouses, and his great-grandchildren made the trip from Toronto, Montréal, and Quebec City. It was a beautiful warm summer day with lots of sunshine and happiness.

***

My grandparents settled into a quieter routine after Jean's golfing days were over. They enjoyed life in their nice two-bedroom apartment at a seniors' complex in Victoriaville. They had their independence along with the option of choosing to use the cafeteria for lunches or dinners or any of the other services that the exceptional complex provided. Now well into their nineties, they had some health issues, including injuries from falling and even getting a new pacemaker so that grandpapa's well-used heart would keep pumping in rhythm. We maintained an annual routine for visits and were always amazed at how their mental abilities and intellectual capacities were both in excellent condition. They read the paper every day, kept up to date on current affairs, watched television, listened to music, and ate quite well (although much smaller amounts). Life was not without some frustrations and challenges, however, as the two of them laboured with the realities of very old bodies. My mother heard all the details of this, and she was instrumental in managing and negotiating with her parents so that a happy relationship continued. She did not share the particulars of these challenges with me, as some things are better left unsaid to the grandchildren.

When grandmaman became very ill in January 2019, she was not up for the fight. At ninety-seven, her lack of a will to battle and her weak body impacted her decision-making. When the doctors presented the treatment options and what they would mean to her lifestyle, she took a pass.

After she was admitted to hospital, my brother went to visit her first and then reported back to me. His update convinced me to jump on a plane the next day and fly from Toronto to Montréal, then drive with Steve to see her. We arrived just after noon and made our way through the hallways of a hospital that we knew well after many years of visits to my other grandparents and other family members. For a regional hospital, it has a great reputation, and the staff have always treated our family with excellent care. My grandfather, mom, and dad had taken a break that day, so only my Aunt Marie-Claude was present. I was not nervous as we approached the room since I knew that grandmaman's mental state was good and that her pain was being managed with strong medicine. My grandmother was not new to illness, and she knew the inside of the hospital very well given her other battles during the last forty years, including cancer.

When we reached the door to her room, Steve told me to go inside first as he followed closely behind. The moment I said, "Allo, grandmaman," she bounced up in her bed in happiness and surprise.

"Mon Daniel!"

We hugged and then I sat next to her for the next hour. There was laughter, small talk, stories about the past, updates on my family, and minimal conversation about her health. It was like we were resigned that this would be her last battle and that there was no reason to discuss her illness.

After a wonderful visit, she began to doze off, so we decided it was time to leave. I was at peace when I told her for the last time that I loved her, that Linda and girls were thinking of her, and that I treasured all that she had done for me during her long life. I was leaving with the knowledge that her love, positive spirit, and generous soul would follow me. She died peacefully a few days later, on January 13, 2019. Madeleine had a long, wonderful life, and she closed her eyes for the last time knowing that she had contributed to her children and grandchildren's constant happiness.

The funeral was one week later, and this time Linda, Emilie, and I made the road trip from Toronto with a pit stop in Montréal to pick up Julia at McGill. That Sunday, the area was hit by the biggest snowstorm in years, but nothing could stop us from attending the small service with family and the few friends of hers who were still alive. Grandpapa almost looked relieved that day, knowing that his wife would no longer suffer. It made us feel good to see that, and it demonstrated that when a person reaches ninety-seven or older, only a celebration was required, not mourning. He was stoic at the funeral and maintained his composure. However, a few weeks later, the enormity of his loss caused him great pain. My Grandpapa Jean is one tough soul!

Postscript

On November 26, 2022, one day before my Grandfather Jean's one hundredth birthday, my niece, Camille, gave birth to Amelia Elise Robitaille. She represents the fifth living generation for our family. On the day of her birth, Linda and I went to visit the newborn and attend grandpapa's birthday celebration in Victoriaville. Seeing someone over one hundred and a baby only hours old from the same bloodline within the same twenty-four hours is incredible. In his usual comedic way, when we asked my grandfather how he was doing on that iconic day, he said, "I'm in pretty good shape. But I'm starting to wonder if I haven't been forgotten."

His reference was to how the Good Lord has maybe overlooked him and decided he should stay as long as he wants.

Honoré Demers 1816–1900, My great-great-great-grandfather.

Emile Demers at his barbershop, circa 1940s.

The Demers extended family on Victoriaville's centennial celebration,
circa 1961 in front of my great Grandfather Emile's home and barbershop.
Notables: Grandmother Réjeanne sitting second top left, my dad and Emile to her
left. My aunt Ginette is standing with the white purse to the left of my very happy
grandfather, centre in a dark suit.

The treasured Demers cottage on Lac Elgin, circa 1960s.

My Great-Grandparents Paul Baril (circa 1920s) and Odelie Pinard (into her 90s).

My Great-Grandfather's Restaurant Café Jos Hinse, Plessisville, circa 1930s.

My favourite picture of Linda and her dad, Stanley.
The early years at the cottage on Lake Eugenia, circa 1966.

Dad getting ready for slalom water skiing. He spent
countless hours at Lac Elgin either on the water making
waves or driving the boat for his sister Louise, circa 1960s.

Mom and Dad (in center) with their parents on their wedding day. June 24, 1967

Mom at a young age with her immediate family in Victoriaville. From Left: great aunt Annette (who lived with them), grandmother Madeleine, uncle Luc, grandfather Jean, mom, great uncle Marcel, circa mid-1950s.

Dad with some of his cousins. Dad is standing top right, aunt Louise is kneeling below him bottom right, aunt Micheline is kneeling on the right of my sitting great grandmother, circa 1965.

Grandparents Jean Hinse and Madeleine Houle on their wedding day. October 26, 1946.

CHAPTER 4
NOUVEAUX CHEMINS

Mom and dad on the shores of Lac Elgin, circa 1965.

The rigid chairs in the waiting room were empty as the early spring day came to an end. My father, Claude Demers, was nervous and unprepared for the news to come. It was still the 1960s, and he was not permitted to join his wife of less than two years for the parturition. Even at a young age, he was already a very patient man, not prone to get angry or break the rules. But his new suit, which he purchased for the occasion, was starting to wrinkle due to hours spent sitting in the hospital waiting room. He decided to wander around a little to see if he could find someone who might be able to shed some light on this growing concern. His eyes shifted as he noticed a doctor walking by in the adjoining hallway. The obstetrician was surprised to see Mr. Demers standing there.

"What are you doing here?" he asked.

My father replied with a puzzled look. "I'm waiting. I was told to wait here hours ago."

The man in the white scrubs shook his head in surprise. "Well, congratulations. You're the father of twin boys. They were born just before midnight."

To this day my father doesn't know why no one came to see him after the delivery to share the news with him. The birthdate of his two sons, which were later confirmed as monozygotic (completely identical) twins, was March 13th, the same date as their father's. He was also the first in his entire Demers family lineage, going back hundreds of years, to have twins, which is quite incredible.

The mystery of why my dad never got the news immediately has never been solved, although I have concluded that it was because of the condition of my mom, Martine, after the difficult Caesarean delivery. The medical staff at Fleury Hospital in Montréal would have been focused on her, not my father. She was only twenty-one when her body had to overcome life-threatening conditions because of my brother and me. The complications of the delivery resulted in my mom being separated from us for over a month, so she could recover and regain her strength before taking on the task of motherhood without respite. Although it was a monumental task to handle two babies at once, mom tells me that she and dad never really thought of it that way. They just took it one day at a time and felt blessed to experience such a unique phenomenon. My dad was not a traditional father. I'm not sure if it was because there were two of us and he needed to handle one boy while my mom had the other or if it was just instinct, but he was all in. In the early 1970s, fathers still mainly stayed away from the dirty work of raising children and only involved themselves for the glamorous aspects like sports and formal events. My dad was the opposite of that, a glowing example of what would be expected of fathers decades later. There are multiple pictures of my parents completely involved with us: changing diapers, feeding us, playing games with us, bathing us, and laughing with us. I guess sharing the same birthdate as his sons was one of many reasons to be the best father he could be.

I've often asked my parents how they did not mix us up when we were so young and looked the same from end to end as identical twins. My dad is less certain, but my mom vows that she always knew which one was Daniel and which one was Steve. I believe her, but I always have some fun with this "certainty" since we were with our grandparents and a few caretakers during the first thirty days of our lives. They must have switched up the babies a few times! Being the older of the two by minutes is also somewhat by chance. I guess it means I'm the one the obstetrician pulled out first and tagged immediately as baby A. To me it makes no difference at all. Only later in our first year did we start to develop our own characteristics and solidified the link of name with baby. Being monozygotic means that a single sperm fertilizes a single egg to form a zygote, and this zygote splits into two masses of cells that give rise to twins. Even with this complex scientific occurrence, my mom insists we were always different with unique behavioural aspects. Having said this, when we were young my mom did partake (a bit too much based on the hundreds of pictures) in the routine of clothing us in identical outfits that were only differentiated slightly by one or two colours. This was the "show" part of being a twin. It lasted for quite a few years until we got old enough to realize what was happening and rebelled in a big way, never to wear the same thing again.

Let me do a bit of myth busting about all the different theories out there on how one has identical twins naturally. It is entirely luck! Some have reported that age, height, weight, and even diet (oh, gosh) can increase the chances. Others have stated with confidence that twins skip a generation and that they can predict when the next set of twins will arrive. Good luck with that! Like it is for us, other identical twins have shared that there was not a single set of twins in their ancestral line for as far as they could research. So, enjoy natural conception to the fullest, and maybe you'll be lucky enough to experience the magic of getting a two for one deal!

***

Both born and raised in Victoriaville, my mother, Martine Hinse, arrived on October 9, 1947, with my father, Claude Demers, arriving two years earlier, on March 13, 1945. Their upbringing was family focused, with grandparents, uncles, and aunts all very involved. Unlike mom, dad enjoyed school and obtained good grades. Mom was much more independent and disliked the discipline that her father tried to impose on her. While dad was busy building things and painting to make extra cash as a young teenager, mom was sent to a convent in the hopes that the nuns would set her straight. It didn't work. She was a rebel. I love that about her childhood!

This was the time of Elvis, JFK, the Beatles, and television. Everything was changing. Parents were having a tough time understanding and adapting to the needs of their kids, who were seeing the world with a much larger lens. My mom was just looking to have fun, and my grandfather was treating his eldest the only way he thought was best, like his mom had done with him. After a few difficult years, things settled down substantially when my mom said one summer afternoon to her friend Ginette, "Is that your brother riding his bike without holding the handlebars?"

"Yes, that's Claude trying to look cool. Why?"

That was the moment their relationship started.

My parents married at a young age; she was nineteen and he was twenty-two. As teenage sweethearts, it was only normal that once work started for dad and school ended for mom, it was time to tie the knot and start a life together. They had a traditional wedding in Victoriaville on June 24, 1967. Seeing as they were the oldest children on both sides of the family, many in attendance were younger siblings, cousins, and friends. Their parents were also young and although they approved of their love and dedication to each other, there was the overwhelming feeling that it was too soon. My parents' fifty plus years of marriage has proved my cautious grandparents wrong.

My dad's work at the time of their wedding was with General Electric in Montréal. Having lived their entire lives in Victoriaville did not deter them from taking on this new journey and diving into a new life. This willingness to take a chance or just go for it has been a central approach to their lives together over the last six decades. Call it blind innocence or foolishness, they were the pioneers within their family of moving many miles between different cities. Even before working in Montréal, my dad's first job was in Peterborough, Ontario (located 600 kilometres southwest of Victoriaville and 150 kilometres northeast of Toronto). The amazing part of this career move was the fact that my dad did not speak English at all. They hired him and then told him that the job was located miles away from his home and that he should not worry since he would learn English on the job. Even more incredible was that my dad said yes. He drove his car along with some personal belongings for eight hours on small roads to his new home (leaving my mom behind, as this was before their wedding) and settled into a rented room to start what would be a super-successful twenty-four-year career with this giant multinational company. He looks back on it now and laughs when he shares the tales of that first adventure, including the multiple meals at the same local café because cooking was not his thing, and he only knew how to order a few meals in his newly adopted language. He also recalls the epic winter drives when snowstorms and cold could not deter him from making the trip home to see his future wife. This initial risk appetite and resilient approach to change cemented their desire for discovery, new adventures, and what some would call an addiction to moving.

Once the Peterborough test was complete and dad proved that he was multitalented, he was relocated to Montréal. After the wedding, he found a little apartment in Montréal-Nord where they spent their first few years of marriage. They both worked in the first year and enjoyed their metropolitan life in the city that was hosting the giant 1967 International and Universal Exposition (Expo 67). It was a landmark moment for Canada and the main celebration during its centennial year. Those living in Montréal at the time felt a sense of pride and unlimited optimism for the future.

Although my parents enjoyed their independent life, money was short in those days, so there were no luxury items in the house or special trips. They developed friendships with people at my dad's work, spending most weekends back in Victoriaville. With mom's pregnancy during their second winter in Montréal and our arrival in March, things quickly moved from a carefree couple's life to a family of four. The regular road trips to visit their parents gave them a little reprieve from parenting their growing and demanding twins full-time, not to mention that their siblings and parents needed to see us! Avoiding Victoriaville would have been blasphemy given that Steve and I were the first kids of the next generation. Our presence was also enjoyed by neighbours, friends, great-uncles and aunts, and pretty much anyone who was interested in seeing this magical duo. Suffice to say that identical twins were not at all common in the town of twenty-five thousand. Summer visits were to the family cottages, including whatever vacation time dad could negotiate. Since my parents were still in their twenties, they also found a way to maintain an active social life and enjoyed spending time with friends, siblings, and cousins. This is another reason why having the grandparents fight for time with the twins was a good deal for them.

As dad's career continued to progress and he was recognized by upper management as someone with potential, he was offered a promotion in Hull, Quebec (now called Gatineau, located across the river from Ottawa). Without much discussion, they packed their bags in 1972 and headed two hundred kilometres west to live in a duplex at 88 Perros Street. My father was so busy with work and taking care of his three-year-old sons that the entire time there was just a blur to him. He also did not fully recognize how much my mother found the experience a total failure. When I asked her recently about their life next to our nation's capital, she just waved her arms in the air and said it was awful. They had zero friends, it was the coldest place they had ever lived, and my mom was completely overwhelmed with two small kids who were always hungry, occasionally fighting, and filled with limitless energy in a small apartment. On top of it, the trips to Victoriaville were now about four hundred kilometres long and took around five hours of driving. Once dad gained a bit of experience, he told his boss he had to get out of town or quit. They obliged and sent him back to Montréal. He had completed just a little more than a full year in the job.

Moving back to the big city also meant we would finally have our own house, a little three-bedroom bungalow in Candiac, which is a small suburb on Montréal's south shore. It was the start of a wonderful time for our family. Happiness reigned. It was also better financially for us, as my dad's hard work had given him enough promotions to start earning a decent salary. This was also when my mother, who was still in her twenties, started to thrive as a confident independent woman. With her boys in school, she finally had time to build solid friendships with many in the community and started playing sports like never before. Tennis in the summer and badminton in the winter kept her active on the courts and also on the social scene. She joined the social committees of the sports clubs and was involved in all aspects of organizing events and participating in fundraising. The Saturday-night badminton parties were especially hardcore. The club would organize a full-out event with dinner, a live band, drinks, and dancing until the sun came up. There were many Sunday mornings during those winters that we would not see our parents until late in the morning. They needed some recovery time!

Steve and I were also thriving and beginning to experience life without parents around us every minute of the day. We gained trust and freedom from our parents and became active with all kinds of sports and, most importantly, discovery. It started with long bicycle rides across the numerous suburban streets and vast empty fields of Candiac. We would leave on our bikes (sometimes our good buddy Eric from across the street would join) for epic rides that would only end when we were hungry or one of us got hurt. This included stopping at rivers and entering forests to investigate or play whatever games our wild imaginations could come up with. The cold winter temperatures did not stop us either. Instead of bringing our bikes, we would leave with a hockey stick in one hand, a puck or ball in the other, and ice skates around our necks to find a patch of ice in the fields nearby. Unfortunately, some of those winter adventures on our private poorly maintained ice surfaces finished abruptly when one of us would break through the ice or get hurt from a puck bouncing off a crack or bump in the ice (I have a scar on my right eyebrow as evidence of one such incident). The beautiful thing about having a twin brother is that I always had a partner. We liked it when others would join us, but it was never a requirement. During all that time, my mother never seemed to be worried about us. It was like she thought we were invincible even though we were under eight years old. I think after having been with us non-stop for all that time when we were babies, she felt relieved to be able to do things for herself with the knowledge that, regardless of what happened, there were two of us, and one of us would help the other.

My dad was also very supportive of us and contributed to our adventures by acting as our "dealer." He was confident that we would handle things with care, and in addition to sports gear, he bought us electrical tools and other supplies, so we could build go-karts, fix old bikes, and start our own treehouse-building enterprise. It was the real deal. We had gathered enough tools and experience that it was time to expand to more complex projects. We started small by finding old treehouses that had been abandoned by other kids and fixing them. Then we moved up to finding a location and then bringing wood and scraps to complete different models. I still can't believe my parents allowed us at that age to take real tools (hammers, nails, handsaws, screws) on our bikes to our secret destinations in the forest. Like all things, it was great fun until it came to an abrupt end in the summer of 1979.

We had found an existing tree house that was at an ideal location and supported by large trees that allowed it to be high above the ground. There was no one around the structure that afternoon, and it looked like it was abandoned and in need of repair. Steve and I had found it by walking in the woods after leaving our bikes nearby on the road. With our confidence at a high level, we started to move pieces around as we made our way up the damaged ladder to the platform above. It had a door, a window, walls, and to our amazement, carpet on the floor. We were impressed with this find, but given its good condition, we were also rethinking our initial conclusion that the place was available for new owners at no cost.

Not more than an hour after we arrived, we heard voices in the distance and looked at each other with fear. Were those voices coming our way? Had we just invaded an enemy's fort?

We made our way down the ladder to find ourselves surrounded by a group of older boys (I can't recall the number, but it felt like there were a dozen of them).

"What are you doing here, kids?" they asked. "This is our place."

"You'll regret coming here," another said.

All I remember after that is running like hell through the woods to get away from what would have been a good whipping. Unfortunately, our fear overtook our sense of direction, and we ran straight into a pond. Despite the swampy water rising above our knees, we carried on, as there was no question of going back to face the enemy.

Eventually, we made our way to dry land and wandered in haste until we found our bikes and headed home to safety. It was my first good judgment call of choosing flight over fight, which has been my lifelong rule. The event also proved to be the end of our promising treehouse-building enterprise because during the emergency exit, we left behind all the tools dad had given us. It was time to shift all that energy to street hockey!

Life at home was grand, with mom and dad participating in social events and getting the entire family involved in sports, mainly cross-country skiing, badminton, and tennis. Steve and I also moved from the frozen ponds to playing ice or street hockey outside on a real rink in front of our house (we never played organized hockey) and soccer during the summer. Since my parents were so young, they were quite talented at all these sports. We also had an above-ground pool in the backyard, which made our place the gathering spot for all the kids and tennis moms after the sporting activities ended. Those were also the days when people did their own yard work and built their own fences, outside fireplaces, decks, and pretty much everything a group of five adults could manage to put together during a weekend. I don't need to look very far to understand why I know how to fix and build things. The freedom that my parents provided for us at a young age continued as we got older. Mom would even leave to play tennis without supervision for Steve and me. She trusted us, and we never did anything horrible or got into trouble. This was the backdrop for incredible creativity and imagination. Steve and I would play games and invent activities that did not require any adult input. We broke a few things and wrecked my mom's gardens or made messes in dad's garage, but were never punished for it. Their style of parenting prepared us well for all the changes to come.

***

In the late 1970s with over ten years of solid experience, my father's career prospered and grew to levels that he would have never imagined when he was completing his electrical apprentice certificate after high school. His father and grandfather's business acumen were within him, and he combined it with a superior emotional intelligence to achieve professional success. His secret weapon was hard work. Since he did not have a university degree or any other formal academic business schooling, he put countless hours into learning things that others had as core skills. This resulted in staying at work past 6:00 p.m. almost every night, followed by opening his briefcase full of work after 9:00 p.m. on most nights after Steve and I went to bed. He had a basement home office in all of our homes (long before the days of working from home), so he could put in some extra work on the weekends (but truth be told, his favourite "home office" location was the lounge chair in the family room). I always joke with him that on paper he had a long career of close to forty years, but in actual hours worked it was more like sixty years! The incredible thing is that during those years, dad was there for us unconditionally. My mother would maybe dispute this since she spent countless nights alone, but for my brother and me, it never felt like he was away that much. Our sentiment was that he spent every available minute outside of work with us. He never went out with the boys, never watched sports on TV alone for hours (apart from his beloved Montréal Canadiens hockey team), and rarely participated in hobbies that did not include my mom or his sons. His promotions kept on coming during those fine years. He obtained good results, and as a previous senior executive told everyone at the end of my dad's career, "Claude always got things done."

It was during these years that he also improved his English language skills since all of the business meetings and customer interactions outside of Montréal were in English. It was also a time when the political situation in the province of Quebec escalated to a going concern for multinational companies. The rise of Jean Lesage and the Liberal Party of Quebec in 1960 marked the beginning of the Quiet Revolution. Drastic changes in social, economic, and legal values were accompanied by a strong nationalist sentiment that continued into the 1970s. Once the Parti Québécois gained strength and eventually won the provincial election in 1976, their constant talk of separation from Canada made the risks of operating with ease in Montréal very real for large companies looking to grow and invest for the future. There is nothing more deadly for a business strategy than political and regulatory uncertainty. Industry leaders from outside the province feared that the government would change policies and regulations without proper consultation and diminish profitability or force a change to proven operating models. This mood (right or wrong) caused countless large corporations and financial institutions to shift their head offices and other corporate operations from Montréal to Toronto. Montréal still hasn't recovered from losing thousands of executives, corporate head offices, and business investment during the late

1970s and early 1980s. On the other hand, the shift helped Toronto become a super-growth city during the 1980s and eventually the most important business centre in Canada. Even families who were new to Canada (who had predominantly been arriving in Montréal after WWII) started to shift their plane tickets to Toronto Pearson Airport (YYZ). For a young business leader like my dad, the writing was on the wall.

***

"We're moving to Toronto," he said one day.

Instantly, I ran out of the house, crying, leaving my mom and dad alone in the kitchen. I was ten years old on that life-changing day in the late summer of 1979. It took me months to recover and years until I realized that my dad had given me two of the greatest and most important gifts of my life: the English language and the ability to embrace change.

For my parents, informing the kids of the move was the easy part. Telling friends and family (especially their parents) was much harder, requiring a map in hand to show people where Toronto was located. And then there was trying to explain how a family who only spoke French would live in a town not known for its bilingual status. To this day, I'm surprised and impressed that my parents made the decision to move five hundred kilometres southwest down the 401 Highway. To make matters more dramatic, the Mississauga train derailment (also known as the Mississauga Miracle) occurred in November 1979, which was only one month before we moved there. If the extended family didn't know where we were moving before that event, they sure knew where it was afterward. Our first house in Mississauga was in the neighbourhood of Erin Mills, located at the western edge of the city, bordering Oakville. It was a three-bedroom, two-storey home, which was pretty much double the size of what we had before. Because the real-estate prices between the two largest cities in Canada were significantly different (mainly due to the political unrest mentioned before), dad had to get a special allowance from the company to be able to buy a house. The price was more than double what they sold for in Candiac.

What occurred next and how we lived for the next eight years in Mississauga defined our path for decades to come.

My dad continued his career and solidified his reputation as a fair and effective leader who respected every individual around him no matter their level in the company. New roles continued to challenge him, along with the stresses and added pressure of the complex business politics that come with any management team. He will confess that he didn't always sleep well as he managed some difficult issues. The good news for us was now that he was based at the head office where there were thousands of employees and various leadership roles, relocation was no longer required. We even got involved as a full family unit with visits to the large offices on multiple Sunday afternoons when dad needed to do extra work. Our roles during such visits were clearly defined.

> Dad would tuck himself into his office and tackle the mountains of paperwork.

> Mom would settle at the desk of dad's assistant and make calls to friends and family. Many calls. For hours!

> Steve and I would roam the massive empty office space and avoid anyone who might be there. I loved the feel of a business office: the smell of it, the piles of paper, and the massive equipment. It's no wonder we both became corporate office geeks!

While dad was busy at work, mom quickly built new friendships with our French-speaking neighbours, Sandy and Monique. They became her best friends, and they still are today now that they're all in their seventies. My mom also wasted no time re-establishing her love of tennis, and she met dozens of ladies who helped her integrate and learn English. Badminton slowed down for my parents and was replaced by added time trying to manage two sons in their early teens who were super active and needed to be driven everywhere at all hours. Only later did I realize how valuable it was to have my mother present during those critical years. She worked part-time jobs but tried to be at home after school, always making sure the fridge was full of food and serving as our driver to sporting events, socials, Boy Scouts, and record stores. And most importantly, she was there to make our house a home with a rich, loving atmosphere.

My parents' love of travel started to flourish during this period. They began to embark on their first real trips to Europe, the US, Canada's West Coast, and one of their favourite destinations, Hawaii. Mom started to accompany dad on some of his business trips to attractive locations. This was great fun for Steve and me since our grandparents or great-aunt would come to babysit in Mississauga. If school was out, we would go to Victoriaville instead.

My parents' weekly social activities slowed down compared to when they were in their twenties, and with that came a bit more money for family vacations during the summer and school breaks. Dad rented cottages for one or two weeks at Lac Elgin, and we even went to Banff, Alberta during one March break for our first introduction to downhill skiing. We actually went there to do cross-country skiing but quickly realized that it was such an amazing place with "real" hills that we had to try downhill. There we were one spring morning, arriving at the bottom of gigantic Lake Louise to rent equipment and take on the slopes. Let's just say that we did not light it up that day and that my mom almost never made it up the T-bar lift. After a good dinner and some ice on the sore muscles, we decided to try again this time at Sunshine Village. Building on my experience from the day before, I decided to stretch my abilities and kept taking lifts high above the treeline until I saw a sign welcoming me to British Columbia. Skiing back down to the base took hours! I was either crazy or completely clueless. For all four of us, that week in one of the most beautiful places in Canada was the first step toward a lifetime of skiing.

After six years in the house on Oak Row Crescent, mom and dad wanted a change. The moving bug bit again! The real-estate market had been good in the mid-1980s, so the value of our home had increased to a level that created some equity for them to use toward an upgrade. I'll always remember when our pleasant and effective real-estate agent (who also spoke a little French) came to the house to discuss the sale. He was all dressed up with a nice suit and a distinctive cologne that was difficult to miss. He let Steve and me sit at the table to listen to everything that we did not understand as kids and numbers that made no sense. He was a superb agent and such a nice man, and he sold the house in no time.

The move to a new neighbourhood, located in the north end of Erin Mills, was awesome. We didn't need to change schools, and Steve and I kept all of our friends and sports clubs since we were in the same catchment area. Dad decided to go all the way and had a beautiful pool installed just after the house was finished being built. It took up almost the entire backyard, but it allowed for us to have great summers enjoying the warm heat. The new house had four bedrooms upstairs, a double garage, good living spaces on the main floor, and an unfinished basement that Steve eventually renovated into his bedroom and drumming space. It was the perfect suburban life for a family of four.

For my dad, the start of 1988 meant that his boys would likely be gone to university by the fall, so he began to think about different career opportunities. He was in his forties by then, and if the right opportunity presented itself, he would consider it. Following what I'm sure were important discussions between my parents, dad made a big jump and took an ownership stake in a small business. To my surprise, the role he assumed as General Manager of Operations was in the small rural community of Saint-André-Est, located forty-five minutes west of Montréal. It was a return "home" after close to ten years away. They settled on a lovely raised bungalow in the town of Lorraine just north of Laval. It was a beautiful neighbourhood with tall mature maple trees, quiet streets, nice green spaces, and easy access to the highway for the daily commute to work. I loved that house. It became my home base for each of the next three summers and Christmas breaks when I had time off from university. While the move was exciting and aligned well with the start of university, I don't think my mom realized how hard it would be to leave her friends and two boys all at once. The demands of her husband's new job didn't help. She has only talked about it a few times, but it was probably one of her most difficult years. I had no clue at the time because I was off to university and loving my new life. This was before any real technology, so our only contact was our fifteen-minute (thirty if she was lucky) phone chat each Sunday to make sure I was alive and not spiralling down a dark hole. Mom spent countless hours in that home in Lorraine as she tried to build new friendships and construct a new life once again. The lack of connectivity with other parents now that she had no kids in school augmented her feeling of isolation, and it was tough during the first months without her sons coming and going every day. My mother is exceptionally strong and resilient, but I regret during those late teenage years and into my early twenties that I was blind to her needs as a mother. It sounds horrible, but I never really gave it much thought. I was becoming an independent adult, and in my mind, my parents were together, happy, and enjoying a good life. Why would I have to consider their needs? Fortunately, I matured and came around when I started my career.

After some stable years in Lorraine, the next few years were a bit of a whirlwind of relocations and job changes. Dad continued to be the leader of operations, but he had a stressful time with one of his partners, who was trying to run the place from Toronto. He was not really happy after the third year, and he took the opportunity to get out when a larger private lighting company in Cambridge, Ontario asked him to run their operations.

This was in 1992 at the low point of the real-estate market, and since they could not find a buyer, they swapped their house in Lorraine for a cottage in the Laurentians and moved into a condo in Mississauga. Dad had a long commute to work each day once again, but mom was back to an area she knew very well.

Then one day two years later, dad appeared without notice at my work-place to inform me that he had just met with the owner in Montréal and that he was out of a job. He was heading back to Toronto to tell mom and was in shock. I had no clue this was coming since nothing had been mentioned about any dissatisfaction or problems. We chatted for a few minutes, and I tried to comfort him. It was the first time in his long career that someone else had made the choice for him. I can only imagine all the thoughts going through his mind as he drove the five hours home.

It was the start of the most difficult year in my dad's life. It took him almost twelve months to find work and when he did it was to join a national transportation company and become the general manager of the Western Ontario garbage division, a little different than what he had done before! The eternal optimist, dad enjoyed the job, and he loved telling us all the stories and secrets of the garbage industry. He even spent a day with the guys on a truck picking up garbage to learn the business close up. It was not his first choice, but he had a leadership role, and they did not need to move to another city as a condition of taking the job. He could have held out longer for the perfect job, but it was the mid-1990s, and Canada's economy was poor. More importantly, the bills were starting to pile up.

Having passed through some challenging years professionally, my parents settled into a good routine with dad committed to his role. But then the phone rang, and he heard the following winning words: "Would you be interested in coming to Montréal to meet the owners of a small company who need a president to run their business?"

I think dad left his office immediately and jumped in his car to drive to Montréal. When he met the owners, they loved him, and he served as their president until he retired on his birthday in 2003 at age fifty-eight. His time leading the small growth-oriented company from a few million in sales to multiples of that in just a few years was the pinnacle of his professional business career. He enjoyed the people, the customers, travelling, and the ownership group's complete confidence in him. Why wouldn't they? He was making them a fortune. The company's success culminated in the company being purchased by the behemoth where he started his career in the 1960s. A complete full circle!

***

Retirement has been very good to my parents. Before the official start, they had already become grandparents to four girls and one boy, had purchased a condo in Boca Raton, Florida, and continued to have an active social life with new and old friends in Montréal and Toronto. They also began to increase the frequency of their visits to their parents, who were now into their eighties and required attention and guidance. They made two voyages to their condo in the south each year: the autumn warm-up from late October to early December and the winter hideout from January to April. They also encouraged their dear old friends from Mississauga to buy or rent places in the same area. With other family members visiting their warm place on an annual basis, it was the best of times. Linda and I also took full advantage of this and made an annual trip with the girls either in November or March to spend a week with the grandparents. It was lovely and will always be one of the things that Julia and Emilie remember most and treasure dearly.

Early into retirement, my parents tried to live at the cottage full-time when not in the south. That did not work very well, however, as the seasons outside of the summer are not really that nice in the Laurentian mountains. There are clouds of bugs during the spring and well into June, and snow flurries would start in late September during evenings or mornings when the wind was howling. It came as a shock when mom told us they were selling the cottage and buying a condo in Montréal as their primary residence. Mom and Dad never looked back. They treasured the decade of family enjoyment by the lake but were ready to move forward and build new experiences. Like the old Demers cottage on Lac Elgin, I can't help thinking about the fun we could have had in later years if they had kept it.

***

A small hand tapped my mother's forehead ever so slightly. She had not heard the little one approach, so a gentle touch was required in addition to the little voice saying, "Grandmaman . . . Grandmaman."

The gentle smile was bright and joyful, and it warmed my mother's heart as she stared into the eyes of one of her grandchildren. This happened on hundreds of mornings just after 6:00 a.m. for many years when one or more of the grandchildren stayed with my parents. It started with my niece, Camille, and ended when my daughter, Emilie, began to make her morning drink and food without any assistance. My mom cherished every one of those mornings. My parents have been the best grandparents imaginable, selfless in every action and generous beyond description to their five grandchildren for the last twenty-five years and counting. There is nothing more important to them than their grandchildren's well-being and happiness. Like her mother, my mom has taken to new technology and social media to stay connected with all of them, including their spouses or partners. Each Sunday she sends a text to each of them to wish them well, ask a few questions, or just say that she loves them. During the pandemic lockdowns, as physical contact was reduced, this routine provided my parents with a constant connection with their extended family. More impressively, my mom is now an avid user of Snapchat and Messenger and interacts each day. The best part is that the kids love that they have cool (and funny) grandparents.

My parents' lives into their midseventies has continued to be active and positive. They are a little slower than before (as expected), but it has not diminished their passion for movement and travel. Their love for each other is as strong as ever, with a continued respect for all of their funny habits. They always have plans for visits with friends and family, and longer trips abroad will be occurring soon. They are very content and accepting of the evolving limitations that are to come. Dad will continue to monitor his prostate and fight off the cancer if it ever returns, like he did during the entire summer of 2021. At the time I never had a doubt that the treatment would be highly successful given that he is strong and has maintained a healthy lifestyle for decades. Illness is a funny thing; you can do everything right and never abuse your body, but there is no guarantee that something will not come and bite you hard. My parents have been lucky enough to avoid hospitals for the most part and had parents who lived long lives, so the odds are in their favour. I actually never really thought of illness for mom and dad until dad told me about his prostate cancer prognosis. I was outside enjoying a lovely spring day when I answered the phone, and it was dad. (I always know something is up when he is the first one to talk since mom has been the lead for decades.) When I hung up, I told the news to Linda and then I started to cry. It was like suddenly an invincible barrier had been taken down for him and in a weird way for me too. For good or bad, hereditary powers cannot be denied.

As they head into the next few decades, my parents intend to live full lives without hesitation or fear. They are realistic about what their bodies can deliver, and they're good at making choices regarding what they want and don't care for. They are very independent and informed about every-thing around them and all things involving this complex world. Dad loves to watch hockey, and they both have eyes on the television for golf tournaments and tennis matches like they did forty years ago. In addition to playing golf, something else that has never disappeared (and never will) is walking. Unless the sidewalk is coated with ice or it's freezing cold, they go for a walk (or sometimes two) each day. More than being good for their health, it symbol-izes a lifetime of movement and adventure. They go out looking to discover something new or to observe a beautiful part of nature. Since my grandfather is still living, they travel two hours to Victoriaville every few weeks to visit him. It is amazing to me. Like the young married couple they were over fifty years ago, they continue to go home. A force keeps pulling them back.

CHAPTER 5
SALT COD AND PATYCZKI UNITE

Hibbs Cove, Conception Bay, Newfoundland, circa 1983.

Capturing my family history and the people who shaped my life would not be complete without the inclusion of Linda's mom and dad. Along with their Newfoundland and Polish ancestors, they endured hardship before they eventually flourished. Their impact is immeasurable as pillars within their extended family and stands as a shining example of determination and adaptability. While Linda's dad, Stanley, died before I met her, Irene holds a very special place in my heart.

The winter morning was frigid in the small cove in the outskirts of Port de Grave, Conception Bay as Irene Bishop pulled the small rocks out of the bed before her younger sister woke and turned on the lantern while trying to stay warm as she layered the only warm clothing she had. Born at the start of the Great Depression, mere days before the Black Thursday market crash on October 24, 1929, she had lived her young life with the bare minimum. She used the rocks (heated in the woodstove each day) to warm the bed during the night or at least at the start of her sleep. As the second child of four, she knew all too well how to share food and the meagre supplies with her older brother and younger siblings. As the eldest girl, much of the work and care was focused on helping her mother. She was only a child herself, but lamenting was not part of her character and never would be during her long life of eighty-eight years. Quite the opposite, she would be remembered for her unrelenting generosity and love for all her friends and family.

Born Elsie Irene Bishop on October 3, 1929, in Hibbs Cove, Conception Bay, Newfoundland, Irene (her first name, Elsie, was never used) knew only her small hometown community for the first fourteen years of her life. She attended the school down the hill from her home until grade eight, which was considered a good accomplishment in the day. At that time family was a constant in the small fishing community. Her direct ancestors went back to 1650 in Conception Bay, so almost everyone she encountered was a cousin. It was not an area with lush farming land and numerous vendors to provide food throughout the year. Proper planning for the winter months included storing potatoes, carrots, and turnips in the cellar (it was actually more of a hole under the floor) and ensuring that salt cod was plentiful. The Bishop family house was located on a small hill only a few feet from the gravel road leading down to the water and school on one side and up to a rocky cliff on the other. Built of grey wood, it stood two stories high but only measured a bit more than twenty-five feet in diameter as a perfectly square structure among the scattering of homes that made up the rugged community. Since there were no trees on the windswept land that bordered Conception Bay, the building had to constantly resist the wind, rain, and snow. Therefore, it's surprising that the family home withstood decades of weather and was only taken down late in the last decade of the twentieth century after standing strong for almost a hundred years. It was a symbol of the Bishop family's resilience and adaptability.

***

A small purse hung on the back of the bedroom door. Irene told her daughter, Linda, that there should be a penny inside for church. As Irene looked around the room, which she had shared with her sister, Marjorie, as a child, Linda opened the purse and found a penny dated prior to 1948. Linda was stunned by the discovery and filled with amazement as she followed her mom around the house, which had been abandoned for over thirty years. The calendar on the wall was dated 1951. The saltshaker was on the table next to the chairs. Her grandfather's fishing boots were stored at the back of the house next to the door. Coats were hanging behind doors. All the signs and remaining objects of a life grounded in fishing were scattered throughout the home and inside the small wooden storage sheds at the back of the property. It was as if their departure was only to be temporary, like a family going on an extended vacation. But quite the opposite, their departure was much more than that.

Irene's return in 1983 to the family home and community where she was born was a joyous one since she was joined by her eldest daughter, Linda, to celebrate the wedding of Cousin Joyce. It was the first time that her grown daughter of twenty years of age had visited the historical family treasure. The buildings and scenery were magical, but they were no match for the warm welcome and generosity of the hosting family members. It was Linda's first time meeting the aunts, uncles, cousins, and friends who had shaped her mother's young life before she had departed west to Toronto.

Cod fishing and salt fish markets were dominant in Newfoundland, especially in the communities on the shores of Conception Bay. By the middle of the nineteenth century, Newfoundland had a surprisingly large population of over a hundred thousand and had secured itself as the world's largest exporter of salt cod. The Bishop family lived for centuries with fishing and salting as their only way of life. The men sailed or rowed in small crafts from the shores of Hibbs Cove or Port de Grave to near (and far) fishing areas and returned with the day's haul to be processed by family. Throughout the centuries it was always a risky affair, and the ones left behind on land always worried about the return of their loved ones until the boats entered the harbour. Many would wait for days after their loved ones were expected due to poor weather or lack of fish. The "voyage" referred to the entire fishing season, not a particular trip. It was a good life, and no one thought the fish supply would ever end. By the dawn of the twentieth century, traditional fishing was supreme, and around two hundred thousand people were spread along six thousand miles of rugged coastline in small outpost settlements.

But the inclusion of Newfoundland in Canada in 1949 marked the start of the decline of salt fish markets. The peak had passed, and the new realities of an industrialized post-WWII world were redefining fishing. The illegal fishing activities by other countries and the difficulty of monitoring the volume of catch by large boats inside and outside international waters was the catalyst for the critical depletion of cod. This new economic wave did not go unnoticed by Irene's father, Herbert. Born fifteen days before the start of the twentieth century on the shore of that beautiful bay, he had laboured all his life in the fishing industry and knew that with a family of four, he needed to ensure they would have a bright future as they headed into the second half of the century.

Herbert Bishop's first move to build a future outside Newfoundland was sending his eldest son, Claude, to Toronto in the hope that fruitful work would be available and provide a real option to relocate the family. Word was received from Claude soon after he arrived in the Queen City that pay was plentiful, so Herbert soon followed and headed westbound. By then Irene had already left the family home in Hibbs Cove at age fourteen to work as a full-time caretaker for rich families in St. John's. Travel was difficult in those days, so the family did not gather as a group for a few years as each member took a different path to what became a new life outside of Newfoundland. They were one of the first Bishop families to leave the Port de Grave Peninsula since their ancestors arrived in the seventeenth century. While Herbert found work at a leather factory in Toronto, his wife and children continued to live on the rugged coast of Conception Bay for many months. Irene continued her work in St. John's until 1948 when she decided to join her father in the big city. It was becoming obvious that their future would be on the shores of Lake Ontario, and it was just a question of time (and money) until the others followed. Although it had been a few years since Herbert and Irene had left the family home, Irene's mother, Annie Dawe, and youngest daughter, Marjorie, did not act like they were leaving for a new life when they finally made the long voyage in 1951 to join the other members of their family.

They left the house with all of its furniture and belongings for other family members and friends to oversee. The home stood empty for the next several decades until it had to be taken down due to damage by a car crash and almost fifty years of neglect. The family didn't even visit for the demolition, leaving it to the extended family who still lived in the community to handle. While Herbert and Annie continued to be linked to Hibbs Cove, the physical structure was no longer of importance.

Their new home became the modern city of Toronto, which was fully expanding as it entered the core years of the post-WWII economic boom. Reaching a population of over one million, it stood tall as the second-largest city in Canada behind Montréal, which continued to hold a special status as the hub of culture and corporate head offices in Canada. Labour was plentiful, with unemployment at low levels and investment in new infrastructure sprouting everywhere. Such Toronto staples as Union Station, Maple Leaf Gardens, and the Royal York Hotel were already present amid a flurry of development. It was not a surprise that the Bishop family members were quickly able to find work and establish themselves without financial difficulty. However, given that they had only completed elementary-level education back home, manual labour would have to suffice.

Irene worked at different manual labour jobs for over ten years after she arrived in Toronto. The family gathered on the shores of the great lakes, with each of the children working in manufacturing plants. Those were joyous years as they discovered their new, large, and dynamic city. The hourly paid work was structured and sometimes repetitive compared to what they had experienced back home, but the stable income and the guarantee of full weekly shifts allowed for a better lifestyle. It was not big pay, but it was enough to provide a home, food, and a little extra cash for enjoyable times with friends and family. It was evident that returning to Newfoundland would not happen, as the children also started to meet friends and ultimately their future spouses.

It was during this time, in the 1950s, that a young man of Polish descent born in southern Manitoba fell in love with Irene. Their mutual friends decided it would be a good match and made the introduction at a social event. Stanley was steeped in tradition when it came to money and providing for his family. There was no option to get married, start a family, or have children until he had the cash in hand. So, they waited years before getting married in June 1959 and starting a family. But these "waiting years" were good ones for them. My evidence of this is rock solid and captured on Super 8 films that I found in the basement of the family house about twenty years ago. I was looking for a game in the crawlspace when I found a box with little film cases in it. My curiosity was piqued, so I decided to set up the old projector. First, it seemed to be only some lovely home videos of when Linda and her siblings were young, but as I continued to insert more films, a more revealing one appeared. It captured Irene and Stanley having a good time with drinks, food, and multiple friends at a house party. After the brief viewing ended, I called Linda over to watch it, and she was again reminded how her late father loved filming and taking photos. Once I had completed my discovery, I walked upstairs to the kitchen and asked Irene about the "secret" videos. A big smile appeared on her face. "Oh, yes," she said, "we had a lot of fun back then!"

***

Stanley Michael Szarga was born on August 4, 1929, in Griswold, Manitoba. It is located two hundred and fifty kilometres west of Winnipeg and about a hundred kilometres north of the North Dakota border. His parents were both born in Poland and emigrated to Canada in the prosperous 1920s. His father, Michael Szarga, was born on August 24, 1899, in Gorliczyna, and his mother, Victoria Jakubiec, was born on November 26, 1905, in Tryncza. Their hometowns are just ten kilometres from each other in southeastern Poland, bordering western Ukraine. Their lives would have been very different if they had stayed home. Once WWII started, the area was quickly invaded, and the most horrific violence and cruelty that could be imagined occurred. By the start of 1940, numerous concentration and labour camps had been established in the forests surrounding the homes and villages of their extended family and friends. Stan was a teenager during these years. Those events shaped his conviction to provide for his loved ones and to live in peace.

Although Stanley was born in Manitoba, he did not stay there for long. His parents decided to relocate to Toronto soon after his birth, arriving in February 1930. The new Canadians had no intention to return overseas, which Michael solidified by getting his Canadian citizenship on June 28, 1933 in New Toronto. That neighbourhood in Toronto's West End became their home base for years to come.

Stanley continued attending school but did not particularly like it. Once he completed grade ten, he was done and began to work. The family grew to four children as they lived a modest life with no extras, supported by wages earned through manual labour that supplied only the necessities during the Great Depression. It was during those years as a youth that Stanley established his unwavering rule that loans and debt were to be avoided at all costs. Throughout his life he never borrowed and only had a credit card for convenience and travel. One might conclude that this approach to personal finances would result in someone who would build a career on a steady job without any risks. Interestingly, the opposite occurred. He became a highly successful entrepreneur, developer, and business owner.

By the 1950s, Stanley was in his twenties and had started to work in the electricity sector. Since he had limited education, he started in the shop and worked at different jobs with a power company. He was doing well and enjoying life outside of work with his new love, Irene. He saved every penny possible, so he could get married and buy a house. His entrepreneurial spirit blossomed during those years as well, and he started to discuss other opportunities with colleagues and acquaintances. One of these opportunities included a body of freshwater a hundred and fifty kilometres north of Toronto owned by Ontario Hydro. But before he could make a move on that front, he needed to solidify his family life for the future and establish a family home. He made the big step in 1959 by marrying Irene and buying their first house on Iris Road in New Toronto.

This is where their first child, Linda, was born on June 9, 1963. By then the work was good, and Stanley no longer had to slave away at manual tasks. He had moved to an office job, which paid more and provided him with critical experience in business operations, relationship building, and sales. But he was never one to enjoy working for others, so a parallel path of work and ownership outside his main career started to develop. He had the best of both worlds: a stable job, a decent income to provide for his family, and time for other business interests.

He moved to another electric company and started to travel abroad to Europe, particularly Germany, as part of his responsibilities. These were formative years, and the experience of meeting and doing business in other countries with different companies and business leaders was priceless. He was thriving as a business leader and cementing his confidence for what was to come.

Stanley's first serious foray into entrepreneurship occurred on the shores of that body of water north of Toronto. Lake Eugenia is an artificial lake that was created in 1914 when Ontario Hydro dammed the small river that flooded the two hundred hectares that had recently been purchased from farmers. The hydroelectric power station was finished in 1915 and still stands today, producing power mostly during the winter months. Back in the early 1960s, Stanley's Lake Eugenia development project started in partnership with the Baragar brothers and resulted in the creation of a new company, called Resort Developments. The concept was to buy land on the lakeshore, use summer weekends to build wooden cottages that sat on cinder blocks, and sell them for a profit. The simple business plan worked so well that they bought multiple waterfront lots over the years and built dozens of cottages. Some of the vacant land was even available for building into the 1990s. It proved to be a huge success. Unknown today to most of the cottage owners who fill the lake's shores, Stanley and his business partners are responsible for much of what was developed on the north shore of the lake. Many of the original cottages, which he built with his own hands, are still standing today, including the Szarga family's cherished red cottage located on Stanley Drive.

Stanley worked for many years at the same company until he made the jump in 1976 to self-employment and part ownership of G.T. Wood. He was part-owner and operator until his untimely death in 1994. He loved running that business. He was passionate about treating the employees with respect and ensuring that everyone was well taken care of, with good compensation and rewards when the business performed well. He provided annual trips like cruises for employee recognition, which partners could also join, and gave a little something to everyone at Christmas. He had learned in his prior career how to treat customers and suppliers well, and he did it with enormous success. His generosity did not take away from his shrewd business acumen or his focus on making money and maximizing returns for the ownership group. This was a time before cell phones and digital platforms, so being physically present in the building and involved in the work was critical to a prospering enterprise. He was at work by 7:00 a.m. each morning, returned home by 5:00 p.m. to have dinner with the family, and always returned for a few hours of light work after 7:00 p.m. from Monday to Thursday—after a post-dinner nap on the couch. Weekends were dedicated to family as the responsibilities for three active children in sports along with summer at the cottage were more than enough to keep him and Irene busy, with few idle hours. His hard work had paid off.

Years before, at the start of their marriage, Irene would go to the bank and cash their weekly paycheques, then place the proceeds on the kitchen table, so they could split it into little piles that represented their expenses. Sometimes there was a little left for pleasure, and sometimes there was not enough for essentials. Now that he was doing well and his ongoing projects like the cottage properties on Lake Eugenia were providing some decent returns, they were able to save a little. Then it was a little more, which satisfied Stanley and enabled him to stay debt free. Their savings did not amount to a fortune, but it was enough to avoid having to count every dollar on a weekly basis. It also allowed Irene to have a full fridge at all times, something that she enjoyed greatly. They had finally made it!

Beyond love and affection for their children, Irene and Stanley extended their generosity to family and friends. Once they felt that they were on solid footing financially, it was only natural that others who needed help should get it. This included brothers and sisters, friends of the kids, and even business associates. For the twenty-two years that I knew Irene, she was most generous and always willing to help Linda and me with anything. Just like when we were with my parents and grandparents, there was no question of paying for anything at all when staying at the Szarga house in Mississauga or at the cottage on the lake. I was never even allowed to buy ice cream for the kids. Irene would hand me a twenty on our way out the door or through the car window before we made our way to Jolley's in Flesherton next to the lake. She funded hundreds and hundreds of ice cream cones over the years!

As much as Stanley was entrepreneurial in business, he remained conservative and prudent in his personal life and financial planning. The home they had on Iris Road was good for two kids, but when Linda and Mike were about to be joined by Laura in 1971, he made the move to a new suburb and purchased a larger home in Cooksville, Mississauga. The home was newly built, and they never moved again. The same was true of the cottage. While an extension for a new kitchen, water well, and basement was made in 1974, the cottage remained pretty much the same until a few more renos were done in the late 1990s. Irene also kept change to a minimum but was incredible at adapting to consequences imposed on her later in life. Stanley's death forced her to become the matriarch of the family. She started to travel regularly when a banker (me) took her daughter away to Eastern Ontario and Quebec for more than a decade. She handled the deaths of close friends and family with a strength that always impressed me. And lastly, she endured side effects and illness as a result of her unrelenting bronchial asthma and osteoporosis battles. While most people would have complained about their deteriorating state, Irene never did. I don't think the grandchildren even knew she was going through some of it until maybe the last year of her life, which is amazing.

My daughters spent countless days and hours with their grandmother from the time they were born to her last day in the spring of 2018. She was ever present. Irene was there with us at the hospital for both of their births, and my girls were with her during the last few hours when their grandmother was gasping for air. Before her decline, she shared her bed with them when we visited, always got up with them in the early morning hours, read them countless books before bed, and always made meals that the girls adored. Their combined happiness made Linda and me the happiest parents in the universe. They miss their grandmother dearly and will always remember her warm smile, limitless love, and soothing embrace.

For me, Irene remains the most generous person I have ever known. And that's saying something coming from parents and grandparents who gave me the world and having a wife who rivals her parents' giving souls. There was something about her presence that always calmed me and made me feel at peace. I miss that special power that she had over me.

Postscript

Rugged terrain and sea water surrounded the entire landscape. I was surprised by the lack of trees except for a few small bushes and spruces that stood no taller than a few metres. The visit with Linda on a windy Tuesday on September 6, 2022 was my first on the narrow Port de Grave Peninsula in Newfoundland's Avalon region. I finally got to experience what her mom talked about when she described her childhood, usually delivered with funny stories and laughter. Life was simple with daily routines such as walking down the hill from the house a couple hundred metres to attend school with brothers and sister, helping with meal prep, cleaning, washing dishes, and wondering if her father would make it back from fishing. The small school she attended still stands today and is now a museum filled with the original furniture and artifacts from the children who attended almost a century ago, including some items from Linda's immediate family and ancestors. We found the small piece of land where the Bishop family home was located and where Linda's mom lived for her first fourteen years. The house was gone, but as we walked on the property, we found a few old things half buried that belonged to the family: first a teapot, then a bucket, a few metal rings that had probably held together some small barrels, and (incredibly) a leather shoe that was clearly from the time the family still inhabited the wooden structure in the early 1950s. Tears flowed from Linda's blue eyes as she informed a curious older man in his car that it was the location of her mom's childhood home. The man smiled. "Oh yes, I remember that little house before it was torn down," he said. "How things change."

We finished our visit at the bright red and white lighthouse that sits at the edge of the peninsula a little less than two kilometres from Hibbs Cove. It has constantly accepted the strong waves and wind that for more than one hundred years have eroded the rocks and soil that once surrounded it for dozens of metres. It was Linda's first visit to the end of the peninsula mostly because her mom had never mentioned the lighthouse and Linda did not even know it was there. This puzzled me, but it was maybe because, to the locals eighty years ago, those were insignificant transportation tools like streetlights and highways. But today it still stands tall, beautiful, and strong.

Daniel J. Demers Genealogy

FULL NAME	DATE OF BIRTH/DEATH	MARRIAGE DATE/LOCATION	PLACE OF RESIDENCE
Jean Demers	1600–1669	1627 in Normandie, France	Mers, France
Barbe Maugis	1600–1669		
Jean Demers	February 6, 1633 to July 3, 1708	November 9, 1654, Montréal, Canada	Quebec City, QC
Jeanne Vedie	1637 to Dececember 1, 1708		
Jean Demers	July 6, 1661 to July 11, 1736	May 2, 1696 Sainte-Famille, Canada	Quebec City, QC
Jeanne Arrivée	March 13, 1669 to June 25, 1748		
Louis Joseph Demers	November 12, 1703 to After 1777	February 11, 1730, Château-Richer, Canada	Saint Nicholas, QC
Thérèse Gagnon	March 21, 1705 to May 21, 1777		
Louis Demers	April 1, 1731 to July 9, 1775	June 16, 1761, Saint Nicholas, Canada	Saint Nicholas, QC
Françoise Paquet	January 17, 1741 to May 24, 1819		
Basile Demers	June 12, 1769 to August 3, 1834	October 28, 1788, Saint Nicholas, QC	Saint Nicholas, QC
Charlotte Douville	April 5, 1752 to November 17, 1838		
Frederic Demers	December 5, 1792 to May 6, 1874	November 9, 1813, Saint Nicholas, Canada	Saint Nicholas, QC
Suzanne Frechette	February 19, 1796 to July 30, 1834		
Honoré Demers	January 3, 1816 to April 6, 1900	January 14, 1840, Saint Nicholas, Canada	Saint Nicholas, QC
Marie Ester Bergeron	February 4, 1821 to April 20, 1856		

FULL NAME	DATE OF BIRTH/DEATH	MARRIAGE DATE/LOCATION	PLACE OF RESIDENCE
Thomas Demers	November 10, 1851 to June 11, 1931	January 30, 1894, Saint Nicholas, QC	Victoriaville, QC
Rose Roberge	December 30, 1854 to December 13, 1924		
Emile Demers	December 21, 1895 to October 26, 1961	February 25, 1919, Victoriaville, QC	Victoriaville, QC
Evelina Beauchesne	April 25, 1897 to December 25, 1960		
J Raymond Demers	July 11, 1920 to September 20, 2006	May 20, 1944, Victoriaville, QC	Victoriaville, QC
Réjeanne Baril	August 26, 1917 to January 22, 2013		
Claude A. Demers	March 13, 1945	June 24, 1967, Victoriaville, QC	Montréal, QC
Martine Hinse	October 9, 1947		
Daniel J. Demers	March 13, 1969	May 30, 1998, Prince Edward County, ON	Oakville, ON
Linda Szarga	June 9, 1963		
Julia Demers	May 12, 1999		Oakville, ON
Emilie Demers	May 21, 2001		Oakville, ON

BOOK 2

CHRONICLES OF A RIPENING FRENCH KID

PROLOGUE 2

The music was loud as the next song selection was being considered from among a wide array of genres and years. It was almost midnight, and I was sitting closest to the speaker and getting the pleasure and the eardrum pain of the music selections, which were now getting into the mostly heavy hard-rock songs of our youth. With Steve sitting in the chair to my right and my other "brothers" (Gil, Rémi, and Frapps) on my left and across the table, it was pure elation at the end of a wonderful autumn day.

For almost a decade we had been meeting for a golf weekend at a "cabin" tucked into the woods one hour north of Ottawa on Lac Perreault near the town of Gracefield. Steve built it in the early 2000s with a strict rule that no trees would be cut unless completely necessary to retain the natural privacy that the cedars, fir, and spruce provided. The long slope from the cabin to the crisp clean water was steep, and the staircase was wrapped in small trees, making each trip down to the lake a well-planned affair with proper considerations for food, drinks, and bathroom breaks. The new front deck was a welcome addition, which my oldest niece had to negotiate vigorously with her father to convince him that cutting a few small trees would be worth the benefit of a large gathering space outside. I'm a tree lover too, but we kept reminding Steve that to sacrifice a few was acceptable given that there were literally thousands of other trees on his property, which he had expanded with more land purchased from the family who had owned acres around the lake for more than a hundred years. The expansion ensured that the cabin would remain free from close neighbours. Only two other cottages were at the end of the small lane that passed on the south side of the property, so we usually saw more animals than people during our visits. I loved the smell of forest and the sounds of the wind passing through the tall white pine trees. It was the perfect escape.

On that late September weekend, we were blessed to gather once again with our closest friends of more than a few decades. And that year we added some young golfers to the group, which allowed for the addition of another foursome. Since we were now in our fifties, it was the sons of the senior golfers who were joining the fun. Few of us were great golfers, and the rounds were friendly with small wagers keeping things exciting. There were no egos, no serious competition, and complete respect for everyone, which was constantly kept in check with uncontrollable laughter and storytelling. It was pretty simple: anyone who couldn't laugh at themselves didn't belong. It was made a little easier since we knew each other so well and had essentially grown up together since our teenage years. There was a magic to these friendships, although I must admit we each had a secret weapon helping us along this unique friendship adventure: our wives! Their encouragement and respect for this special bond between us created an environment that allowed us to be ourselves. Linda knew the pleasure I got from spending time with my friends and regularly asked me when the next gathering was occurring since she knew it was not only good for me but also for our relationship. And she quite enjoyed the funny stories I shared after each event.

It was in this context that I found myself singing along with my best buddies to some rock songs while Steve assumed the DJ duties. In his usual collaborative way, he polled the guys for song selections and then picked up my phone to investigate and make a pick. This was not our most productive time of the day, and a few evening drinks had only amplified the incompetence. To say that it took him a few minutes to scroll and punch into the phone the letters of a potential song would be an understatement. At one point I inquired about his progress, and he replied with a frustrated tone that the phone had locked again. He held the phone up to my face to unlock it and then continued his research. But the next time it happened, he left it on his face as he barked at me that my security lock timer was too short. Incredibly, that time when he looked back at the phone, it unlocked without my intervention.

"No way!" Steve exclaimed. "Wonder Twin powers . . . activate!"

Our faces can unlock each other's phones.

As the other boys laughed uncontrollably at the security breach, Steve and I were once again reminded of the uniqueness of our lives as identical twins. I have taken steps in my lifetime to ensure that I am distinctive and have characteristics that are different from my brother. I have lived in different cities and sometimes not seen him for months because of our work and family priorities. We both cherish our wives beyond imagination and love them for their shared and different qualities. And we have raised children to become successful young adults who will do incredible things. In my everyday life, I don't dwell on the fact that I am an identical twin. The reason why this moment in my fifty-third year was so important is that it made me realize how lucky I am. Everyone on the planet who looks at me when my treasured brother is next to me asks me questions, knowing I have stories to tell. The following pages contain some of them.

CHAPTER 6
CAN'T SHAKE HIM OFF

With my brother Steve playing at the Demers cottage on the shores of Lac Elgin.
Mom did not want us to reach the water since she could not swim, circa 1972.

"Come visit when you can. The blue babies are here for the weekend."
This was said to friends and extended family members multiple times by my grandparents, aunts, and uncles during the first few years of my life. They were referring to my brother and me during our visits to Victoriaville. My mother frequently dressed us in the same colours (often blue outfits) when we were babies, which amplified the fact that we were identical twins. It became a bit of a show for those who had never seen twins. Sometimes I think mom and dad should have charged a viewing fee! So, there we were, in our little baby beds or car seats on top of the dining room tables of our grandparents' houses, on full display for everyone to see, touch, poke, and pick up. Of course, I don't remember these times, but the story (along with pictures) has been shared with me so many times that it is ingrained in my memory. We even have extended family who still refer to us by that name when we attend funerals or celebrations of old family members. This love and attention was amazing for my parents and grandparents in those early years. Everything changed for them with the start of a new generation. It was like they were beginning a new life, which brought them the pleasure and pride of seeing what their hard work and dedication to family had created. The focus was no longer on their daily tasks of work and paying the bills but on the future and how they could give more to ensure success for these newborns. Incredibly, since my mom and dad had got married so young, my grandparents were still in their late forties when I was born. They had immense energy and a willingness to be involved and provide breaks for my parents whenever possible. As the oldest children on both sides of the family, my brother and I developed a closer relationship to my four grandparents than my cousins did. I was with them so much that it has never been like a visit or a formal occasion to spend time with them. It is completely comfortable and genuine.

Since I had a brother who was always with me and provided a full-time partner for all the fun (and trouble) we wanted to have, I never thought about needing or wanting another brother or sister as part of our family. It was like the nucleus of the four of us was perfect, and nothing else was required to be happy. Only much later as a teenager did mom share that the decision of having more children was taken from her once we were born because of all the complications she had following our birth. She has always said that we are all that she needs and has never given it a second thought. I believe this with all my heart, but sometimes I wonder if they would have had another if Steve and I had been easier on mom during the delivery. She was only twenty-one years old at the time. Dad has never really talked about it.

My early life as a baby and young child must have been pretty comfortable with continuous love and affection because I can't recall anything negative or shocking from those years. I know others will talk about an event or a moment of fear that has been hardwired into their brain, but I have none of that. There is nothing bad from those years that causes me to reflect or try to understand how it impacted me later in life. I was one of the lucky ones. The everyday words, actions, reactions, and engagements must have been grounded in genuine care and love. Incredibly, they continue to this day. I have never seen my father really angry or yell at anyone. That is just crazy. It's not to say he never gets upset or unsatisfied with a specific situation, but he has incredible patience and complete respect for the views and actions of others. My mother is a bit more on edge (it comes from her dad), and while she has also never been witnessed to yell or be visibly angry at anyone, she does share her views and opinions more openly and without a second thought. Because they never scream at or disrespect others, they have built an environment of positive attitudes and love around all their friends and family. A treasure to protect.

My first memories as a child are of me playing sports and adventuring outside. I don't remember many moments from school, family events, or even vacations before age seven, but I remember playing, competing in sports, and riding my bike everywhere until snow covered the ground. With Steve acting as my full-time friend and partner, playing and being active was always available and became a constant in my pre-adult life. As a young boy, I played soccer, baseball, hockey, badminton, and tennis, went cross-country skiing, and even joined swimming clubs, which I disliked because the lessons were early in the morning when the temperature was cold and the pool water even colder. The swimming instructors, who were really just young teenagers, would stand by the pool in their hoodies while we would be in our little bathing suits as they forced us to get into the water.

"Let's go. Jump in. The water's fine."

There was no limit to the things I tried to play or the games we created when traditional sports became less interesting. There were super-competitive Ping-Pong matches in the basement, and we even developed a game where we would make a small ball from scrunched-up aluminum paper. The objective was to throw it and score on Steve by getting the little "ball" past him. The wild thing is that the net or goal was different parts of the house or a piece of furniture. Oh, how my mother was patient. During the 1970s there were no electronic games, videos, or children's television shows to keep us glued to the couch during the day. It forced me to be in motion and seek out games and adventures to pass the time and spend all that energy, and I had a lot! The only thing that would bring me back to focus and some sort of a schedule was lunch and dinner when my belly would be calling for more fuel to continue moving.

My love for riding a bicycle during those early years evolved into a full-blown addiction to repairing and building bikes. I had a very acceptable bicycle, which I oiled and cleaned with superb attention (a classic red ten-speed), but on my long rides in Candiac and a little later in Mississauga I would see other boys who had dirt bikes with big fat tires or older one-gear models with banana seats and extended handlebars, which looked to be six feet high. As excellent as the ten-speed was, when I needed to get to soccer practice or to a friend's house, it was not adequate. *I need a cool bike,* I thought. *Actually, maybe a few.*

Since dad had put up the money for the ten-speed, which I wanted to keep, I knew there would not be any other money coming my way to solve my "problem." This is when Steve and I decided that we needed to look everywhere and anywhere for bike parts and start a new production shop in the garage. We became obsessed with the goal of creating new bikes and becoming amateur mechanics. Each and every garbage day, we would ride along streets close to our house to look for parts (or sometimes we even got entire bikes) before the garbage trucks picked them up. We let it be known to everyone that we were in the bike-building business and would be happy to take any parts or old bicycles off their hands. Incredibly, we gathered substantial amounts of parts in the first few weeks, which we kept updating for several years. We had tires hanging all over the garage walls, frames, handlebars of different sizes, tire tubes for puncture replacements, different seat styles, and most importantly, we had a lot (I mean a lot) of bolts and nuts. The latter were the most important ingredients to enable our wide range of bicycle styles. With different sizes of bolts and nuts, we could put any tire or handlebar on a frame, which resulted in many design opportunities. The only thing we purchased from our own savings was paint (it had to be Tremclad rust spray paint), which allowed us to put a professional final touch on the numerous bicycles we created. Working on bikes and building tree houses in the woods as a young boy provided me with the base knowledge and the chops to become quite an effective renovator and assembler later in life. To this day I adore fixing things and will accept any challenge from my wife or daughters to repair or install something.

Spending countless hours with Steve either outside or playing multiple sports were the dominant activities, but I also needed some solitude to enjoy another developing passion: music. My mother listened to the radio in the house and usually had some easy-listening pop station playing in the background on most days. She has never been an avid television watcher, preferring the sound of lively music instead, which was likely influenced by her mom's love of the piano. Along with the exposure to my Grandpapa Demers' master musicianship on full display during his living-room concerts, it was no surprise that an inner need for music was evolving. My grandfather was a spontaneous player who would sing and pound the piano keys to create loud engaging songs. When he played the violin, it was also loud but with a fast jig style well known in Quebec for parties and dancing. His foot would pound the floor as he moved the horsehair bow with lightning speed up and down the four strings. Conversely, my grandmother had obtained formal training and played more classical piano pieces with a light touch and great precision. She was able to read music and played wonderfully for us at Christmas or on other occasions. When we encouraged her, she would also sing in her slight voice to enrich the ensemble of popular and well-known traditional songs. I recall sitting on the piano bench with each of them from time to time and trying to make some kind of music, but I never seemed to have the feel for it. Luckily, one day my grandfather held out his violin to me and asked, "Would you like to try making some noise?"

That's when it all changed. I was completely engaged at how easy it was to make a sound that was acceptable. I was not making any real music, but once he showed me how to hold the bow and slowly move up and down the strings, I felt like I was getting somewhere. His positive reinforcement and big smile at watching me try to handle one of his favourite instruments played a big role in developing my new confidence. None of his four children had taken up any instruments, so for his young grandson to show an interest was a proud moment.

At one point a few months after my initial "audition," my grandfather offered me a priceless gift. "I would like to give you this smaller violin that I have, so you can learn and start playing on your own," he said. "If you don't like it after a while, just give it back to me. That's all I ask."

It was not a new violin, and the case had definitely been through many different hands over the years, but it was mine, and I was thrilled. I still don't know how much the violin would have been worth at the time or what it's worth now. (I still have it with the original bow and case that he gave to me over forty years ago.) Its monetary value does not matter to me since it will never be sold or given away unless I have the opportunity to pass it on to a grandchild in future years like he did. I took that violin to dozens of lessons, several music recitals, and a few family visits where I would show off my newfound talent. The unfortunate part was that I did not have the natural ear and melodic feel that my grandparents had. I worked hard to build to a certain level of proficiency, but it still felt somewhat mechanical compared to the flow that I see in the best musicians. The challenges did not stop me, and I persevered with more lessons and practice until it all came to a sudden stop when our move from Montréal to Toronto occurred. I think it was just too much change and the hurdle of learning English and continuing the lessons caused me to pause and never formally pick it up again. Regardless, the gift of music had arrived.

***

"It is very important that the boys are not in the same class and that this continues until they finish grade eight."

These words from my mother were directed at the vice principal of René Lamoureux School in Mississauga on a gloomy Monday morning on December 3, 1979. We had just arrived from Montréal, and Steve and I had yet to recover from the shock of leaving our beautiful suburban town of

Candiac on the south shore of Montréal. We had left behind many friends and sports teams in addition to our grandparents, who were now more than eight hours of driving time away from us.

My mom was not finished. "It is also very important that you assist them in finding their bus at the end of today, so they get home without any issues. They have never taken a bus to school, and they don't know this city at all."

That second statement caused me to sink down into the stiff square armchair that was located in the corner of his office. I still recall the empty feeling I had and the fear of having to walk into my new class within the next hour. I don't think I said a single word the entire time we were provided the orientation of how things worked at the only French elementary school in the entire city of more than three hundred thousand people (it was thirty times bigger than Candiac).

Most kids have the chance to start at a new school with all the other kids in September. Not many have to do it in the middle of a school year when all the friendships are already established and social circles are well defined. On that first morning, I was engulfed in fear, and it continued when my mother left me with the vice principal and he walked me down the hallways, outside through the cement recess area, and into a portable classroom with a class full of grade five kids. On top of having to survive that nerve-wracking experience, I was in an enclosed square portable, which I had never experienced or even seen before. The VP introduced me to the class by saying, "Daniel just transferred from Montréal. He does not speak any English, so please support him. Oh, and he has an identical twin brother in the other class."

Well, now I feel like a real loser, I thought.

The desks were positioned in a U shape around the class with no space between them. I was asked to sit at about the middle of the U toward the back of the class but facing the teacher. I don't know if the teacher was a mastermind at helping new kids or if it was just luck, but the student next to me immediately introduced herself with a big smile and made me feel at ease. Her name was Caro, and she saved me that day. Her welcoming attitude was the single most important reason I avoided panic and came away from that day without any lasting emotional scars. Caro also introduced me to my longest-lasting friend, Steve Frappier, on that first day. She also made sure I knew the routine for the buses at the end of the day, and she was just super nice. Thank God!

René Lamoureux was a school of about five hundred students from kindergarten to grade eight. It covered the entire city of Mississauga and had grown exponentially from 1976 to 1980 with the exodus from Montréal of all the head offices of multinational companies. The school's capacity in the main building (which still operates today) was only about three hundred kids with only one gym, so the Peel Board had to increase capacity by adding more and more portables in the back and on the side of the school. When I left that school after grade eight, there were more classes in portables than inside the main building. The student population was not very diverse. It was composed of two main groups of students: those who had moved from Quebec and had to attend this school because they only spoke French and those who grew up speaking English but had either a mother or father with francophone roots (therefore allowing them to send their kids to this French school, so they could learn the language). This mixture made for an interesting recipe of teaching and curriculum content. It was normal to have the teacher insert some English words into the lessons, so the less francophone kids could make sense of the content. Most interesting and surprising to me and Steve was that everyone spoke English the moment they left the classroom. The teachers and the school leadership team had to remind kids constantly to speak French in the classroom and in the hallways and went as far as issuing detentions for those who broke this rule. This dynamic between the use of the two languages was quite fruitful in helping me learn English, which I grasped within one year of our arrival in Ontario. Once my fears subsided and I made friends, the rest of grade five went well, and I moved on to grade six (although I don't remember anyone not passing at that school) in much better condition than I had thought would be the case on that first morning in the vice principal's office. In addition to the blessing of having Caro next to me on that first day, the boys at the school played sports outside every recess throughout the year, which was aligned to my core strengths. The hours of baseball, football, and soccer that were played by a bunch of young boys in the schoolyard three times a day from 1979 to 1983 is in the hundreds. Again, thank God!

Over the years, many people have asked me how I was able to learn English with ease. In addition to school, this priceless gift of full bilingualism was given to me by two critical influences: Jack Tripper and Arthur Fonzarelli (Fonzie). Along with their friends—Janet Wood, Chrissy Snow, Mr. Roper, Richie Cunningham, Ralph Malf, Potsie Weber, and of course, Arnold—they are responsible for introducing me to a new language with comedy. I'm not kidding! My early impactful listening occurred for one hour each day after the school bus dropped me off at home. I would sit in front of the tube eating my afternoon snack (Rice Krispies with lots of white sugar on top or two slices of white bread covered with caramel spread) before heading outside to play road hockey until dinner. The routine was simple, with thirty-minute reruns of *Happy Days* and then *Three's Company* without any inter-ruption (supplemented on rainy days by another round on another channel). I found Henry Winkler and John Ritter just brilliant and crazy funny with their physical comedy and trademark expressions. John was just like Jerry Lewis, and Henry was cooler than Elvis. In addition to being exposed to a new language, I was also observing and learning about American culture, which had not been part of my upbringing due to the isolation of the French language in Quebec. I watched hundreds of hours of both shows from grade five to eight, augmented by weekly nighttime viewing of some of the most popular sitcoms, including *M*A*S*H* and *Family Ties*. I have always been a better student when listening and viewing versus only reading. Looking back, it is not a surprise that watching those numerous television programs during our first years in Mississauga paid back in spades. Credit also goes to my English teachers in high school who were excellent and helped me refine my writing skills.

In that first home in Erin Mills, our family became immersed in a new culture, and we enjoyed the benefits of a good home and a great neighbourhood. The single-garage home with three bedrooms featured a vaulted ceiling at the back, which was the width of the house. It opened to the staircase and hallway that led to the three bedrooms, which were at the front of the house. It made for a bright home with good sunlight. The house overlooked a large community park called Woodhurst Heights. The park had two soccer fields, tennis courts (which turned into an ice rink in the winter), a playground, and a small hill that was superb for sledding. All that was missing was a pool. Our yard was very simple, with a small deck, patio, and BBQ. Anyone who has lived in southern Ontario during the summer knows that it can get hot and humid. Suffice to say we became very good at inviting ourselves to our neighbours who had pools to splash around in on hot days. My mom also loved the water and obtained summer passes to the public outdoor pool at the Erindale Campus of the University of Toronto in order to cool off when other families on the street got tired of their new French intruders. That house and the surrounding cycling trails and parks offered me everything I needed as a young teenager.

With the national sport in Canada being hockey, and as a kid growing up in the 1970s, almost everyone either played hockey or had friends who played. There was no way to avoid the sport. I mean, what else was an ordinary super-active Canadian kid to do? Even if someone wanted to enjoy other sports on the world stage, there was no way to watch them. It was an era when we were all a little closed-minded unless someone was lucky enough to have a family member or a friend from another country who was able to inform them (and maybe provide some printed information) about another spot. Hockey's dominance was also greatly influenced by the success of the NHL north of the forty-ninth parallel. During my first twenty years of life, the Stanley Cup was won by a Canadian hockey team twelve out of twenty times. Montréal dominated the 1970s, and Edmonton ruled the 1980s. So, it was no surprise that I played a lot of hockey both on the ice and on the road. Surprisingly, I never played organized hockey, not even for one game. My games took place on the streets and outdoor rinks around our home in Candiac and Mississauga. I never had a helmet, knee pads, shoulder pads, gloves, or any of the other equipment that kids had to wear when participating in league play. All I had was a stick with a white plastic replacement blade at the end. Since we played on the street most of the time, a regular stick blade would be reduced to a thin piece of wood in a couple of days on the rough pavement, so we just used old broken sticks and put a white plastic blade on the end—simple! The routine was pretty repetitive. On weekends from September to April, I played for at least a couple of hours each day with whoever could be convinced to come out. I always knocked on the door of the boys who had nets or goalie pads first, so we could have something close to a formal game. The entire exercise was quite fluid as kids came in and out of the game since we played for so long, and their moms or dads called them home for other things (to this day I don't know what those "other things" were). It didn't matter if we were three, six, or ten players. Steve and I always played, and we adjusted the game and team sizes according to the available roster. Then on weekdays we supplemented with games for one to two hours before dinner. Steve or I would open the garage door, then we would take out our sticks and tennis balls and begin playing with some passes and shots on the road in front of the house, always trying to make as much noise as possible. This initial ritual was the callout to all the boys on the street that it was almost time for the first period to begin. If our noisy enthusiasm did not recruit enough players, we took the next step and went directly to their houses and rang their doorbells with a simple request: "Are you ready to play?"

The kids ranged in age from eight to sixteen. The youngest was Blair, who lived next door and had a great net and a full set of road hockey goalie equipment. The oldest was Drew, who lived two doors down and had the best skills and the most powerful slap shot (even with a tennis ball). I loved playing hockey during those years. The best part was that there were no egos, no fighting, no name calling, and no bullies. We were just boys (and sometimes girls) spending our energy on a sport that was fun and provided us with a platform for teamwork and celebration. I still cringe when I see NHL players yelling at each other and using flagrant violence as part of the game. I support intensity and competitiveness but not when it goes beyond respecting one another. It is a big reason why I have not really watched professional hockey very much for over twenty-five years, except for the playoffs when the Habs or the Leafs are competing.

The other great sport in Canada that is played by hundreds of thousands of kids every summer but does not have television or decent media coverage is soccer. Like today, there were leagues of all ages everywhere back then, and it was by far the most popular organized summer activity in the country (it still is). I started playing at a young age in Candiac and kept it going until my teenage years. Most hilarious was that my dad, who knew nothing about the sport, was our first coach. Sometimes he would arrive at the field in his suit directly from work and lead all of us into something that looked like soccer. After those unstructured early years, we began to have formal practices, competitive games twice a week, tournaments on some weekends, and best of all, a year-end festival with food and games. Being on a team was great since I did not play organized hockey. It was the only real structured sport that I participated in. I made some great friends and was blessed to have solid coaches, especially in Mississauga. Though I never made the rep team, it was still competitive within the house league, and I learned technical skills with good sportsmanship and respect for my opponents and teammates. Although I played soccer for almost ten years, I was a very average player. Unlike racket sports, which I mastered, I found myself mostly running around without ever scoring more than one or two goals per season (sometimes none). My strategy was simple: kick it out of bounds when in trouble on defence and pass it to a wing as fast as possible when on offence. I never missed a game or a practice unless I was away for a family vacation or Scout camp. Looking back now, I must have learned a few things because I was asked to keep coaching year after year when my daughters played house league. The parents said I was enthusiastic and fair with all the players.

The first time I put my hands on a racket was on the outdoor tennis courts in Candiac. Mom had started playing the sport regularly and decided (wisely) that her sons should take it up in the midst of our already active schedule, which included soccer, swimming, and cycling. She purchased junior rackets and a couple of sleeves of balls before signing us up for lessons at the Haendel Community Park, located less than a kilometre from our primary school, Saint-Marc. It was the park where we also had our swimming lessons and where my parents had their infamous badminton parties. The tennis lessons were in large groups with kids divided based on their skill level. I was relegated to the beginner cohort but improved at a good pace with the help of my mom, who supplemented the lessons with regular visits to the courts on other days. My mother was a great tennis player and hit the ball hard and flat. Her ability to power into a ball and return it with a precise shot only inches above the net impressed me throughout her playing years, which extended well into her forties. I recall in those first few years how I would hit the ball to her, only to have it come back to me instantly. I don't think I ever beat her in a match. Tennis became one of my favourite sports. I perfected an effective yet simple game, emulating my mother with mostly a flat forehand and a one-hand grip on my backhand (with a slight top spin). Apparently, I had a pretty good style and ease because when we were playing in Florida during a vacation in Isla del Sol near Saint Petersburg, a pro came over and asked if I had ever thought about playing junior pro. Steve laughed openly!

I expanded my repertoire into badminton a little after starting tennis and also ventured into the tough game of squash during high school. That's because one of my best friends at that time, Mark Ducharme, was playing semi-pro as a junior star in Canada. He is over six feet tall with no fat on his body and arms that extend to allow for an above-average reach. His ginger hair and kind smile fooled his opponents into thinking he would be an easy competitor . . . wrong. Mark is talented at all racket sports (tennis included). He has won dozens of squash tournaments, won the exclusive Ontario Federation of School Athletic Associations (OFSAA) singles in tennis and badminton during high school, and continues to play squash at a highly competitive level into his fifties. But for me it was badminton that became my passion. The badminton club I left in Candiac was immediately replaced with the excellent Erindale Club, which gathered on Saturday mornings at Erindale High School from September to May. The club was extremely well run, with semi-pros teaching the kids for the first sixty minutes, followed by competitive games for the next ninety minutes. We were ranked each week based on our wins and moved up or down the ladder, which included close to fifty kids from ages seven to eighteen. The weekly competition prepared me for the high school team and the OFSAA championships in grades eleven and twelve. I played on the Loyola team and qualified for singles and mixed doubles. During my grade twelve year, I got beat pretty badly in the first round of singles but made a good run in mixed doubles with my strong partner, Andjela. She was tall and fit with dark hair and superior agility when moving from side to side. Her precision on serves and drop shots always took our opponents by surprise. Andjela never feared the smashes from the opposing team even if they were frequently directed at her. Sometimes I had to approach the net during matches to warn the opposing male player that continuously smashing at her was not cool. She carried us into a few wins and eventual elimination at OFSAA, but we left with our heads held high.

I didn't use my rackets much in my twenties, apart from a match here and there with a friend. I've continued to play a bit of tennis, but I have mostly enjoyed hitting the ball with my daughters on the local outdoor courts over the last couple of years. I think I've officially retired from squash given that I have not stepped onto a court in more than a decade. Luckily, badminton has come back into my life with weekly competition against Mark (yes, my lifelong racket partner!) and other adults at courts nearby. Those who play racket sports know that to remain competitive requires strong, healthy knees, back, and arms. The feared tennis elbow is a real risk for most in their forties and fifties; therefore, many people slow it down to save their body from serious injury. I've decided that I will be cautious, but once I'm on the court, there's no slowing down my fierce competitive spirit. Just recently Mark and I looked at each other after ninety minutes of badminton and laughed. "That was a lot of work," I said, followed quickly by, "And it was great!" If I get hurt, so be it!

***

My brother's presence during my childhood was constant. Steve and I had the unique and rare benefit of having a friend the same age living in the same house, eating the same food, having the same parents, and looking exactly the same. In those years we never gave it a second thought. It was not like we thought, *I'm tired of this guy. I'm going to go find a new friend* or *He's changed recently, and I don't like his new attitude.*

Interestingly, we also never gave it a second thought that we were identical twins until someone reminded us of it or made a comment like, "Wow you guys look the same" or "As a twin, do you know what the other is always thinking?"

Let me address this last question—and I consider myself an expert on this topic. There is no such thing as being able to read another person's mind, feel the same emotions, or know what the other is thinking by just looking at him or her. If you happen to have those talents, it is most likely not because you are a twin but because you have developed something beyond my understanding. There is no cosmic power or magical psychological connection that exists between twins. This is a complete myth, and those who claim to have it are making it up! What does exist is a deep knowledge and understanding of the other person. This develops over many years just like it does for someone who has a spouse or partner of many years, a close brother or sister, or even a dear friendship that has lasted for decades. The level of closeness and time spent together are the variables that define the extent of "knowing what the other is thinking." As we grew out of childhood and into our teenage years, an additional force captured our imagination: autonomy.

CHAPTER 7
FIRST ESCAPES

Receiving a Scouts badge of merit during one of our camping trips, circa 1981.
From left to right: Me, Michel, Jacques and Diane Belisle, and François.

"A twenty-four-hour survival adventure to the top of the mountain will occur this year as part of the annual one-week camping trip," Jacques said. "You will be bringing only matches, a sleeping bag, dry food, your walking stick, rope, a small tarp, and a compass. Everything needs to fit into your backpack, which you will carry. No tent!"

At that moment I realized that adventures from then on would be much more than the bike rides or hikes in the woods near my suburban home. I also soon discovered that *real* adventures would become a driving force in my life. I was eleven years old.

Jacques Belisle was our Scout leader, and he made this statement as we began to plan our summer camping trip, which would take place north of the Gatineau Hills in Quebec. He was the most informed person about nature, survival, and the environment that I knew. It was amazing the things he would teach us and how he had an immense respect for animals and the bush that surrounded and protected them. In 1981, he was well ahead of his time on environmental issues. Best of all, he was the dad of one of my best friends in grade six, François, whom we nicknamed "Çois" (pronounced "Swa"). Our friendship took off at the start of my first full school year at René Lamoureux, where I was becoming a bit more confident after almost a full year since our move from Montréal. Like me, François enjoyed playing sports, was very active, and especially liked discovering things. It's because of him that I joined the Boy Scouts. I had no knowledge of this organization or what they did or stood for until he started telling me about it during breaks in class and at recess. One day in September when we were chatting, he asked if I'd like to come to the meeting on Monday night to see if I liked it. "No pressure, just come and check it out," he said.

Steve laughed at me when I mentioned it to the family during dinner. He was quick to judge on anything that was not sports related or considered cool. This did not discourage me from at least trying it out. As always, my parents were very supportive and offered to drive me. The following Monday, I was dropped off at the front doors of my school (the Mississauga French Scouts Troop held their meetings there), and I made my way down the hall to the staff lunchroom where I was greeted by François with a big smile. He introduced me to some of the boys who had arrived and, more importantly, to his dad, Jacques, and mom, Diane, who were the leaders. Only later did I appreciate why having both parents participate made sense given all the planning that was required and the time away from home.

The first hour of that first meeting with that new group of young boys was brutal. The Scouts movement has certain traditions and formalities that take place at every meeting, and it felt like a board of directors meeting (I also know first-hand how those can also be dry). I was seriously reconsidering my decision as I looked around the table and stared at the posters and newsletters on the walls, which were targeted at the teachers of my school who spent breaks and lunches on those stiff metal chairs. I don't recall any of what was said or if I even spoke a word for the first seventy-five minutes of that gathering. I was quietly planning my exit. Then Jacques said it was time to close the meeting and start the activity.

"What activity?" I quietly asked François.

"Tonight it's sports!" he replied.

"Really? Awesome!"

Given my love of sports and my above-average athletic abilities, I was excited as we made our way to the gym. The best part was that this was not gym class with structure and a teacher telling us what to do; we could play anything. The next thirty minutes was an intense game of dodgeball, which was enough for me to accept the other boring rituals and join. I learned later that not all activities were sports. They included a mixture of discoveries on nearby nature trails, lessons on survival in the forest, and my favourite, scavenger hunts.

Jacques and Diane Belisle were the reason for that group's success. They were so nice to the boys, and they had a way of managing our energy and early teenage behaviours so that we focused on the right things. There was no yelling, intimidation, playing favourites, or any of the horrible sexual comments or incidents that have, unfortunately, scarred many youth clubs since then. Jacques's focus was on teaching us about nature and how to use it responsibly while respecting everything around us for a better world. We were encouraged to help others (do a good deed each day) and work well with people to accomplish tasks. The discipline and respect came naturally through the routine and structure of the weekly meetings. The other part of what Jacques included, which also made me stay for six years, was camping—real camping. We had two weekend camping trips in the fall, one during the winter, two in the spring, and a full week at the start of every summer. It was during the planning of that first summer camping trip that I found out I had to survive for twenty-four hours in the woods.

The Awacamenj Mino campground measures seven hundred and fifty acres, and nearly two kilometres of its territory borders the waters of Lac de

L'Île, Quebec. This location, where I attended my first one-week camping trip, was founded in 1955 and is located about sixty minutes north of Ottawa, just west of the town of Low. The name of the camp is an Algonquin term meaning "Better than the Better." It is located on the territory of the Omàmìwininìwag (Algonquin) First Nation. It was and still is a secluded oasis of deep nature full of wildlife and vegetation. The lake is deep and pure, with its dark water only warming up to a suitable temperature in July and August once the sun is high in the sky for more than eight hours per day. Another endearing feature of this peaceful place are the blackflies and mosquitoes, which are usually in full force and very hungry by the end of June. The larger and more damaging horseflies come a little later and feed off the campers during the hot summer weeks. Suffice to say that you obtain the complete package of real camping when you stay at Awacamenj Mino.

After completing five weekend camping trips in my first year as a Scout, I was quite confident in my abilities to take on the challenge of a full-blown week of camping without power, a proper shower, or air conditioning to keep my seasonal allergies under control. The camp's location also made for a long trip of over six hours from Mississauga along Highway 401, then north to Ottawa on Highway 105. Part of the planning was a robust fundraising program that lasted all year so that we could make the trip without having to request big money from our parents. Even though our fundraising provided for everyone, not everyone attended since it was a full week away from home. Some did not attend for reasons of homesickness or parental insecurity, others because it did not align with their family's summer vacation plans. This left a bit more than half of the troop members to attend, which made it easier for the Belisle leaders to manage. The good part of this thinning out was that only the ones with a passion for adventure were joining the annual pinnacle. The core group of boys for the years I participated included François, Jacques, Michel, Stephane, Steve, and me (my brother joined the Scouts once he realized I was having a blast at the weekend camping trips).

Our transportation that year was an ancient passenger bus from what looked like the 1950s, which I think Mr. Belisle rented for a real bargain. It had no air conditioning, old torn-up seats, a standard transmission, and no bathroom. Its exterior colour was army grey. While our parents almost rescinded their agreement to send us away when they witnessed this wreck pull into the school parking lot that Saturday morning, we didn't mind at all since we were so excited about our upcoming week of freedom. It felt like a well-earned trip since our fundraising efforts were so effective. Back in those days we could make real cash selling chocolate bars, having people sponsor bikeathons, and collecting newspapers for recycling (a full container of newspapers could fetch around $500, so we did multiple collection days during the year). That morning we packed the inside of the bus so full that we had to sit in the front half, which was fine with me since it reduced my carsickness. Once on the road, we sang songs and played music until the hum of the road put a few of us to sleep in the afternoon heat and the wind of the late-June day. The overall travelling time was good, and we were on the last stretch, approaching McNichol Road, which led to the camp entrance, when the bus just stopped.

"Hold on, everyone. Let me see what has happened," the driver said. Seconds later, he came back inside, looking less confident. "Might be overheated," he said. "I'll try again in fifteen minutes."

Nothing could get it started. My excitement dropped immediately. I started to think how this could be the start of a bad week. As much as Diane and Jacques put on a good front, we were all a little disappointed and shaken as we waited outside with the bugs in the summer heat for hours until another bus came to rescue us. The redeeming factor was that when the bus did arrive, it was a new model with all the luxuries of a 1980s rock band tour bus—minus the booze, drugs, and girls!

With the drama of our travels behind us, we woke up the first morning to a beautiful day and finished the installation of our gear. Our campsite was secluded from others, and it felt like a spacious paradise. We had two larger beige canvas tents as sleeping quarters for the boys, one canvas tent for Diane and Jacques in their own private area, a kitchen tent with netting for food prep and dining, a storage tent, and finally, a small nylon tent near the kitchen/storage area for our cook. Yes, we had an older retired Scout leader whom Jacques admired who joined us for the trip and was put in charge of cooking in addition to supporting the leaders when they needed some down time. He was more than a cook; he told wonderful stories and taught us everything about the plants and mushrooms we could eat in the forest. Interestingly, he had a glass left eye, which he was very comfortable with. To impress us, he would remove it around the campfire at night as part of his stories.

It was my first experience seeing how fun a well-organized trip with the right people could be even without the comforts of home. Each day had a schedule and chores to complete. There were formal Scout customs and routines at the start and end of each day, which included raising and lowering the flag, praying, singing songs, and sharing about the most important moments. The critical part was focusing on the lessons and activities that would be tested later to earn points or merit badges. There were badges for fire starting, running obstacle courses, cooking, climbing, canoeing, swimming, and more. You name it, there was a badge for it, although the gold standard was the survival badge.

After four nights and three full days in our new environment, the group was humming along. Daily routines were all done with ease, our early morning swims and afternoon canoeing were close to perfection, and the fires at night were joyous with singing, laughter, and storytelling well into the late hours. As Wednesday morning arrived, it was time to prepare for the long-awaited survival adventure. The schedule for the next twenty-four hours was as follows:

1. Pack and prepare before lunchtime.
2. Have an early lunch made by the cook (maybe our last meal?).
3. Depart with gear and load the canoes.
4. Paddle across the lake, heading northeast to Black Bay at the bottom of Black Mountain.
5. Unload the canoes and store them along with our life jackets and paddles for the return trip.
6. Load our gear in our packs and climb to the mountaintop.
7. Prepare our individual cooking and sleeping areas.
8. Eat, sing, and sleep without a tent.
9. Have breakfast and descend back down the mountain.
10. Paddle back to camp.

To pass the test and get a badge, we had to do everything ourselves without help from anyone. We had to carry our gear, start a fire, make food, ration our clean water, sleep without a tent, and not get eaten alive by flies. I loved the challenge and the opportunity to do my own thing and show off my organizational skills. I've always been able to plan and execute as per instructions.

I'm also a good listener, which ensures I don't miss anything important. On that first afternoon, the physical demand of climbing the mountain (it was *big*) was more than I had expected. There were setbacks with regular slipping on wet rocks and roots, along with constant warfare with the flies, who were dive-bombing my sweating arms, neck, and head. I don't recall how long it took to reach the top, but it was a real challenge for sure. The most satisfying part was finding my little corner in the woods and laying my sleeping bag under the little tarp that I was able to fit into my backpack. It was an A-shape shelter held in the middle by a piece of wood, leaving both ends open to the elements—and the bugs. The ground was not flat, so it would be a bumpy night with no cushioning to protect my bones.

Things went perfectly until the first roar occurred. There are two types of roars that scare campers: the roar of a bear and the roar of thunder. On that Wednesday night at the top of Black Mountain, it was the latter that raised our eyebrows and created doubt in our hearts. Looking back now, it might have been better if it was the roar of a bear that we heard, so we could sing and chase it away.

The day and early evening had been calm and without wind but quite warm. I suspect the moisture had something to do with the first roar from the distance, then another and another. Just before dusk, a powerful thunderstorm with strong winds from the east hit us hard. We were all scared at first, but then we gathered in small clusters under the best tarps until the storm faded away. Like all summer thunderstorms, it was relatively short but the damage to our gear and little village of shelters was serious. The leaders quickly did a head count to ensure everyone was fine and realized without delay that all our sleeping bags were wet and that it would be difficult to restart our fires. Unbeknown to all of us, Jacques had an emergency walkie-talkie stored in his pack to reach the base camp in case of an emergency. After some chatter on the radio, he asked us to gather as he shared the news. "We are not able to stay due to the circumstances and our inability to provide safe overnight conditions. We're going to go back down, get in our canoes, and paddle back to camp for the night."

Immediately, we started back down the mountain, our way lit by a few flashlights. I remember that difficult descent mostly because Jacques had ordered us to grip a rope, which he held at the front and Diane held at the back, so none of us would get lost. He also decided to leave all the wet gear behind, which we would retrieve the next day.

Reaching the bottom of the mountain and seeing the calm waters of the lake was a relief that quickly turned into an incredible surprise. Once the tree cover was gone and we could see the night sky, we witnessed a wallpaper of bright stars. The storm clouds and wind had disappeared by the time we paddled back toward our base camp. Our heads turned upward constantly to witness the dozens of constellations that we had been studying over the last several months. There are no pictures of that evening, but I vividly recall the moment and the feeling of our canoe floating quietly. Escape.

We glided the canoes on the sandy shore next to the camp's swimming area, then climbed into the warm, dry blankets that the base camp staff had for us. Jacques had asked for help, which included snacks and water, but most thoughtful was the request for dry beds with sheets inside the main chalet since our sleeping bags were soaked at the top of the mountain. The special attention that Jacques displayed during those hours was exemplary and proof that all leaders in any industry, sport, or business can both challenge teams *and* care for them.

The Scout movement continued to be a passion for me well into my high school years. When I turned fourteen, I was too old for the Scouts, so I continued under the Venturer status until I turned sixteen. We continued to have seasonal camping trips each year along with the week-long summer camping adventures. After two years at Awacamenj Mino, we shifted to Ontario for the remaining years. We had the privilege of using the Haliburton Scout Reserve, which is the largest Scouts camp in Canada. With its twenty-two square kilometres and many lakes and islands, it is a mecca of nature and untouched beauty. It opened in 1947 and has been operated consistently by Scouts Canada ever since. The team runs a perfect operation, and with many lakeside campsites for troops to select, each year presents a new experience. We were lucky to utilize different lakeside sites for each of the years we went to Haliburton. Another unique aspect of the camp is that access to individual camping sites is only by canoe, with the help of a barge to bring initial supplies. It made for an epic week. Funnily enough, one year we experienced a thunderstorm that rivalled the one on Black Mountain a few years earlier. The wind blew all of our tents down, lighting hit close to the main kitchen tent while we were all hiding inside, and we got soaked! At least this time we were at our base camp and didn't have to descend a mountain. Discovering this area three hours north of Toronto was incredible and started me on many journeys of travel and adventure in north-central Ontario, including a multi-day canoe trip on the rivers of the legendary Algonquin Park in my midtwenties.

During my third year, the Greater Toronto French Scouts Council decided to redesign their logo and open a contest with all Boy Scouts in the association to design the next logo for years to come. I submitted my drawing and a few months later was honoured to have my design selected. It was a big deal, which included recognition by the executive committee, all troop leaders, parents, and of course, hundreds of boys. There was a big event with speeches and media, which I attended with pride. The new design would be represented widely, and a patch featuring the design was worn on the shirtsleeve of all Scouts in the Greater Toronto chapter. To this day it is the only formal recognition I have ever received for anything relating to art or drawing. I'm also proud to share that the logo and badge is still being used today.

During my fourth year in Scouts, the Belisle family relocated to Montréal. I missed them dearly, and it was never the same after their departure. Our next leader, Alain, took over with enthusiasm and was great with us. He was funny and respectful, vested in our success, and donated countless hours to making the group successful. Although the number of boys shrank to just six under his watch, we continued to respect the traditions and do many good deeds for people in the community. By then I knew the end was near, and the wonderful road of being in the Scouts soon ended without drama when our leader decided we were more interested in listening to music, talking about girls, and trying to sneak small quantities of booze into our camping gear instead of focusing on being Scouts. By then we were sixteen years old, driving ourselves to meetings and camping trips, and had no interest in fundraising. We agreed with our leader that it was time to move on. I still have the badges, awards, plaques, some supplies, and various pictures from that time. I'm thankful that François asked me to join and loved the experience.

***

The subway car bumped and squealed along the tracks as the lights flashed and dimmed along the eastbound line. There was something so very much Toronto about boarding the subway and letting it take me east, west, north, and south to the limits of what used to be defined as the outskirts of a relatively small capital city. These days the end of the subway lines barely touch the outer edges of the newer suburban cities and towns that define the Greater Toronto Area (GTA). The project to build the first subway line in Canada began in 1949. It was ambitious and represented an enormous effort of engineering expertise and construction discipline. The official opening of the Yonge line was in 1954, with the number of stations and lines continuously expanding for the next few decades. The Kipling station where my journey into the big city began opened in 1980. It was relatively new when I boarded it for the first time to attend my inaugural big arena rock concert. I was excited but also apprehensive since we rarely went into the depths of the city, where streets were full of specialty shops, restaurants, bars, and people. It was very different from the atmosphere that my quiet neighbourhood offered. Our family treks into the heart of Toronto since our arrival in 1979 were mainly to visit the main attractions and to bring our extended family to tourist landmarks when they visited from the province of Quebec. The regular spots included the CN Tower, Casa Loma, Centre Island, the Science Centre, and the Eaton Centre. This time was different. I was going without my parents and would return late in the evening after a night of loud music and visual amazement. Looking back, I should have been much more familiar with the city's downtown nightlife than I was. But life in suburbia kept me content and away from Hogtown during my early teenage years. It was an escape to the unknown nighttime mystery of downtown, far from the subdivisions I knew so well.

A large number of long-haired teenage boys in jeans and black leather jackets dominated the sidewalk on Yonge Street when we exited the subway station. Surprisingly, many young women with long hair, tight jeans, and concert T-shirts were also partaking in the event. It should have been no surprise to see so many since the star of the band I was about to see was an attractive (and super-talented) blond guitar player. The crowd was moving as a herd with anticipation and youthful energy, which made me feel part of the gang. There was one destination for this clan, and it was impossible to get lost as everyone channelled toward the legendary Maple Leaf Gardens. Located just east of Yonge Street at the corner of Carlton and Church Streets, it was home to the iconic Maple Leafs Hockey Club from 1931 (when the building was completed) until 1999. Along with the Forum in Montréal and Madison Square Garden in New York City, it stands as one of the most important hockey buildings in NHL history. After the Leafs moved to their new home in the financial district, the arena continued to be used for concerts and some sporting events. Other Toronto teams also used it until it was closed and fully renovated into a modern retail and commercial space. In addition to being a legendary sporting venue, it was a majestic place for music. Hundreds of epic concerts have occurred there, with some still remembered by artists as their pinnacle performances. Name any musical group or performer, from the Stones to Neil Diamond or to heavy metal bands like Black Sabbath, and they have performed there. Acts who were favourites of the Toronto music scene also sometimes performed multiple consecutive nights and set attendance records year after year. Like the Forum in Montréal, it was a structure with character.

So it was on that spring night that I found myself looking up at the massive building as I prepared to enter that temple of music concerts. As I approached the entrance, the large illuminated sign above the front doors announced in big letters "Triumph—with special guest Honeymoon Suite."

Entering the arena, I immediately felt transported into a new world. I kept looking at my ticket and the signs to make sure I was heading in the right direction.

"Concert shirts here! Programs!" was being heard from every direction.

I couldn't resist, and I had to buy a classic three-quarter-sleeve shirt with the logo of the latest album on the front and concert dates for Canada on the back. (I still have it. I know, I'm a geek!) Then finally I found the small tunnel that led to my seat. I couldn't stop looking at the stage, the monstrous lights, and the speakers. Nothing else mattered; I would finally see a live rock show.

Honeymoon Suite did a fine job and played songs that I knew pretty well. But I was a little puzzled since many people didn't pay attention, and the sound wasn't that great. It was during their performance that I started to smell a lot of different things. When the house lights came back on, the place had a massive cloud of smoke in the rafters. This was before smoking was banned in buildings, and the illegal stuff was tolerated by the ushers. A moment after Honeymoon Suite's equipment was whisked away, the house lights went off, and the crowd went wild.

As Rik Emmett hit the first notes on his guitar, we all stood in excitement. Then it happened: the full power of the massive sound and light show filled every inch of the place. It was so loud and bright; I had never seen or heard anything like it. The three guys from Triumph put on an incredibly energetic musical performance. In return, they received more than a hero's welcome from their hometown crowd. My emotional connection with the band and its music was more than I had anticipated. My focus was uninterrupted, my escape pure.

Although my ears rang for days afterward, I decided to repeat the experience as often as possible. That first concert was soon followed by ZZ Top, Rush, Kim Mitchell, Red Rider, Bruce Cockburn, Toto, and countless others.

***

The low water level created additional ripples and softened the sound of the rapids since the spring volume from the north had dissipated to a steady stream of warmer liquid. The canoe was laid gently upon the shallow shore on the northwest edge of Forge Park in Terra Cotta as three boys began to load their supplies with help from one of the fathers who had driven them there. The temperature was warm with a light wind and the water was clear in that section of the winding Credit River. It was a stark difference from the brown shadowy texture that the popular river adopted as it approached Lake Ontario. Straps and bungee cords were attached to the canoe's gunnels to hold the gear for the overnight paddle, which would include sleeping at a yet-to-be-determined location on an island or on the riverbank. It was the first such independent and unaccompanied adventure for the boys. Once our life jackets were clicked, François' dad, Jacques, addressed us. "Okay, boys, looks like you're ready. Good luck, and call me when you reach the big lake."

Before joining the Scouts, I had never imagined that I would paddle a canoe down a fast river full of rapids, wood, and rocks. I also never imagined that I would be excited about it! I don't recall if it was me, Steve, or François who had the daring idea to ask our parents if they would allow us to embark on such a wild adventure at thirteen years of age. Regardless, with some recent summer camps under our belts, we had the courage for anything involving water and forests. Our daily canoeing lessons at camp and structured technical practice, which was required to attain a steady control of this unruly method of transportation, gave us the confidence required. And our healthy level of innocence and lack of appreciation of the risks kept our excitement level high. What could possibly go wrong? Luckily for us, we had all the equipment needed between our own personal supplies and the gear from the Boy Scout troop, which was conveniently stored in the basement of François's home, including a tent, paddles, cookware, coolers, an axe, saw, ropes, life jackets, and of course, the canoe. Never to go anywhere without music, we also included in our survival gear an assortment of cassette tapes and Steve's large portable radio, which was secured with duct tape and rope to the canoe's bow. Our original highway for the next two days was (and continues to be) a fixture for anyone who has lived in the GTA and travelled to the west end of the core. The Credit River and its tributary streams are over fifteen hundred kilometres long as it flows through Orangeville, Halton, and Mississauga to Lake Ontario. Its original name was Missinnihe (Trusting Water), and it was used by the Indigenous people when they began fur trading to meet the expanding demand in Europe. The river flows through the territory of the Mississauga of the Credit First Nation. They were the first experts who travelled the river and respectfully cohabitated with the rich environment with great care. Interestingly, the English name comes from the time when French fur traders supplied goods "on credit." The French name, Rivière au Crédit, was later translated, and a formal trading post was established at the mouth of the river in Port Credit during the early eighteenth century. These days the river is mainly surrounded by urban housing developments, golf courses, and parks, and it's crossed by dozens of bridges. Salmon have had some difficult years there, but they continue to make their most important run each fall up the river with the hope of minimal disturbances from curious onlookers and fishing enthusiasts. Numerous bylaws and regulations have been implemented by environmentally minded politicians over the last forty years to protect this important natural treasure. It has become a respected asset within a highly populated area.

Back in the early 1980s, neither me nor my two paddling partners had any appreciation for the significance of the waterway we were about to tackle.

As we waved goodbye to Jacques and turned up the volume to our favourite song, we were thrilled.

The first few hours of the journey were calm and without any real portages or important rapids to challenge us. We paddled with care and avoided the rocks that were visible due to the lower water level. The river was calm, and we never saw anyone else on the water for the entire journey. Although it was not our initial purpose, the sense of abandonment and natural escape overtook us.

Lunch was on the shore where we found an opening for the canoe. We relaxed and even went for a swim before heading back out. The number of bridges we went under and the noise of passing cars surprised me later that afternoon. Since we were moving through the edges of Georgetown, Norval, Huttonville, and north Brampton, many roads followed the river, and there were several old bridges to manoeuvre around. If it had been spring, we would have had to portage because there would have been no way our canoe could have been able to pass beneath the bridges. I was also surprised that so much of the river was in wide-open farmlands or open spaces. My assumption was that we would be in the woods with trees overhanging the river and providing us much-needed shade, but that was only in a few areas, mostly when the rapids were more pronounced. The need to paddle constantly was also something we did not expect. There were long kilometres requiring good rhythm to advance to our destination and avoid being pulled into distributaries and dead ends.

The moment that defined our first afternoon was crossing under the mighty Highway 401. The cement structure was huge, much higher than it seems when driving on top at a hundred kilometres per hour. It was also very noisy, so we decided to get as far as we could from the constant humming of engines and tires for our overnight campsite.

The highway was in the distance once we identified an island in the middle of the river. It was perfect, as it would give us natural protection from larger animals and any troublemakers who might want to scare or bully us during the night. We did not want to have to deal with older teenagers or adults finding us and giving us a tough time, scared little boys that we were! There were no trees of any size on the island, but the grass had grown high, and we needed to flatten the location for our tent and find an open area for our fire. Since it was warm, we only needed the fire for cooking. Once our camp was established, we swam and then prepared our dinner as evening took the sunshine away. We quickly learned that an attack was not going to come from humans or animals but from bugs! That evening was one of the worst ever for me. All types of small and large flying creatures decided that we were the best thing they had seen in weeks. The heat of the day intensified the volume of bugs that roamed the river. By the time we realized our war would not be won, it was too late to pack up and find a better location on the shore of a park or an established campsite. Our only option was to lock ourselves in the tent, kill all the bugs inside, and try to sleep despite the heat. That night we failed on all three fronts!

Day two started as soon as the sun hit our tent. The heat level inside rose within minutes. The bugs were still swarming outside, so all we did was pack up as best as we could and then get on the water for relief. We ate breakfast in the canoe. What had been a relatively calm river with minimal dangerous rapids on day one turned into a full-on affair of paddling through heavier rapids and portaging the canoe hundreds of metres in the water due to shallow areas. If you have looked down at the river while crossing the large bridges of Eglinton, Highway 403, and Dundas, you will notice significant rapids. Our movement was also much faster on the second day as the rapids carried us without a need for constant paddling.

Our early lunch was basic and mostly involved dry goods, which we ate in the canoe. By midday our minds were focused not on canoeing but on getting home, which is probably why an unfortunate event happened.

As we passed under the Dundas St. bridge, we floated past the large sand dunes on the southwest side and let ourselves ride the wave and relax into the final stretch to Lakeshore Boul. It was all going well until we hit a large rock and capsized. It happened so fast that none of us saw the rock beforehand. Instantly, all three of us were floating in our life jackets as we watched our gear (along with Steve's radio) travel along with the sinking canoe as it made its way down the lower section where the water was calmer. Luckily, we were not hurt, but our pride was bruised, and we were angry that we had let such a thing happen during the last kilometres of our trip. Now we had to repack everything in the canoe to finish our journey, and without music!

I remember looking around as we settled back into the canoe, realizing we were in the section of the river that is surrounded by two private golf courses. The members at the Credit Valley and Mississauga Golf and Country Clubs had surely witnessed our plunge and would have had a good story to tell their friends and families after their round that day!

Once we arrived at our destination, wet and tired, we called Jacques at a payphone next to Lakeshore Boulevard, and within an hour he arrived to hear our stories. He laughed for a long time when he heard our response to his question of, "Why are you guys so wet?"

CHAPTER 8
INDEPENDENCE

I'm ready for my high school graduation party.
Mississauga, 1987.

"What are you planning for school next year? You should go to university. You've been very good in this accounting class."

This recommendation in late spring of 1987 changed my life. I was packing up my books at the end of class when my high school business teacher, Mr. Yarema, decided to give me a nudge. I can still hear his tone and picture his slow walk toward me as he said it and the look he gave me to emphasize his words.

Loyola Catholic High School in the 1980s was a large two-storey building with multiple portables in the Erin Mills neighbourhood of Mississauga, just a short walk from the South Common Mall at Burnhamthorpe and Erin Mills Parkway. My first visits to the English-only secondary school were a few years before grade nine when I attended French grade school and we had an exchange program with Loyola that allowed grade seven and eight kids to take a class in arts or mechanics or woodworking. Since René Lamoureux was small, it had a limited curriculum outside the core requirements, so this was a chance to learn more things and experience another facility. Along with my mates Steve Frappier and François Belisle, I decided it would be cool to take home economics and sewing. All the other boys did shop class. The three of us loved it and enjoyed learning important family skills and, of course, hanging around with all the girls. Loyola had great teachers and was a relatively new school with big hallways, clean classrooms, and a full-service cafeteria. The other advantage of that high school was that it was only a ten-minute walk from my house. Without forcing it, the regular visits during those two years planted an idea in me. Maybe it was time to leave the French system, eliminate the long bus rides (which would have been almost one hour each way to attend the only public French high school, Étienne Brulé, in York Mills), and jump into a new path. Once again, with support from mom and dad, in the late spring of 1983 I decided to attend high school at Loyola. The difference this time, apart from the obvious language differences and an entirely new group of students, was that Steve was not going to be with me. He decided to stay in the French system with everyone we knew and make the long daily travels for the next five years. For the first time, I would be alone.

Interestingly, I was not the only one to notice this new high school on the western edge of the GTA. Some of my classmates had similar impressions of Loyola and made the same decision. What I was foreseeing as a very painful entry into high school without my brother or any friends (apart from a handful of local soccer team acquaintances) suddenly became much less stressful. The first to disclose his choice was François. He was one of my best friends and my partner in the Scouts, so I was thrilled that he would be with me. We stuck to each other for that first year and shared a few classes, but most critical, he was my regular lunch buddy. Second was Richard. He was the toughest guy in grade school and always wore jeans and a rock T-shirt wrapped in a leather or jean jacket. His jackets had studs or large patches on the back with a picture of one of his favourite heavy metal bands. He had had long black hair and a moustache since grade six. I always liked him and respected his fashion choices, and our shared love of heavy rock created a strong bond. I was glad to have him as a close friend going into a new school. Truth be told, right away I made sure everyone knew he was in my court. I even made acquaintances with the rocker gang he joined at Loyola and would have lunch with them in the cafeteria from time to time. My strategy of inclusiveness worked, as I never got into a fight or was bullied since everyone knew that gang would avenge me. Richard was a tough guy and did not have it easy as one of the youngest kids in a difficult family. But he worked hard and graduated from high school with pride.

Third was Mark Ducharme. He was a great classmate, and we shared our passion for sports from the first day I met him in grade five. Mark was the most social and adventurous of the four of us, and he opened doors to new relationships and participation in extracurricular activities. He was and still is the ultimate athlete who played all sports and joined as many teams as possible. Everyone wanted him on their team, and teachers would recruit him to ensure success. Our relationship grew during high school, and I still play golf and badminton with him. With this core group of friends and some positive soccer teammates who opened doors for me, I was set for a good transition to high school.

When Mr. Yarema approached me in 1987, I had no clue that teachers had superpowers. His intent was true and well timed. He made me reconsider my decision to attend community college after grade twelve. Instead, I signed up for grade thirteen and obtained the credits required to apply to business school at a Canadian university. I can only imagine how many hundreds of other students were guided to a successful career path by thoughtful teachers like him. I frequently think about the importance of belief in people and sharing with an individual how you feel about their talent or any other aspect of who they are that makes them special. Many people think about it, and some of them share their observations with a partner or friend, but few tell the person directly. In life, you can choose to be a multiplier, a diminisher, or a bystander. If you stay quiet and indifferent, you will be an invisible bystander and won't make a noticeable impact on others. Diminishers give negative feedback, are never satisfied, and think that if they tell someone they are special, it will go to their heads and contribute to an inflated ego along with possible lower performance in the future. I keep diminishers out of my life unless required due to family or other connections. The multipliers believe in others, encourage them, and celebrate their successes. They help drive others to greater accomplishments and elation in life.

I was lucky to have a few multipliers in the Loyola faculty during my five years there who had a big influence on my success and career path. Mrs. Warthall and Mrs. Walsh were fantastic English teachers who helped me get my English grammar rules in order and write to a strong proficiency. Mr. Clancy came along in grade thirteen and used a hyped-up approach to engage us and bring our writing structure and discovery of the English language to a higher level. I made a step change in that class with Mr. Clancy. The mathematics wizards, Mr. Mercurio and Miss Ermellini, kept my natural number skills at the top of the class. Mr. Wright dictated his way through each class, but the repetitiveness made me learn all I needed about geography (I still adore maps and travelling). Lastly, our business teachers, Mr. Stack and Mr. Lajoie, prepared me for a relatively easy first year of my bachelor of commerce (BComm) degree. Teachers don't need to say it every day, but a proper word or a well-timed piece of advice can change a life for the better. I'm living proof!

Today I'm surrounded by high school teachers. My wife, Linda, was the only woman in the math department at the tough Westwood High School in Malton. She still tutors students in mathematics and loves it. My great friend, Rémi, is a teacher and now holds senior roles with the Ontario Francophone Teachers Union (AEFO), having served as president in the late 2010s. My close friends Marc, Harold, Ron, and Sylvain recently retired after exemplary careers as teachers, positively influencing thousands of kids in academics and sports. Linda's close friend, Andrea, is still teaching in Milton after more than thirty years dedicated to getting the best out of students. I could go on.

***

Constant pain; monitoring of dietary intake; abdominal symptoms; weekly visits to health centres; endless tests; long stays in the hospital; extended time away from school, friends, and drumming; unimaginable weight loss . . . survival.

Darren Leigh is one of the most courageous individuals I have ever known, and I was lucky enough to have him as a close friend during my teenage years. His disclosure to me in 1984 that he had leukemia was shocking. I was not educated about any serious illnesses at the time, mostly because I had been lucky enough not to have anyone close to me experience such a thing. But when he explained that it was a serious type of cancer, his mom beside him with tears rolling down her cheeks, I realized he was entering a scary period. I didn't know what to do or how to respond to this situation, which was impacting my board game and music buddy. I would play dozens of hours of Risk or Monopoly with him each month. Even my dad and Steve joined our marathon games during the winter on Saturday and Sunday afternoons. The games took place on the dining room tables of our houses, with the addition of special "custom" rules, which made the games last for hours. As if those games aren't long enough already with the standard rules! If a board game was not happening on a certain day, it was all about his drumming and the love for music that we shared. In fact, he's responsible for Steve becoming a drummer. He introduced Steve to the instrument and gave him his first lessons. Steve still talks about how Darren helped him with his technique. "He used to make cymbal, drum, and hi-hat sounds with his mouth while coaching me. Psst! Ticchh! Splash! Boom! His love of drums was contagious."

Darren and I met while walking on the trail in a nearby park on our way to Loyola. He lived on a crescent two streets away from our place, so we would run into one another whenever we walked to or from school using the adjoining trails. The ten-minute walk was mostly alone for me in grade nine, so when I noticed this tall guy with longer hair walking the same route day after day, I made the first move and greeted him with a simple "Hey."

Our friendship started with conversations about music (not board games since it was not cool to admit you liked that stuff in high school—it remained our little secret). My first visit to his house after school one day turned me on to Don Henley and the album *Building the Perfect Beast*. His older brother, Darryl, would blast that album and the hit song "Boys of Summer" continuously from his basement stereo system. (Funnily enough, it is one of my wife's favourite songs of all time!) Darren showed me his drum kit and pounded on it with a bluesy approach while we listened to some tunes in an attempt to drown out his brother. He never mentioned his dad and was being raised by a single mom who worked two or more jobs to keep a roof over the boys' heads. I never saw her much during my visits over the years, but when she was home, she was usually sitting at the kitchen table eating something and having a smoke. It was very different from my traditional family lifestyle, and it made me really appreciate for the first time what so many single parents sacrifice for their families.

Since Darren's cancer diagnosis occurred within the first year of our friendship, I only knew his family a little, which made it difficult to help or know what to say during his treatment. My mom said, "Be present, and treat him like before."

That is what I did. I visited him frequently when he had long stays in hospital and brought him new cassette tapes of music I thought he might like. He was always listening to music, using his small cassette player with headphones when he was in the hospital. He continued to come over to our house to play board games when he had enough energy. I visited him regularly at home, and we'd do what we had always done: play drums, music, and games and watch music videos.

As things got more serious and the treatments started to take a toll on him, he decided to live full-time in the basement where he could have easy access to a bed, TV, stereo, bathroom, and his drum kit. The decline in his health included physical changes like full hair loss and weight loss (followed by bloating), which was noticeable at every visit. To my amazement, his mom and brother went through similar changes in weight, attitude, and general health. The stress of Darren's illness caused side effects in them that I still have difficulty comprehending today. What I do know is that he was fighting for his life, and they were fighting to stay positive and keep working to pay the bills. From the time I first met his mom to when he finished his battle with cancer, she looked ten years older even though only two years had passed. It was a lesson in unconditional love. It gives you elation, but it can also give you misery.

Months into his ordeal, Steve and I did not think Darren was going to make it. He was no longer able to keep food down, he was skin and bones, and he had lost all of his hair. He never left the house apart from hospital visits, and he spent all of his time watching movies and music videos and listening to music. Even our regular board games became challenging as we adjusted the format and played on the little table next to the couch in the basement. I would call him before my visits and then enter the house through the side door and make my way downstairs to his "cancer cave." If his mom was home, she would peep out of the kitchen to say hi and chat for a second (mostly ending with tears in her eyes). For several weeks, our friendship consisted of these little visits. The most difficult part for me to witness was his constant need to excuse himself, go to the bathroom, and vomit bile. There was nothing in him to throw up, as the treatments were so wicked that his body could only respond in this instinctive manner. At first when it happened, I asked if I should leave, but he just smiled and asked me to stay. I don't know if it was a power to defy the illness or just a conviction to survive, but Darren was never negative or remorseful about what had attacked his body and caused him so much pain. He was always smiling and excited to see me and never declined an offer to do something, even if his body caused frequent interruptions. Someone once said you shouldn't allow an illness to define who you are, and Darren lived by that principle. Eventually, the lows turned into a few highs, and hope began to build. The doctors who had prescribed the strongest treatments that his young body could handle are to be thanked for his triumph over leukemia.

Darren's great laugh and his love for jokes and tricks is another thing I adored about him. The jokes were so lame sometimes that it was funny to laugh together at the outcome of the response versus the joke itself. The culmination of his positive attitude and courage was demonstrated to me and every other student at Loyola on a morning in 1985. The school administration had followed his journey, and many of the students knew him or at least were aware that one of our own was battling cancer. Darren was also aware that kids would be very curious to see his physical condition (mainly his lack of hair) when he finally returned to school. I had seen the full transformation and had told him as a joke that the end state of no hair was pretty much the best he had looked in over a year (he never wanted to cut or shave his long hair during the hair loss period, so he looked similar to Gollum from *Lord of the Rings* for a few months).

As I entered the school that morning and made my way down the hallway toward my locker on the main floor, I noticed that the kids were louder than usual. It was also evident that something was happening at the end of the long hallway. Like everyone else, I was curious and continued walking past my locker until I finally witnessed the top of a large red clown wig above the crowd. Then I overheard one of the kids exclaim in a jubilant tone, "It's Darren! He's back, and he is wearing a big red wig!"

I walked faster to see his big smile as he gave handshakes, high fives, and hugs to all the students around him. It was incredible.

***

There is a line in one of the most famous songs from the Canadian rock trio Triumph that I treasure and has helped define who I am: "I got the magic power of the music in me." It was written by Rik Emmett for the song "Magic Power." Those are simple ten words, but they deeply define what many are lucky enough to experience when music enters their soul. Having music in my life allowed me to fight all the negative thoughts and emotions that are part of every teen's life. It allowed me to win the battle with anyone who bullied me without the use of my fists. It allowed me to be elated when love was found and rescued me when love ended or disappeared. It also allowed me to rage against the world in my bedroom with the volume turned to maximum without hurting a soul. It opened doors to new friendships, helped me build an invincible positive attitude with all of the optimistic lyrics I have read, and enabled me to be open to all types of music without judgment. Music has also allowed me to be myself and act completely natural when the power ignites in me. Sometimes it has allowed me to shut out the world when needed. It has allowed me to celebrate with my closest friends and build an unbreakable bond with my daughters, and most of all, it has given me happiness.

It all started with the influence of my Grandpapa Demers and Grandmaman Hinse with their infectious love of songs and musical instruments. This was followed by my mother's habit of always having the radio on in the house. When I hear soft rock or pop songs from the 1970s and early 1980s, I can recall the lyrics because of her. For some reason music was never complete for me without the lyrics. I have always been able to remember lyrics to songs even after hearing them just a few times. The power of the lyrics and the melting of the singing into the melody is a combination I adore. It is likely why I have never been a big fan of jazz or classical music. All of my friends know that hardwired into my head are pretty much all the lyrics for any popular song from the 1980s and 100 percent of the lyrics of any song from my favourites, including Rush, Triumph, Supertramp, Tears for Fears, Bruce Cockburn, Richard Séguin, and many others. Never being a big reader (mainly because during my entire banking career I was reading work-related documents and either preparing or reviewing countless meeting slides), I used whatever free time I might have to learn the new lyrics to an album or to play back a classic. This has created a bias for me in the music I add to my playlist. If an artist or band doesn't write their own stuff, I don't listen with real enthusiasm. To me, a real musical talent is someone who writes the music and the lyrics—collaborations included. When my daughters introduce me to a new song or a new artist, they know the first question I will ask is, "Do they write their own stuff?" I like the power of music to be pure.

I got serious about music when I was ten years old. The only way to listen to music in the early 1980s was either the radio or by purchasing a cassette, vinyl record, or eight-track tape. I didn't have a lot of money at the time, so my main supply was from FM radio in Toronto. Q107 was the station that played the rock I liked, so we always tried to convince mom and dad to tune the car radio to that station. As always, they were willing to oblige, which made us very happy—and quiet. Later on, dad told us that he liked the station so much that he listened to it on the way to and from work. We were never a family that listened to talk radio or AM stations; it was all music all the time. To supplement my radio intake, I got my hands on a small portable cassette tape player just after my eleventh birthday. I don't remember if it was gifted to me or if dad got it from work (they had older equipment that he was sometimes able to take home instead of it being thrown out). Now let's be clear: this machine was not a stereo or anything that a real music lover would use to listen to the latest hits, but it was all I had, so I optimized that little unit. My first tactic was to record songs that I liked from live radio onto blank tapes, so I could listen to my favourite songs whenever I wanted. This involved tuning in at 10:00 p.m. for the "top ten at ten" and trying to time the start of the song so that the announcer's voice would be gone before I pressed the two little buttons to begin recording. This lasted for years since even in my teenage years it was pretty much impossible to have enough money to purchase all the albums I wanted. I would fill a tape with songs on both sides and listen on that little recorder with limited sound quality. But it was a start.

The first cassette I purchased was *Breakfast in America* by Supertramp. I would play it on my little tape recorder, in the car, which had a tape player, or on a friend's boombox. Don't judge me (I know I'm a music nerd), but I still have that original cassette tape in a box in my basement. It is tucked away with dozens of other cassettes that I purchased in the 1980s. My cassette collection includes classics such as *Pyromania* by Def Leppard, *Back in Black* by AC/DC (I think all teenage boys from my era had that one), *Just a Game* by Triumph, *Moving Pictures* by Rush, *The Song Remains the Same* by Led Zeppelin, and multiple others of the hard-rock genre. Eventually, I moved on to CDs, and I have that collection next to the cassettes. My addiction intensifies every time we relocate them from one room to another or I take them out to show friends or curious kids. Since people can now stream the entire collection of the world's music for about ten dollars per month, there is a belief that physical albums were cheap forty years ago . . . not! Most were between five to twelve dollars each (equivalent to over thirty dollars today). Unbelievably, the initial cost of my old music collection was almost more than I spent on my first used car!

I listen to music every day and have done so since age ten. For years when I had more free time, I would close my bedroom door and play albums as loud as the speakers would allow without breaking. It was especially deafening in our house after school and into the evenings when Steve and I would blast our favourites from within our individual bedrooms. It caused a few arguments when one of us became unreasonable with the volume, but mostly it was civilized. It is not Steve I should thank but my parents for their patience and understanding. They never told us to stop or discouraged me from enjoying music and singing at the top of my lungs (including heavy stuff like AC/DC and Iron Maiden, which must have seemed dark to them). Again, without my parents' open mind and support, music would not have become a critical outlet, and maybe other bad habits would have taken up my time. Later, they shared that they had decided it was better to endure and know where we were versus wondering when we would come home. This all-encompassing "noise" was amplified when Steve started playing the drums and practising for hours with his high school rock band. I would watch them and act as a critic. They played really well. It was awesome.

My listening evolved from that crappy recorder to high-quality head-phones, which the family appreciated since the noise was reduced—apart from my singing, of course. I'd pull the lyrics out of the cassette or CD case, so I could follow along and take in their full meaning. Some lyrics were pretty basic, but some were excellent and helped me expand my thinking and appreciation for strong writing. To this day I have never discovered lyrics more positive than the ones Rik Emmett wrote with Triumph. He is an elite guitar phenom, and he wrote lyrics with the intent of making listeners feel confident and optimistic. An equally important lyricist for me is Neil Peart of Rush. His writing was more than lyrics to a song. They were short stories, poems, and essays. More than the GOAT for drumming, he is a talented author who influenced my thinking and burgeoning writing skills. Lastly, I must mention Bruce Cockburn for his masterful song writing. The words and wisdom found in his hundreds of songs are often overlooked. People like Rik, Neil, and Bruce who are admired in the music industry have been able to combine their music with powerful words to deliver an experience of joy.

It is no surprise that once concerts were again open to large crowds in 2021, the number of acts performing and the demand from concertgoers exploded. People wanted to feel that joy again. I was lucky to participate in the great concert revival year by attending a Genesis show in Toronto. It was their final tour since Phil Collins's aging body is finally giving out on him. Incredibly, after the first two warm-up songs ended, he lifted the crowd with a powerful vocal performance of their hit song "Mama." It felt good to see him back on centre stage. Steve rightly pointed out at the end of the evening that Phil is probably one of the most successful and accomplished songwriters, drummers, and singers of the 1980s. Reflecting on this observation, I realized that Mr. Collins combined music and lyrics to epic levels on dozens of massive hits. To his credit, he has recently been mentioned by legendary musicians as one of the most influential drummers of all time. It is good to now see his son carrying the flame and acting as a strong ambassador for his dad.

***

The heritage of hard work from my dad and both grandfathers continued to the next Demers generation with my brother and me starting to work at jobs once we turned thirteen. It was never a question whether we would work; we wanted some financial independence as soon as possible. The first few jobs that supplied much-needed money for music cassettes and various supplies for Boy Scout camping trips included babysitting and grass cutting. I have always enjoyed working, and the innate motivation to get things done and accomplish tasks has been a constant throughout my professional career. I just like taking action. My first real job was with Pizza Pizza on Queen Street in Streetsville. It was (and still is) a small franchise located in the northwest neighbourhood of Mississauga. Back in the 1980s, the Pizza Pizza restaurant chain dominated the GTA. With their little radio jingle, the same phone number for all locations, and an innovative thirty-minute delivery guarantee (customers would get their order for free if it was late), they ruled the city streets with thousands of delivery drivers dressed in orange. Since I did not own a car when I turned sixteen and got my driver's licence weeks later, working as a delivery driver was not something I was considering as I headed into the summer after grade eleven. But that changed when we moved to our new home on Phoenix Park Crescent and a school friend named Donofrio (a.k.a. Dono) who lived a few streets away started giving me rides to and from school. He was a year older, had a car, and kept talking about his part-time job making deliveries on weeknights after school and late into the evenings on the weekends. "I'm making hundreds a week, man!" he would declare frequently. This claim of riches got my attention, so I agreed to shadow him on a short shift after school one evening.

My first impression was not good when I saw what Dono had to wear for the job. It included a bright orange baseball hat and jacket, black pants, a white collared shirt, and a black clip-on tie. They took pizza delivery seriously in those days! Dono had a four-door beige car that I think was a Ford Granada. He took excellent care of it, and it had a powerful stereo system.

As we pulled up behind the pizza shop, it was obvious that this was not a quiet operation given the number of delivery cars parked in the tight laneway waiting for the busy dinner period to start. Once inside, he introduced me to the other drivers, who were mostly men and much older than I had anticipated. These were fathers, husbands, wives, and a few older teenagers doing delivery to supplement their main income with a cash-paying tax-free part-time job. They were very nice, liked to tell stories and jokes, and loved to talk about cars. Brian was the owner and adored his new Corvette, which was always parked in the space directly in front of the store, so he could show it off and answer all the questions from customers about his little beauty. As the owner-operator, he was there every day, only taking time off during the afternoon between the lunch and dinner rushes. The place opened at 11:00 a.m. each day and closed after midnight, with extended hours to 3:00 a.m. on Friday and Saturday. Brian was mostly chill and loved having good tunes playing on the store stereo when customer traffic was slow. The entire crew operated like a professional sports team. When it was quiet, they could fool around like during practice, but when it got busy, it was time to perform to keep Brian happy and not give away orders by taking more than thirty minutes to arrive.

Once that first night of shadowing was complete and I witnessed that the "hundreds of dollars" was a real thing and not an exaggeration by my new job recruiter, Dono, I wanted to try it. The only way to do the job would be to borrow mom's four-door 1981 red Honda Accord, pay for the gas from my earnings, and maybe contribute to maintenance costs. The pay structure dictated by Brian was simple: $5.00/hour or $1.50 for each delivery, whichever was higher for the entire shift, paid in cash. On busy nights with longer shifts, if a driver completed over fifty deliveries, the $1.50 paid off nicely. Add to that the tips of plus or minus $1.00 per order, and Dono's math theorem proved correct. In the mid-1980s for a high school kid to make over $200 per week was exceptional.

The negotiations with my parents were not difficult since the Accord was five years old and dad was planning on replacing it soon. We made a deal that I could use it for delivery during school on a part-time basis and then review the situation for the summer months. Once again my biggest supporters provided the initial seed funding, and I took the job. Pizza delivery is great. You listen to your favourite music all night long, drive a car, which at sixteen years old is nothing but a joy, and hang out and chat with others when it's quiet. Brian kept us busy between deliveries with in-store chores like doing the dishes, mopping floors, kneading and cutting dough, and general food prep. On unexpectedly slow nights, he sent his least favourite drivers home early. I worked hard in the store, so I was usually retained for all of my scheduled shifts (unless I wanted to leave and volunteered to go home). Most of the delivery customers were nice with a few rude people here and there who didn't tip or who took forever to answer the door. It was an all-cash business back then, so I made sure not to carry more than $100 in small bills to discourage robbery or threats. The most important rule that was ingrained into my brain before my first shift was never to enter a home under any circumstances, especially between midnight and 3:00 a.m. There were no cell phones back then to call for help, so we were on our own out there. I was lucky never to have any incidents apart from drunks joking around or using foul language. I knew Brian would not tolerate any of his drivers not getting paid, and I witnessed him leaving the store a few times and returning to a delivery location with his driver to collect. He got his money every time! I had my share of late orders in the first few months because I got lost and didn't make it in thirty minutes. Brian tracked all departure times, so he knew which orders could be late based on distance, traffic, and his incredible knowledge of his territory. He made drivers pay for late orders that were their fault, so suffice to say I studied the map carefully (no GPS back then) until I could almost draw it in my head.

I delivered pizzas for two and a half years between grades eleven and thirteen. It provided me with good work experience and enough income to buy the Accord from my parents (at a discount), pay all car expenses, and fund all of my hobbies, including tons of music cassettes, concerts, and a most excellent Harman Kardon home stereo system. The number of shifts I requested after grade twelve was reduced by about half as I decided to get a job at a golf and country club to reduce wear and tear on the car. The golf club had me cut grass all day or sometimes drive the four-wheel mower for the greens on the weekends when the full-time crew took days off. Our shifts started at 7:00 a.m. on weekdays and 6:00 a.m. on Saturday and Sunday. I made $4.25 per hour, and I was at the bottom of the experience and seniority ladder, resulting in the worst tasks being assigned to me. I didn't care, though. I took it all in stride, never complained, and was happy to be outside all day for the few extended summer months that I worked there. Pizza delivery and golf course maintenance officially ended at the start of the summer before university when I got a generous referral to work in the Canada Packers (a.k.a. Maple Leaf Foods) factory in Toronto. I was so happy with the pay of $11.25/hour plus lots of overtime opportunities. My job was in the cook room with dozens of older and more experienced workers. Again, as a student I did anything they asked without complaint. I mostly did all the grunt dirty work, though I finished the summer replacing the hot dog production line operators for several weeks during their vacations. That was the hardest physical work I have ever done. I'll leave the details of what goes into hot dogs out of this book, but let me tell you that lifting racks with over a hundred and fifty raw sausages every two minutes is demanding. The guys who did it full-time were hard workers, and I respected them.

The lesson I took away from the different jobs I had during high school and into the summers of my university years (I did four consecutive summers at Canada Packers) was that you must stay in school for as long as possible to give yourself the best career options. I realized that the better my education, the more choices I would have during my lifetime to select work that fulfilled me. This is not a new revelation, and it is quite evident to most, but the time I spent in those positions doing hard work made it real for me and gave me the extra drive during university and later in my career to give it my best effort.

Looking back on my high school years, I wish I could have overcome my shyness toward girls and apprehensive traits in group settings. Steve was much more advanced and open than I was. It took the start of my final high school year for me to break out and leave behind my relatively quiet social network. Sure, I had big crushes on girls and took detours along the corridors at school to see them in the hopes that they would look my way and make the first move . . . as if! I talked to a few and sat at their table during lunch or attended the rare basement gathering in their presence, but I lacked the confidence to take things to the next level and take risks. I don't know what the risks really were since I had nothing to lose! In the end, maybe I have a strong resemblance to my Grandfather Hinse and his serious nature. It took him time to shed the layers and allow for emotions and vulnerability.

The most dominant impact on my life during high school was my new-found independence. My decision to go it alone by changing school systems and leaving my brother behind was critical in the building and moulding of our individual personalities. Our personal needs, priorities, emotional intelligence quotient, and approach to challenging situations grew differently and allowed us to be unique as identical twins. Interestingly, the separation for five years also deepened our dependency on each other, though in a mature way. Instead of depending on each other for playing games, doing sports, and going on adventures, we now needed each other to share difficult situations, ask for advice, and be there when the other was down. We also wanted to be together and have fun. (We still do!) Our independence never eliminated our closeness and love for each other. It is like our time apart as teenagers allowed us to better respect our differences and learn to appreciate the things that bring us together even more. Our core values continued to be as identical as our physical features. During high school we made a step change and elevated our friendship with each other beyond what I thought was possible as a young boy. Since then we have never had a fight or a serious argument, raised our voices at each other, or disputed each other's choices. We do keep each other in check, however, and we have a pact to always nudge the other if something isn't right.

CHAPTER 9

INSEPARABLE BROTHERS

My brothers. From left: Gil, me, Rémi, Steve (twin), and Frapps. August 2005. Group family vacation in Shediac, New Brunswick.

Steve woke early after a Labour Day long weekend that had been relatively quiet, spent at the house with our family. Being big tennis fans, we spent a lot of time in front of the tube watching our favourite tournament of the year, the US Open in NYC. As teenagers we never had any grand trips during the last weekend of the summer, and we tended to stay home, as on many other summer weekends. On that Tuesday, September 4, 1984, Steve woke up just after 6:00 a.m. to begin his second year of high school and the daily long-haul travel that took him to his high school, École Secondaire Étienne Brulé (EB) in the north end of central Toronto. The travel time was about one hour each way on a lucky day with a bus transfer in the middle of Mississauga at Square One. This was not with the public transit system but with the educational school system since he attended the only public French high school in the entire GTA.

After a quick shower, he threw on some jeans, a T-shirt, and his jean jacket, then walked out of the house and headed up our street to make it on time for the 6:55 a.m. bus at the intersection of Council Ring Drive. He had perfected the timing in grade nine and had the routine mastered with little time to spare, even down to his regular seat on the bus. Since not a lot of kids were going to EB from the western edge of Mississauga, it was a small minibus that picked him up, and he was usually alone for the first part of the ride, with other kids joining as they headed east. Many mornings he would rest and get some shuteye until he boarded the larger regular-size school bus and travelled the final leg to EB. It was a routine he disliked but endured to be able to attend EB, be with his friends, and get some freedom from suburbia. I thought after a few months of the gruelling regiment in grade nine, he would resign and join me at Loyola with the much shorter ten-minute walk, but he never did.

On that cool early September morning in 1984, he stood on the street corner just before 7:00 a.m. and turned his head to the left as he heard the rumble of the bus coming down the street. An insignificant greeting to the driver followed as he walked up the three steps and then made his way to his usual back-row seat. To his amazement as he looked left to the back of the bus, he saw two tough-looking older teenagers (almost men) taking up the full space of both seats without any inclination of moving. As shock and fear took hold, he took the first seat on the right without any salutation. There would be no sleeping on this morning ride. Little did he know that the teens were brothers and had recently relocated from Montréal just like he had five years earlier. The bigger of the two had short red hair (almost ginger), was fit and tall, and had shoulders the size of a linebacker. He did not look friendly, and his dark leather jacket completed the look of a tough hard rocker. His brother had no resemblance to him, with dark hair down to his upper shoulders, a slightly thinner frame, and a tight-fitting leather jacket. The redhead, Gilbert, was seventeen, and Rémi was sixteen when they relocated to Mississauga from Brossard on the south shore of Montréal. Although they had left five years after us, the exodus of talented business leaders from Montréal was continuing at an alarming rate. Their dad, André Sabourin, worked at Maple Leaf Foods and, like my father, needed to move or get out. Like many others, he and his wife, Nicole, made the hard decision, and along with Gilbert, Rémi, and their youngest son, Pascal, they moved the family of five to Ontario. They purchased a four-bedroom home on Council Ring Drive about two kilometres from our home and had the added luxury of a large above-ground pool, which was a critical negotiating tool to get the boys to accept the relocation.

Their July arrival made for a miserable summer without any friends or jobs to keep them busy. Music and sports kept them going until they could start at EB and hopefully find a few Quebecers to build a new gang. What they didn't know was that their size, clothing, and general façade projected an unwelcoming first impression for potential friends. However, the close confines of the minibus eventually encouraged Steve to listen to their conversation and build up the courage to talk to them. It was their shared love of music that initiated the first words, in particular an exchange on Rush's recently released album, *Grace Under Pressure*. They all adored that album, but when the Sabourin brothers told Steve that they had tickets to the concert at Maple Leaf Gardens, he was devastated.

How did these new guys get tickets? he wondered. *I must be a fool to not have tickets.*

The moment also proved to be a turning point in Steve recognizing that these two guys seemed to be on top of things, and sticking close to them might be rewarding! As they shared backgrounds and things they liked, they realized that road hockey was another shared passion. One day a few weeks after the start of school, Steve accepted an invite from Rémi and biked to their house with his hockey stick to play what he thought would be some light passes and shots. To his surprise, his new linemate had him strap on some "light" goalie gear, put him in net, and began taking wicked slap shots from the bottom of the driveway. A few hit the garage behind the net, but many hit Steve directly without him having the chance to move due to their speed. After almost an hour of this abuse, Steve had several bruises, and Rémi was having a great time. That night Steve could not stop talking about his time with his new friend and how good he was at hockey.

Within months Steve, Rémi, and Gil were inseparable. From 7:00 a.m. each weekday, the three of them would command and control the minibus and, subsequently, the larger bus once they expanded their friend group and became more confident. There was no more sleeping in the morning or resting on the way home. It was non-stop chatter, jokes, loud music, and the occasional addition of food and drinks, which were now the norm. Bus drivers scolded them, and they visited the principal's office periodically to be reminded of the rules, but there was no stopping teenagers locked up for over two hours per day in a stinky box. The stories from that period are remembered fondly, including the good (and sometimes bad) times they had with the other dozens of kids riding with them. The bond that was built during those hundreds of hours on the bus swelled into friendships outside of school. Since Rémi and Gil were older, they were in a grade higher than Steve, so it limited their time together during school hours, but they made up for it outside of school. The brothers also made friends with others at school and enjoyed an active social circle at EB. Since they had experienced a few active teenage years in Quebec where the legal age was eighteen (and very liberal at the time), their party habits were advanced compared to others. Suffice to say that it did not take long for the hundreds of kids at their new high school to discover who the newest Quebecer imports were.

Steve continued to grow his friendship with Gil and Rémi during grade ten as I watched from the sidelines and kept to my friends and routine without much interaction with them. I did enjoy that my best friend from grade school, Frapps, who was also attending EB, had begun to warm up to the new duo. There were informal gatherings, music listening, and other events that I started to attend with Steve and the EB guys later in grade twelve. It was great fun, and our shared love of sports and similar hard-rock bands was at the centre of our conversations. From the basement to the car to the parties to the lazy days by the pool, music was always playing. We also shared a love of humour right from the start. We attended parties where we would just focus on having fun and laughing with others. This created a safe, positive energy and attraction to us that others could not resist. I started to enjoy this new group of friends from EB, as it complemented my time with friends at Loyola. It also gave me more confidence and strength going into grade thirteen. I was gaining experience at social gatherings and becoming more of an extrovert in large groups. My special gift of having two distinct groups of friends with very different backgrounds was awesome. There was something refreshing in this new group that I had not felt before; we could just be ourselves.

Just when we were at a high with our new little gang, it was time for change with the end of high school for the Sabourin boys. Only two universities in Ontario offered extensive French programs, the University of Ottawa and Laurentian University in Sudbury. The boys were both accepted at Laurentian. After only two years in Toronto, they were going to move far away from home to a place they had never heard of before completing their post-secondary applications. Sudbury is a mining community and is essentially the "capital" of northern Ontario due to its relative proximity to Toronto and central location between the mid-size cities of North Bay, Sault Ste. Marie, and Timmins. It is the largest in the north with a population of about a hundred thousand. The rich cultures and diversity of the area since the early twentieth century are a result of Europeans relocating to find stable work and safety for their families. While Sudbury's economic engine spans different sectors, such as healthcare, education, and the service industry, it is a mining town at its core. It is impossible to avoid the numerous smoke-stacks, the dark mining buildings, and the sparse tree coverage.

By the time the brothers had decided to attend school four hundred kilo-metres away, all of the good places and residences were no longer available. With limited inventory available within their budget, their only option was to find a place close to the public transit routes. They eventually found a small one-bedroom apartment on the second floor of a wartime home in the old Donovan neighbourhood. That area of the city was established after WWII and inhabited mostly by Ukrainians, Poles, and Finns. Their strong culture and religious beliefs are still present today with Ukrainian churches and community centres active in the community. The Donovan neighbour-hood is separated by a railroad track and surrounded by rocks. There are almost no trees, and while it is a respected neighbourhood, it continues to struggle with violence and poverty. Back in the late 1980s when my friends made it their new temporary home, using the word "apartment" to describe their accommodations was generous since it was pretty much the attic of the home turned into a livable space. It had only one bedroom, a minuscule bathroom, a small sink and counter, and room for a couch that turned into a bed at night. I never visited them during their first year and was told that I did not miss a thing. Steve went once during the winter and was lucky to not have to stay there since they spent the weekend outside of town at a winter cabin. They developed a few new friendships that lasted throughout university but never really participated in any social activities during that first year since they had no money. Gil and Rémi have shared many times that it was probably the worst winter they ever had cooped up in that little place during a brutally cold first year of university. They went from kings in high school to minions almost overnight.

As the spring of 1987 appeared, I was finishing grade twelve, and our buddies in Sudbury were finishing their final exams and making their way back home for the summer break. We were elated to be together again and spent every available evening and weekend attending concerts, travelling to Quebec, relaxing by the pool, and attending house parties. By then it was becoming apparent to all of us that we were at our happiest state when we were together and able to share laughter and our passion for great music. The guys worked at Maple Leaf Foods on the evening shift, and Steve and I worked at our summer jobs. Therefore, our focus was always on planning the next weekend and maximizing pleasure before the dreaded month of September split us up again. My grade twelve graduation bash was a legendary event along with the EB Soirée des Étoiles (Talent Night) show in which Steve's band performed and Gil served as part of the technical crew. By then it was like I was going to two high schools and participating in all extracurricular activities that were available.

Our participation in the social scene was good, but the glue that held our little group together was composed of music and humour. These two ingredients cemented us as brothers from the start. We never knew when the magic of music or the elation of laughter would consume us. It was this unknown that acted like a magnet and pulled us together. Simply put, I always wanted to be with them, and I still feel the same today.

Once my final year of high school came around and our friends' second year in Sudbury started, it was very different from the year prior. First, the guys found a suitable apartment in a real building closer to the university, with hot water that never ran out. Second, Frapps decided not to attend grade thirteen, so my brother's circle at EB was reduced, and he started spending more time outside of school with Frapps, Charles, Danny, and the super-cool crowd from Oshawa. Third, Gil decided halfway through the year that he had had enough of university in Sudbury. He decided not to go back after Christmas and was accepted into the RCMP instead. Fourth, Steve's girlfriend, Josée, decided to take some time away from him, which left him alone and in tatters for most of grade thirteen. Finally, I went forward with my pledge to continue higher education and attend university once I finished grade thirteen. Time was moving fast, we all felt somewhat separated, and our unit fragmented after a period of inseparable friendship. Unbeknown to us, the fragments would be reunited soon enough.

It was during this transitional period that Frapps and I once again started to spend a lot of time together. He has been a constant in my life since that first day at René Lamoureux School and my brother for over forty years. In the first four years, we spent countless hours playing sports at school, having sleepovers at each other's homes, and making new friends. Actually, it was Frapps who was moving forward on the social scene in elementary school, with me tagging along in the shyest and most awkward way possible. He was generous when he was ten years old, and he is even more generous today. As an only child from a half-francophone family, his extroverted character and passion to bring people together made him the perfect contrast to me during our youth. I have recently assigned him the name of "rassembleur" (unifier). His network of friends and professional colleagues is endless. He enjoys nothing more than making people happy and having fun. Having no children of his own, he has adopted all the kids close to him as his nieces and nephews. Incredibly, they all refer to him as "Uncle." My daughters have been lucky recipients of his generous heart and have a unique bond with him.

Like my other brothers, he has had a great professional career. What is most impressive is his business acumen and relationship skills. He has a natural ability to engage others and the superior intelligence to bring about a positive outcome for complex opportunities or issues. Stringing together many career opportunities with different companies has kept him interested and highly successful. Sometimes out of nowhere he will ask me a question about a person or recommend a product that might be helpful for my work. It always surprises me that he even took time to think about it, let alone have the sharp mind to connect it to my business.

As we've grown older as a close group of five brothers, he has been more reflective on our journey and the significance of it. He's also just as funny as ever and the catalyst for many of our social pleasures. Rightly so, his focus is on continuing to have wonderful experiences at every turn. We've learned that simple things, simply planned, can be the most rewarding. From golf games to concerts to good food, we are lucky to have a magic state that allows for pleasure. There is no naïveté among us. This treasure is to be protected and may be lost one day, but for now we will participate.

The bond I developed with Gil, Rémi, and Frappier during those growing years is everlasting. While we have spent some years a bit more apart than others during our ongoing journeys of marriage and parenthood, the closeness and incredible fun we have when we're together has not diminished. Because of them I have never felt the need to seek out new best friends. No trades are required! My view is that I have the brothers I need, and I only want to grow with them while developing new friendships. We've all been blessed to have multiple great friends from different areas and backgrounds. For example, there are friends of Linda's whom I treasure and with whom I enjoy every minute. Now in our fifties we are so fortunate to have dozens of people as close friends. The cool thing is that many of these friendships overlap and complement each other as we grow older.

***

During the writing of this book, our little rock band, called "Up to 11," performed at the annual friends and family gathering just outside Ottawa in Clarence Creek. Our friends Rémi and Lesley Sabourin host this event called BouBou Fest. It is a gathering of my brothers with our extended families and friends. We first performed a few songs in 2018 as a surprise for Rémi's fiftieth birthday party. At the time we were not really a band, just six guys who decided we should pool our musical talents and give the best gift possible to our friend for his milestone birthday. Nothing would make him happier than to have his best buddies and two brothers play a few of his favourite rock songs. We selected a few tunes and worked ourselves through five songs with moderate success given that we had never really practised together before the actual day. The goal to surprise him was achieved, and something magical also happened for the musicians: we really enjoyed it!

Soon an agreement was reached to do it again, and a new band was created. The band members include Steve and Gil on drums (yes, we have two drummers), Pascal Sabourin on bass guitar, his son Maxime on lead guitar, Marc Fortin on rhythm guitar, and me as front man. Playing with other musicians and driving a song forward with energy for others to enjoy provides a feeling of elation. I felt that back in 2018 for the first time.

The 2022 edition of BouBou Fest occurred on July 30th. It was our fourth time playing as the "house band." We followed our inaugural show with another in 2020 that included just over ten songs for a small crowd and another in 2021 for a larger group with just over a dozen favourites and a few unrehearsed encore jams. This year was different. We had grown as a group and wanted to escalate our song selection and overall musical acumen. I'm not sure if it was the freedom of knowing that there would be no limitations on our ability to gather for practices or the expectation that the crowd would be quite big, but we felt a force pushing us higher. Our musical director and bassist, Pascal, had been tracking some of the requests from the crowd the prior year, along with songs suggested during the winter from various sources outside and inside the band. As much as we want to keep the fans happy, a heavy weighting of self-indulgence always influences the final set list. While the guys are very modest about their musical talents, they've all been playing their instruments for decades and are quite good. One of the reasons is that they have always refined their craft by playing complex songs. This means that they're not interested in playing simplistic tunes. The proof of this was on display when Pascal sent the first list of proposed songs for BouBou Fest 2022, and it included over twenty selections of fast, complex pieces. Looking at the list, I gasped and replied with a few questions. The feedback from the musicians was direct: they were hooked on these songs and weren't ready to change or reduce the number of songs. As the front man, my job is to represent the five talented musicians behind me and do my best to sing with a level of proficiency and timing that complements the music. They need me and I need them. For the 2022 show I felt increased pressure given that we were playing a lot of songs (pretty much like a professional band at a festival or arena concert), and they varied from slow to fast and new to old. Given this ambitious state, Steve felt we needed to find a better sound with more effective use of the mixer, so I could run through the songs with more ease and less "yelling." His dedication to this goal was evident during our last practice and during sound checks. His call to me the night before the show as I drove to Ottawa was encouraging as he shared that he had found the final winning combination for the mixer. This reminded me of the other reality of music: you are never done and can always get better. It's an endless journey.

Our show included a jam in the afternoon when we tested the sound and got warmed up for the evening. The warm-up also provided our families a chance to critique and suggest small adjustments. This time the feedback was limited, as we nailed it with strong playing and the benefits of better mixing for the vocals. Our final set list included classics from many different artists, including blink-182, ZZ Top, the Tragically Hip, the Killers, Pink Floyd, the White Stripes, and Bob Dylan.

With the arrival of darkness and the gathering of the fans around the house, I took a few minutes to relax and change into my concert outfit: comfy shoes, jeans, and a black T-shirt. Once Maxime hit the first guitar notes for "Knocking on Heaven's Door" and Gil pounded the drums to kick it off, we never looked back. My vocals were the best they had ever been, and the musicians were incredible, with a tight feel for every song. Over fifty people were watching, which elevated our energy and created a feeling of intensity. I invited others to sing and dance, with my daughters Julia and Emilie making important contributions on songs that needed additional vocals to support my limited range. I completely enjoyed the musical selection, and it lifted my spirit to new levels of performance and confidence. The band seemed pleased with their front man, which is the best compliment I can receive. The virtual circle of pleasure created by the band and the crowd once again proved that if you are lucky to have the magical power of music inside of you, you will never be alone.

It is incredible that as inseparable brothers we have evolved continuously and now also have this band as a medium for fun and celebration. I can't wait to see what comes next.

CHAPTER 10
FILLING THE FRIDGE

At the Relay for Life, Canadian Cancer Society—Quebec City, June 2009.
Community involvement has been one of my greatest pleasures during my career.

The nudge from my high school teacher made me take action. I applied
to business school at different universities and looked forward to starting that journey. I obtained decent grades, which would be good enough
to get accepted into most programs but not the best business schools in the
province. That was fine with me. As I discussed financial support with mom

and dad, they shared that since I would be going away for school, it would be great if I could attend the same school (or at least be in the same city) as Steve, so we could reduce rent, travel, and food expenses. I didn't give it a second thought since I was super happy to have their support because without it I would not have the cash to start a post-secondary program. The choices were limited since Steve was also applying to business school but in French, which was only offered at the University of Ottawa or Laurentian. We began to receive acceptance letters, and I was lucky enough to get the nod for both the bilingual schools in addition to Brock and McMaster. Steve was accepted at Laurentian but waited for a response from Ottawa before accepting. During this time, I began to accept the idea of being in northern Ontario for the next four years. And since Rémi was already attending there, it was a solid option that would allow me to discover a new area. I completed more in-depth research and confirmed that the BComm degree at Laurentian University (LU) was very strong academically and well respected by banks, accounting firms, and insurance companies. The group of professors in the English and French business programs at LU had received high distinction with most holding a PhD along with related real international management experience. By the time Steve received his rejection letter from the University of Ottawa, we had already started planning our living arrangements, which would now include Rémi, making it even more economical for our parents.

The job of finding a place to live was delegated to our mothers, Steve, and Rémi. They packed into the car on a mid-July day for the drive to Sudbury to find us a three-bedroom place to live off-campus. We were hoping for a house. I did not join them since getting time off from Maple Leaf Foods was a luxury, and I was the selected one to work that night. Their objective was to find a rental in one day and then return so that the guys would not miss two evening shifts in a row. There were no cell phones back then, so I was completely in the dark during their entire visit. They drove to a few options around town, and after a few failures they met with a guy named Frank who owned a small house in the Little Britain neighbourhood just west of downtown. He was moving his family out to a new home and ready to rent year-round only. It was a perfect match as we wanted to limit our moves from year to year. Having the mothers present gave him the confidence that we were responsible boys. It also helped that our moms were the ones with money and signed the lease as guarantors. Steve and Rémi were super excited when they returned home. They couldn't stop talking about how great it was and how cool it was going to be to have our own place with complete independence. There was even a three-season porch with windows in the front and a spacious yard and driveway for my car. It was a gift.

As we entered the last weeks of summer employment, more great news arrived. Gil had not yet heard of an official date for the start of his RCMP training in Regina, so instead of continuing to lift hot dog wiener racks five days a week, he decided to join us for the first semester. He would take courses linked to his recently paused degree and continue until he received an official start date. We were all going to be together. I was elated.

My mother's eyes were filled with tears as we gave our last hugs and kisses before jumping into my little rusted red Honda Accord for the long westbound drive along Highway 17 from Montréal to Sudbury. It was Sunday on Labour Day weekend in 1988, and Steve and I were about to begin our university life in a northern Ontario city to which I had never been. The car was filled with our clothing, albums, tapes, a couple of stereos, kitchen supplies, and of course, some homemade food that mom had prepared for us.

As excited as I was about starting this new life and joining the Sabourin brothers in our rented house, my mother was beginning some of the darkest weeks of her life. Our departure represented the end of family life as she had known it for the last twenty years. Making it even more drastic was the fact that both of her boys were leaving at the same time—having twins has its rewards and disadvantages. Only much later after I started my career and had my own children did mom share how those months were some of her toughest. Dad avoided some of these negative emotions given his busy career and twelve-hour workdays. He was not there for her as much as he would have liked. The option of stopping, relaxing, and taking some time off was a non-starter, as he had bills to pay and two boys who needed his financial support to attain their undergraduate degrees.

Our arrival at the little white house was greeted by big smiles and excitement from Rémi and Gil. They had arrived earlier that day due to their shorter drive from Mississauga. We were thrilled to join them and start our new life. As we unpacked and filled the house with our belongings, Steve's drum kit proved to be the most challenging. He was not going to be without his passion, so there was no question that the kit had to come. Finding a place for it took a few minutes of measurements and discussions.

"Can we put it in the living room?"

"No, that would be silly."

"The veranda then?"

"Please, boys, no. I'll freeze out there," Steve pleaded.

"Then there's only one option: in your room, my friend!"

"Are you serious? It won't fit."

"It fits! I did it! Come and look, boys."

It was during the careful installation of his kit that I was executing the most important task of all in my own room: the setup and wiring of my kick-ass Harman Kardon stereo system, complete with speakers good enough for a pub. Once the first song blasted from the speakers, all four of us crowded into my minuscule room, closed the door, opened some beers, and had one of the most legendary listening sessions of our lifetimes. Bring on the university years!

Since the Sabourin brothers had been in Sudbury for a few years and had already established a circle of friends, our first few days were filled with introductions and social activities. There would be no need to wait until classes started or frosh week activities began to enjoy the fun part of university life. For that first week and almost every weekend until November, there was a party or a gathering of friends at our house. Even our other brother, Frappier, who was still working in Toronto, would make the four-hour drive up and down Highway 69 every second weekend to visit and share in the pleasures that LU was providing us. He was with us so often that he started telling people he was also a student. Oh, the fun we had with that little story!

Although we enjoyed all the people and the beer, we stayed relatively grounded in the routines we had experienced with our families. We made dinner and ate together each Sunday and on most weeknights. The groceries were purchased jointly on a weekly basis and included mostly Kraft Dinner, bread, pasta, rice, chicken, and eggs (with a very small budget, the vegetables and fruits rarely made it). We also never really had any alcohol from Sunday to Wednesday, which to most kids away at school was unheard of. We made our moms proud by doing dishes every evening and taking care of the place with regular vacuuming and bathroom cleaning. We took pride in the little square house that we called home. I took the car each day to school with a short ten-minute drive to campus. Sometimes our schedules would match, and one or two of the boys travelled with me. Otherwise, it was the bus or rides from various friends for my roommates. I quickly made myself familiar with the small campus, which was mostly quiet between classes given its small size. First-year classes for the commerce program were designed so that the same kids were in most classes, and making friends was easy. Since I had a great social situation with the boys at home, I was not highly motivated to make a bunch of other acquaintances, but I quickly realized that in a small school like LU, it didn't take much effort to get to know people. Between time on campus and nights enjoying kamikaze shots at the big downtown dance bar called City Lights, quite a few became close friends quickly. It was fantastic, and I loved it.

I found the academic side relatively easy for the first semester since most of the subjects, such as accounting and economics, tended to be a review of grade thirteen. Stats and computer science were new and interesting to me. The non-business class I enjoyed the most and learned a lot in was psychology. The most valuable realization in the first few months was that I was in the right program and was interested in the content, theories, and business cases. I went to every class (as I did throughout my four-year degree) and participated with some questions and frequent answers. Most of our classes were under fifty students, and the professors, rather than teacher assistants, were teaching us. These were PhD and MBA types who also had real work experience, so their lessons were impactful and interactive. I quickly took advantage of being at a smaller school with great professors.

Classes were from Monday to Thursday except for Psychology 101, which was at noon on Fridays. My routine was to drive to campus for my first class at 8:30 a.m. or 10:00 a.m., then stay on campus until the end of the last class for the day, usually 4:00 p.m. or 5:30 p.m. This time on campus allowed me to complete homework, do research, and meet with classmates to do group work. Since over 50 percent of the kids in our program were local, gathering off-campus outside regular hours was a challenge, so using free time between classes proved most effective for all of us. I liked having my days feel like full workdays, and it reduced the need to complete homework and readings during the evenings and on weekends. As homework and group work demands escalated in my third and fourth year, I maintained my routine of being on campus for full days from Monday to Thursday.

When experiencing full independence while away at university, a person's moral compass is tested early on. I never felt the need to participate in inappropriate behaviour to impress friends. The internal strength, independence, and confidence that I had gained during high school allowed me to flee uncomfortable situations or just avoid them altogether. Steve, Gil, and Rémi were the same, so we were able to keep each other honest and never allowed each other to cross the line. This started with respect for one another. They respected my choices, and I respected theirs, all within the moral lines and shared values that defined our lives. We did some silly things and enjoyed many nights at Sudbury's pubs and dance bars, but our goal was always to just have fun with friends and enjoy the music, never having time or energy for anything else. We held the same standard when we hosted house parties. If someone got out of line, they were thrown out quickly by our big friends. The smartest thing we did was have big strong friends, like the twin brothers from Timmins who became good friends and were revered for their street fighting skills. Imagine that; two sets of identical twins hanging out together. What were the odds?

One evening at a dance bar called Studio Four, some unpleasant guys started to tease Gil's girlfriend. The twins were with us, and the moment they witnessed the situation, they took off their leather jackets and ended their opponents in seconds. I was so shocked that I just grabbed Steve and left the bar immediately. I have my friends to thank for never having been involved in a fight in all my years in Sudbury.

Following the first year of discovery and experiments, university life settled into a predictable routine for the winter months and summer break. The excitement of starting a new academic year was there, although on a diminishing scale during the four years. Summers for me were focused on making as much money as I could. I worked in the meat production and packaging plant and did anything they asked of me for any shift they offered and always accepted overtime. My usual shift was 3:30–11:45 p.m. from Monday to Friday with almost an hour of travel time each way, which resulted in no social life. Having such a brutal schedule and doing such mundane work drove me to higher levels of academic performance. As much as I respected and liked most of the people in the factory who worked hard to pay the bills and put their kids through school, I did not want to do that. Interestingly enough, most workers who got to know me would support my efforts and kept telling me, "Stay in school and work hard. You don't want to do this all your life."

Their conviction to be there for their partners and children provided me with a high level of appreciation for all who contribute in the workforce no matter the task. My Grandfather Hinse had done the same. Working those hundreds of night shifts helped me be a better leader when I eventually had to make decisions that impacted thousands of colleagues.

With a bank account full enough to get me through eight months of personal expenses, I made the trek to Sudbury each Labour Day weekend and began a new cycle. The second year was much like the first with Rémi and Steve sharing the house (Gil had by then started his RCMP training and was soon to begin his career with distinction in southern Ontario). Unfortunately, in September 1989 the teachers were in a battle with the university administration for their labour contract and decided to go on strike the day before classes began. It lasted four weeks. In addition to the sour impacts of the strike, I found my second year less challenging and not as interesting as I had hoped. It was well known that the third year was the "breaker," with more than 30 percent dropping out due to the challenging workload and elevated academic requirements. So, it made the second year kind of a waiting game academically, but thankfully it was full of discovery for all things northern life. Our local friends, Tim, the Barbeau brothers, Vince, and Chris, introduced me to ice fishing, snowmobiling, hunting, winter cabin parties, and local rock concerts. In the late 1980s, prominent Canadian acts like Tom Cochrane, Gowan, the Tragically Hip, the Northern Pikes, the Spoons, and others made Sudbury one of the stops on their way to western Canada. With ticket prices at around $20, these shows had the best quality-to-value ratio I had ever experienced. Steve has recounted countless times his air-drumming exploits during the Spoons concert in which he was rewarded with a drumstick from the drummer. That night was capped by a brief acknowledgement from the band members as they walked by us in the lobby on their way to the tour bus after the show. The non-academic experiences were well worth the drudgery of a transitional year.

I was ready for the third year of my BComm when the new decade arrived, and we moved into a new house on Ontario Street with our new roommate, Chris. Rémi had finished his time in Sudbury and had decided to complete a few more classes for his undergrad at McMaster in Hamilton. Our landlord, Frank, had sold the previous home we had rented but at the same time decided to move out of his existing older home just a mile away. It was almost as old as our previous accommodations, but it suited our needs quite well. Steve and I took the two rooms upstairs, and Chris had a room on the main floor next to the living room. He was a night owl, so we all agreed that it was best to have him close to the kitchen and TV while we slept normal shifts in the quiet section at the top of the narrow stairs. Chris was in all of my classes in second year, and we became great friends. He was from St. Thomas, just south of London, Ontario, had a laid-back approach to everything, and was an all-around positive soul. Our living partnership went very well as we continued to be socially active at the house but only with our circle of close friends and visitors from Montréal and Toronto. The days of regular house parties were gone. Steve and I were laser focused on school and making sure that our significant investment thus far and our parents' sacrifices would not be wasted. The hype of the challenging third year drove us to a higher level of commitment and confidence. The structure of the BComm program was simple for the student purging year. We had five courses that lasted the entire year: Accounting, Human Resources, Marketing, Operations, and Finance. The academic format was also simple, with business cases grounding all the homework, and theoretical lessons from the professors building the knowledge base. Lastly, group work was required in all classes, which meant we selected (or were selected by) five people who would become a big part of our lives for the winter months. Monthly "weekend special" business cases rounded out the demanding year. Because teamwork was critical for success, I was deliberate about my group members and instead of looking for the social contacts or cool people, I gravitated to the hard workers and brainiacs. It paid off!

There is something magical about matching one's innate skills with work. If you are lucky enough to find the perfect match, everything is easier and less stressful. After the first six weeks, I returned from the Thanksgiving break to find our third-year classes had shrunk substantially. The weeding-out process had begun, and I was solidifying my status as a competent business student. The magic of the "match" was playing out naturally, and I had a feeling that what was pegged as a very difficult year would become quite good for me. I increased my contributions during class and was providing sound solutions to business cases in group work, my writing skills were becoming more concise, acknowledgements from profs were more frequent, and my marks were improving. For those who have never experienced the power of the magic match, I can't imagine how they ever thrived in their work. I was lucky. Once October was behind me, there were no more questions about what I would do for my career; it would be business. Like an athlete or an artist who discovers their God-given talent and never looks back, there was no reason for me to even consider other options. I played to my strengths. November and December were pure head-down months with continuous business case readings, weekend specials, and exams. We didn't visit a bar or go out during this time, and our social interactions were limited to having Tim and Chris's girlfriend Irene visit at night to watch hockey. I spent each day from 9:00 a.m. to 5:00 p.m. at school and hours after dinner reading business cases and completing tasks. The newly built library at LU also became my second home as I studied company profiles in large Moody's books or financial statements on microfiche (no Web back then). Again, the work did not feel difficult, but it sure felt heavy. In the back of my mind was the fact that the marks I would get in third year would be front and centre to any potential employer participating in recruitment at the start of fourth year. I set a goal to do my best in the first semester and the mid-term exams so that professors would know me as an achiever and hopefully remember it when I ran out of steam at the end of the second semester and needed their help.

After a well-deserved Christmas break at home with lots of food and family time, I returned to the nickel capital to start a new semester. I was also anxious to get my marks for the December exams. When the five professors started to share the results, I was happy. In all my fifteen years in school, I had never obtained such high academic results. From then on, the tone professors used with me was intelligent and mature, I elevated my profile above the average, and I never looked back for the rest of my undergraduate degree.

***

"Here is my business card. Make sure you submit your resume and apply."

These words came from the HR manager at the TD Bank. It was early October 1991, and I was twenty-two years old and in my last year of the

BComm program at LU. That initial conversation in the empty "bowling alley" hallway during a quiet campus recruitment day set the wheels in motion for a near thirty-year career in banking.

I would not have stopped my walk to class for a guy from a bank on that cool, cloudy afternoon had he not given me a big smile and a cheerful "Hello."

His enthusiasm and apparent interest in striking up a conversation was different from the other quiet recruiters from other companies who were sitting behind their tables looking uninterested. He shared the usual details about the company with passion, gave me some paperwork about the types of jobs available, and answered my questions. Following our conversation, I tucked his card into my backpack and continued my walk. Later, I asked dad about this interaction during our weekly call, and his advice was to follow the lead. I visited the university recruitment centre the next week to get more details from a career adviser. They validated that the recruitment efforts were legit, with up to five graduates hired each year from LU out of hundreds of BComm graduates. I was told that my bilingual language skills would be a real asset for banks since they could use me in different bilingual markets all over Ontario, as far away as Kapuskasing in the deep north. I don't recall thinking negatively about that information, mostly because it was the early nineties and the unemployment rate was over 11 percent. Finding a "grown-up" job in the business world after finishing school the next spring was a priority. The career adviser also gave me the dates when the banks were holding their first interviews on campus, followed by wine-and-cheese events to socialize with top candidates. With all this information I moved ahead and created a proper CV with my pizza delivery and meat packer experience prominently on the first page (I had no hope). At most they would maybe appreciate my work ethic while overlooking that it had nothing to do with financial services. My visit with the career adviser must have paid off, however, and I obtained on-campus interviews with most of the banks and got to enjoy free food and drinks for a few evenings. This included another conversation with the HR manager, which was much more casual in nature, along with introductions to other people, who were all making quick judgments about all of the young candidates. Once this was all done, I was told to hold tight for a few weeks.

The next step would hopefully be an invitation to formal interviews at head offices in Toronto.

My first-ever flight out of the Sudbury airport was on a cold November day. I guess only one bank liked me enough to invest the money to get me down to the big city, complete a robust day of interviews, and treat me (along with a few other candidates) to a nice lunch. I have no detailed memory of what happened that day except that I was nervous and put in front of at least three HR people and a few leaders from different departments. I knew essentially nothing about banking, so it must have been questions and conversations about my experience, my education, my career goals, and my capacity to handle people in group settings. I was aware enough to know that they had had prior conversations with the recruitment folks at LU and obtained good reviews from the commerce professors about my grades and overall work ethic. That day of interviews was really about my values, beliefs, and professional acumen. The one thing I do recall is how every one of them asked me some version of the following questions: "I'd like to confirm that you are committed to moving anywhere in Ontario after graduation?" and "You would be willing to do it again within twelve months once the management training program concludes?"

I didn't blink an eye and told them about the number of relocations I had gone through as a kid. Apparently, they were sold!

In my last year at LU, I was highly focused on academics and spending time with the few close friends who remained. Steve had not returned to Sudbury, choosing instead to finish his degree in Montréal at the very fine HEC school, so he could be close to Josée. After his undergrad he continued at the same school to complete his Master of Science in finance. Chris and I stayed as roommates and lived in a two-bedroom apartment on the second floor above a (loud) family. It was on Lawson Street just a few blocks from the house we had rented the year before. Our good friend Tim visited often, and Chris's girlfriend was a regular addition but only for short visits or to spend the evenings on weekends. At that point I was looking ahead to the next year and could not wait to finish school, leave the nickel capital, and start living as an independent adult. Making things easier for a few months was a new girlfriend—my first serious longer-term relationship—who shared my interests and allowed me to avoid anything having to do with going out to bars and hanging with a bunch of guys. I count myself lucky to have shifted away from all that busy social student lifestyle so easily without missing it. Again, I have my great lifelong friends to thank for that since we had so much fun together that there was no need to continue to live my teenage years well into my twenties. As in high school, I was away from Steve, but this time I missed him a lot. His dedication to Josée was immense, and our conversations and time together were reduced to a few hours during holidays. Reflecting on it now, it was probably one of the most important personal development years for me, much like my time in high school.

I was clenching a large brown envelope in my left hand as I opened the door to our apartment after a good day at school working on projects and attending class. The windows were all frosted in the dim light as the sun descended out of view for the night. It was mid-January in one of the coldest cities in Canada where the sun was long gone by five in the afternoon, not to be seen again for fifteen hours. I'd been feeling punky since my return from the Christmas break in Montréal. I barely had enough money to get through the next four months. My only option was to return home once school ended. My social life was stagnant, and I felt uneasy about my relationship with my girlfriend. But maybe that envelope was my ticket out of that funky mood. The green logo in the corner gave me hope, but the thinness of the envelope made me conclude that it was merely a short decline letter. I had been told by the career adviser following all of the formal interviews in late November that most employers took until after December to inform candidates of their decision (at the time I thought it was prolonged but later realized that companies needed to confirm their budgets for the next year before moving ahead with new hires). As I pulled out the two-page letter (which I still have), I read the first sentence, which started with the word "Congratulations." I was jubilant. Then I continued reading, and it said that my training would start on May 25, 1992 in Espanola, Ontario.

"Where the heck is Espanola?" I muttered.

I quickly exited the apartment and ran out to my freezing car to get my map of Ontario. (No Internet then!) I found the location in small print only a few centimetres west of Sudbury. I would be starting my career in one of the smallest towns where banks still operated a branch, and to beat it, it was only seventy kilometres from where I was standing. But at least I had a job.

Yay! The last paragraph of the letter confirmed my starting annual salary, an underwhelming number but enough to pay for a car and a place to live with some food in the fridge. It was a start!

Once I had that letter in my hands, all I needed to do was graduate. While I focused and kept my head down, my sights were set on the summer and starting my new professional life. During exams I found a little one-bedroom place in the Walford apartment building around the south end of Sudbury near Lockerby. I had decided to travel forty-five minutes each morning and night to Espanola instead of living in the secluded community of less than five thousand people. The bank did not have a formal condition that I live near the branch, so I made my first move of many in a long line of relocations. I temporarily stored the furniture I was going to use from my student days at Tim's place and returned to Montréal for the last few weeks of living with my parents. As usual, they were super proud and supportive, and they offered to give me some furniture from their home and combine it with a few items my Uncle Luc had generously offered. The best part was, dad rented a truck and moved me with my Grandfather Jean as a passenger to Sudbury, and he paid for it (I literally had less than $200 to my name). My grandfather still talks about that drive, moving things into my place, and having a nice dinner in Sudbury. On the morning of May 23rd my father and grandfather wished me good luck, then left me to carry on the family tradition of earning an honest pay without being scared of hard work.

***

I arrived at the parking lot next to the Espanola branch at around 8:00 a.m. on that first Monday, well before it opened. It was a cloudy morning but warm for late May in the remote rural town, which was surrounded by forest. To the east I noticed a large cloud of yellowish smoke spewing from a square smokestack much smaller than the tall giants I was accustomed to in Sudbury. There was a reason why the entire town was on the west side of that stack. As the clock neared 8.30 a.m., I made my way to the branch's front door, thinking that someone would open it and give their newest recruit a warm welcome. What I got instead was some weird looks from inside and an eventual acknowledgement from a staff member, accompanied with a direct order to step away from the building and come back after 9:00 a.m. That was my first lesson in banking: don't hang around the branch and try to get staff to open the doors when there are hundreds of thousands of dollars exposed in the open vault during the critical opening procedures. Got it!

Once I did make my way inside, the welcome was nice, and I spent most of the first day filling out paperwork, completing checklists, and signing off on multiple documents to generate a payroll number and login IDs. As tradition would have it, my first lunch was with the assistant manager, who would be my boss during my time in training.

My first several weeks were great with the small team of dedicated bankers. The staff were all very experienced, all lived in the small town, and were all much older than me. They were very good to me and so knowledgeable. My bias that most bankers were men was quickly corrected as I found myself working with only women apart from the branch manager. My training included shadowing every role and spending at least one week doing the different tasks until I got the thumbs-up that I had mastered it. I found it so interesting to learn everything about how a bank operated, from counting hundreds of thousands of dollars in cash each day to balancing the General Ledger (I still remember the GL numbers). Most of the tasks were completed locally at the branch and manually in those days, so we had to learn everything from end to end. This deep knowledge that I gathered for the first seven years of my career working in branches paid back in spades for years later on by giving me a sound understanding of how banks make money.

The management training program also included two months at the large regional administration centre in Sudbury. It was nice to have only a short drive with more time to enjoy the short summer. Upon returning to Espanola in the fall, I found that the return to a small team was less motivating. Fortunately, as winter approached, the HR team decided it would be good for me to finish my training at the large commercial banking centre in Sudbury. It would also allow me to avoid the treacherous daily winter driving to Espanola. Later, I found out that they were very pleased with my progress and wanted to make sure I kept learning at a fast pace in a big complex banking unit. I was matched with the excellent assistant manager of administration. I learned tons in that large branch of almost one hundred employees spread over three floors. The management team's dedication to hard work resulted in my schedule extending substantially to an arrival at 7:00 a.m. and a departure at around 6:00 p.m. (this became pretty much my daily shift for the next twenty-eight years).

As February came to an end, I found out that some of the other trainees already had obtained their first postings across the province. This made me a little anxious about what was next for me. My manager would tease me almost every week that I was going to be shipped to the far north where there's no summer. I found his jokes discomforting until the day he called me into his office and had a map of Ontario laid out on his desk. He said that HR had called, and I was being shipped out to start my first official posting the following Monday. For additional impact he circled his finger around the map until he stopped over the city of Ottawa. For a moment I was very excited until he shifted a little to the east and said, "You're going to Hawkesbury."

"I've never been to Hawkesbury," I said. "We have a branch there?"

I didn't even know that the small town of ten thousand on the south side of the Ottawa river even existed, let alone that it was one of the only predominantly French communities in Ontario. After saying goodbye to the team and a few friends, I packed my suits and drove east on Highway 17, promising myself that my highly rewarding time in northern Ontario had come to an end.

My career in the greater Ottawa area advanced nicely over the next nine years, with new roles every twelve to eighteen months. I moved to different branches, taking on new roles to learn everything possible about personal branch banking and develop my management skills. The people were fantastic. There was a positive culture and great leadership in that market, and I learned so much from the dedicated and experienced bankers. When I left Hawkesbury after my first posting, I never thought I would return, but in 1997 I was fortunate to be named the youngest branch manager in the region at that same location. Once in the role for more than a year, and without telling anyone, I made myself another promise not to do another branch management mandate after Hawkesbury. I would seek out a broader role to learn new things. By then I was highly interested in having a long rewarding career that would give me the opportunity to do different things and continue learning. My plan of breaking the mould worked flawlessly, and I obtained a new mandate at the regional office in Ottawa following the announcement of the merger between TD and Canada Trust. The next couple of years were exciting as we merged the entities and created a new brand and company culture. By then I had expanded my career plan to a broader vision that, hopefully, would take me out of the region and branch banking altogether. Again, I was lucky to have a supportive regional leader (he became an important mentor in later years) who reluctantly provided approval. Within a few months, I was moving our entire family and starting a new leadership role as Head of Eastern Canada Visa Operations in Montréal.

My time in Montréal was the most stressful in my career. Linda and I had young daughters, and the job was demanding with all of its operational facets, combined with a 24-7 operating model. My learning curve was steep, and my management abilities were tested with labour relations issues and constant changes to the credit card business model. We had over three hundred people spread over five floors inside a worn-down business tower in old Montréal that was a favourite target for recruitment of our experienced call-centre employees, which made for high turnover and constant training. Although I had many sleepless nights, with Linda's support and my dad's counselling, I persevered and became recognized at head office as a competent and patient business leader who was able to get things done and navigate tricky issues. The senior leaders also realized I could be trusted and always put the company's interests first.

After six relocations (three with Linda) over the past ten years, we decided it was time to move back to our hometown of Toronto. Linda had been more than patient and courageous to follow me and support my career, and now it was time to do something for her. Professionally, this was also an important decision since I knew by then that I would never achieve my career goals without working in the big black towers at King and Bay. I will always remember sharing my plan with the leader of credit cards during a visit to Montréal and being completely relieved (and excited) with his reply: "That makes sense. I'm happy to help you make that happen."

A few months later, a "For Sale" sign was on the front lawn of our house, and we were moving fast to complete the relocation before the new school year started for the girls. When we found our new home in our neighbourhood of choice in Oakville, I spent days renovating the inside and replacing all the flooring since we would live there a long time, or at least that was the plan!

I adored working at the bank. The work was interesting and challenging, and best of all, the people were great. I had observed that becoming an executive at a major financial institution (or any large company) was a career milestone. I never thought when I started that it would even be a possibility for me, but as my first six months in head office ended, I felt like I was emulating some of the qualities of an executive, or at least I was trying to replicate what I was witnessing in the best leaders around me.

One day when I was meeting with my leader only eight months after having moved our family into our Oakville house, she told me that they wanted me to interview for a district executive role. I was stunned, mostly because the role was back in Montréal. Then I made a fatal mistake. I took my boss's advice and went home early to start the discussion of this possible relocation with Linda. When I showed up at the door, Linda greeted me with a surprised look (I never came home early) and was less than happy when I proposed that we go have lunch at a local restaurant to chat about an opportunity. She knew very well that if the opportunity was in Toronto, I would have just shared it over dinner, and she would have said, "Congrats, well done," and moved on. Suffice to say that we did not finish our lunch.

Once I completed the interview in Montréal with the regional leader and found out that the job was actually in Quebec City and not Montréal, I came home to tell Linda that it was probably just a courtesy interview after all and that I would most likely not get the offer.

A few days passed, and the opposite occurred. They wanted me to be the first fully francophone executive leader to live in that important growing market for the bank. This time I did not call or go home early to inform Linda. Instead, I let her know that evening that the career opportunity in question was serious and was now mine to decline. We talked about what it meant for our long-term future, the sadness her mom would feel by having her oldest daughter and granddaughters hundreds of miles away once again, and the change of school the girls would have to make (likely twice). Somewhat reluctantly, and with immense courage, Linda agreed that we would do this final relocation, but it came with the condition that we would return to Oakville after two years. That was in April 2007.

With fifteen years of experience and a good knowledge of banking, I completed my first executive mandate and loved every minute of my time in

Quebec City. It was professionally rewarding and validating to obtain sound business results and superior feedback about my leadership and business acumen. The team was passionate about the brand and dedicated to increasing market share. I enjoyed the people and the culture and visiting multiple towns in the province's northeast area. The girls learned to downhill ski and perfected their French language skills in a community that was almost 100 percent francophone. I recall the Quebec regional leader telling me about good English-speaking neighbourhoods to use as a selling point with Linda during the acceptance process, but that was false! Quebec City continues to be a wonderful francophone city with less than 5 percent of its residents speaking only English. We were lucky to find a lovely home with lots of outside space. Linda and I hosted events at our home for the management team and built lifelong friendships that continue today. Our time there also provided family and friends with a chance to visit the beautiful city during different seasons and to better appreciate the history and diversity of our country. The biggest surprise for the four of us is how much we loved living there. We were all a little scared about being far from Toronto and isolated in a colder climate, but once the first few months were behind us and the girls were established at the school, it was wonderful. We continue to visit every year and have started to do extended stays regularly since 2020.

Just like clockwork, I took a role back in head office in the summer of 2009 and joined the retail products team until the end of 2010. Boy, did I learn from smart people in that job. I'm so lucky! Then another move occurred, and I was promoted, now working with the GTA regional team and the thousands of employees who serve the biggest market in Canada. The group's dedication and customer focus was exemplary. Again, I was fortunate to have great people around me along with effective leaders. Next was the business bank, working with one of the best bosses I ever had. She was brilliant, direct, and experienced. My time in business banking was one of my most enjoyable stints. It included deep learning about the business of banking and the power of leading with strong accountability. The leadership team operated at a high level in a complex environment. I even got to meet Wayne Gretzky during that time at a recognition event when he handed me a business leader distinction award!

I left the business bank reluctantly to return to personal banking as the leader of the credit centres. It was the biggest group I had ever managed, and I was pleased with the success we achieved. Some of the best personal credit minds in banking were in that group. The team was impressive. As I entered my second year in credit, I heard rumours that I might potentially assume a senior executive role in the near term. I had dreamed it years earlier, and now it seemed possible. Unfortunately, this also carried a certain level of stress. I was always one to focus on the tasks of the current mandate, and things flowed nicely from simply doing my best. Now it all felt a bit heavier and more serious. For pretty much every new job I obtained, it was someone else asking me to join their team or an existing manager asking me to assume a new mandate. This time I was identified for a senior role and asked to do an interview. I was happy but also a little guarded about what it would involve. The fortunate part was that my many years at the bank had been wonderful, and I had been surrounded by amazing people. I approached any chance to advance with the same excitement I had displayed throughout my career. I was lucky to be working at a great company.

My start as a senior executive coincided with the start of university life for Julia. She was finishing high school, and we were about to begin a new stage of our life with the realities of empty nesters in the distance. Emilie still had a couple of years until she left home for university, but the transitional years had started, which was to change how Linda and I lived. As middle-aged parents with adult children, we felt somewhat awkward thinking about the years ahead so soon. But the possibility of moving to a semi-retirement routine that would allow us to travel and do all types of things was attractive. It was also during this period that some of our friends (and Steve) decided to retire from their full-time careers. Once Emilie settled into her residence at the University of Ottawa, we had already tested a new lifestyle with trips, more golf, and more calories spent on new interests. Ahead was this wide-open space inviting me to discover new experiences, try new things, and "work" differently. Linda and I had been having discussions for some time before the decision in 2020. My last day of work at TD, a distinguished global financial institution, was Friday October 30th of that year.

Since then I've shifted my energy to new business interests and all sorts of projects. I've renovated our home, helped Steve with his real-estate projects, immersed myself in learning how to become a producer for my nephew's independent film production company, Pink Wall Films, dabbled as front man for our rock band, and started writing.

Guess which one is me.

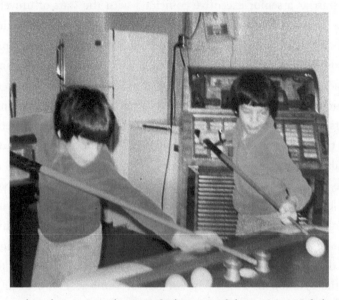

Brother and me listening to the 1950 Seeburg 100 Select-o-Matic Jukebox while playing bumper pool in the basement of my Hinse grandparents' house, circa 1979.

Practising the violin at age nine in front of both of my grandfathers in Candiac in 1978. Grandpapa Demers in his three-piece suit is so very proud that I am playing his favourite instrument, which he gifted to me. Grandpapa Hinse shows off his pride in a more reserved way, as music was never big for him.

I played soccer for almost ten years.
Erin Mills Soccer Club, Mississauga, circa 1980.

A tired group returning from my second twenty-four-hour
survival adventure in 1982 at Awacamenj Mino Camp.
Notables from top left to right: Guide from base camp,
Jacques (second top left), Me (next to Jacques),
Steve (top, second from right), François (shirtless in centre).

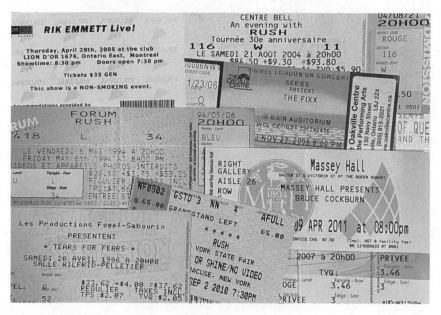

Some of the concerts I attended when paper tickets were still issued.

Hawkesbury, summer 1997.
Living together in our first home.

Grandma Irene with my daughters, Emilie and Julia,
at the Red Cottage, summer 2003.

Julia on the slopes at Le Massif. February 28, 2022.

Mom and dad with my daughters,
Emilie and Julia, in Boynton Beach, Florida, November 2008.

Emilie with Marigold, August 25, 2015.

With Grandmaman Madeleine on the day my grandfather played
his last golf game at age 92. Victoriaville Golf Course, August 15, 2015.

Moments after winning Rugby OFSAA gold,
May 31, 2017. Emilie, Linda, and Julia.

Our family: Julia, Emilie, me, and Linda.
Old Quebec City, September 19, 2020.

CHAPTER 11
I FOUND MY ANGEL

Linda on the Oakville Pier in 2017.
Her love of photography has never diminished.

"There are some beautiful people at this wedding," my dear friend Danny Sokolowski declared as we waited in the lobby before entering for the reception.

"She's too tall for you!" I replied.

Before he had made the observation, I had already seen her in a slim dark blue-and-white polka-dot dress, her long hair lightly curled. She was standing with her back to me as she chatted with some friends next to the door of the dining hall. When she finally turned in my direction before disappearing past the doors, I witnessed the smile that has been with me ever since. It was late-June 1996 at the Stanton House Resort on the shores of Sparrow Lake, Ontario.

Almost one hundred and fifty years ago, Captain Thomas Stanton from England settled with his wife, Ellen, and their young children on the west shores of Sparrow Lake. It is one hundred and fifty kilometres north of Toronto and is the most southerly lake in the popular tourist and cottage region of Muskoka. Mr. Stanton's beginnings on the lake were modest, and he is best described as a pioneer who made regular trips upriver to trade for supplies for his family, who was living in a log cabin. After a few years of rugged living and isolation during the cold winters, they moved to the lake's south shore to be closer to the school. Roads were limited, and almost all travel was on the water or by train in that beautiful area of multiple freshwater lakes and rivers.

As entrepreneurs, the family was involved in steamboats and established the Sparrow Lake Steamer Line to transport lumber, supplies, and eventually tourists during the busy summer months. The location of their new home was also convenient once the Canadian Northern Ontario Railway expanded their services to the area in 1906. Seeing an opportunity, Captain Stanton donated some of his land to have the new track built just a little more to the north on Sparrow Lake's southern shore. The new Port Stanton train stop was ideally located on the lakeshore for summer travellers from Toronto who no longer needed to transfer to access Muskoka's pure waters.

In addition to the campers who already enjoyed the area, Ellen began taking in boarders and tourists during the summer. She was at the leading edge of the booming summer resort economy and built a sustainable business for generations with the creation of the Stanton House Resort. It was a time of rapid growth for the three larger lakes in central Ontario, Rosseau, Muskoka, and Joseph. Rich families from Pennsylvania south of the border travelled up every summer to escape the heat of Pittsburgh and other cities. They built large homes on the water and supported the locals with a vibrant seasonal economy. The Stantons operated a more modest resort and attracted middle-class families looking to enjoy the same landscape and summer pleasures as the millionaires. Eventually, the Stanton sons and grandsons expanded the family's dominance of Sparrow Lake with the creation of other resorts, including Bayview Lodge and Wildwood Inn.

It was on this site ninety years later that I met Linda at the wedding of our friends, Rémi and Lesley. The location was selected because Lesley had worked at the resort during the summer and was very close to the existing Stanton family members, who continued to own and operate the business. Lesley became friends with Linda when Linda started to visit the resort in the early 1990s to spend time with her friend, Carol, who also worked there. Linda and Carol had met in the faculty of education a few years earlier. The funny thing is, both Lesley and Rémi had a feeling that Linda and I might be a good match, but they never said a word about it. And rightly so, for they feared that we would shy away from any such organized matchmaking and took the chance that it would happen naturally. Their bet paid off. The only nudge we obtained from them after my advanced sighting of Linda in the lobby was to sit us at the same table for dinner. Unbeknown to us, all of our friends who were attending the wedding were watching us secretly and quietly cheering. Once I got the courage to invite Linda to dance, we were inseparable. We sat together for the rest of the night and talked until well after midnight. We walked outside by the water on that beautiful night as our friends and Linda's ride waited patiently. Our friends have reminded us many times that they knew it was a successful match when we returned after our walk, and Linda was wearing my suit jacket around her shoulders, which I had given her to stay warm.

***

As fortunate as my grandfathers and father,
I found an angel to love for a lifetime.
One to encourage me, provide advice,
set me straight, and hold the compass.

She's the only channel,
Always bright on my mind.
The only flower in the garden,
Bringing a vital new scent each day.

***

The distance between Ottawa and Toronto did not diminish our passion to connect and begin a life together. Having both established a professional life without any dependencies gave us the freedom to act and make decisions simply for the two of us. I feared early on that being five hundred kilometres apart could create real challenges over time and make us question our future together, but that never happened. Initially, Linda was able to use her time off during summer (she worked as teacher) to travel regularly to Ottawa and to our family cottage in the Laurentians. I did the same with a few Friday evening drives to Mississauga and the Red Cottage on Lake Eugenia.

Only two months into our relationship, we were both back at work and dreaded the upcoming winter weather with all its travel challenges. But Linda decided that this would not be an issue. She started booking flights every weekend, so we could be together and not pause on building what we knew was something more special than anything we had dreamed of only a few months earlier. She would escape Westwood High School the moment the bell rang on Friday afternoon, race to YYZ, and fly into Ottawa, where I would be waiting for her. To maximize our time together, she would fly back out on Monday morning on the first flight before 7:00 a.m., dressed in full teacher attire. A quick transfer to her parked car and a short drive allowed her to enter the school minutes before first class (her teacher friends covered for her when flights were delayed). Although these were serious sacrifices and tedious travel escapades, Linda was always positive and looked at it as more of an adventure. Each weekend was completely enjoyable, and our routine proved to both of us that no matter what the future would bring, we were committed to each other.

Trust and respect are at the core of any worthwhile and valuable relationship, be it with a friend, family, or lover. I have a strong conviction about this after having observed and been involved in many different types of relationships over the last fifty years. These two elements have also always been at the core of Linda's belief system, which is why we were able to live a loving life together for that first year even though we were apart more than we were together. We never had thoughts of jealousy, uncertainty, or doubt. We knew that if trust or respect was broken, our relationship would be ruptured. From that first night at Stanton House, I have always had Linda on my mind with a goal of doing my best every day to make her happy. It is my religion. I'm not perfect, and sometimes I get it wrong, but I'm always trying and adapting. I believe in the multiplier effect of a positive attitude and generosity, which I witnessed with my parents, grandparents, and many others. The abundance of love I've received throughout my life has filled my coffers and allowed me to give back and fuel the virtual circle of love for family and friends. Linda and I recognized these shared values early on in 1996, which cemented our commitment to each other.

As Linda was getting to know her companions on the Friday night and Monday morning flights between YYZ and YOW, I was working as many hours as possible between 7:00 a.m. on Monday to 5:00 p.m. on Friday, so we could enjoy weekends without banking work. I was also continuing to focus on high performance at work, so I could get promotions now that the dream of having a life with a family was becoming a possibility. Linda also continued to thrive and impact kids at Westwood beyond any normal teacher. She was involved in many aspects of the school, with extra time dedicated to coaching basketball, organizing clubs, mentoring, and teaching mathematics to teenagers who otherwise did not really care. Linda had a magical ability to reach kids and build respectful relationships right from the start of the semester. She still preaches today that during those first ten days is when you establish ground rules, enforce them, and build an environment for mutual success. I loved hearing all about the kids and their unique challenges, how some of them would be making progress, and the pride she had in them as they reached their goals. Her involvement in sports was a critical avenue to establishing closer relationships and building a reputation with some of the toughest kids in the school. Along with her coaching partners, they helped develop some great leaders and famous basketball stars who played at professional levels. Some played in Europe, some for the Canadian National Team, and some in the NCAA and the NBA, and a few transitioned as professional commentators on Canadian sport networks. Even twenty-five years later, she communicates with many of them regularly and shares stories about kids, accomplishments, and sports. We have attended weddings, birthday parties, and other events in the last few years with these same kids, who were only a few years younger than Linda when she started her career. When we were in New York City a couple of years ago, she ran into Sherman Hamilton, one of her former students who was a renowned member of the Canadian men's national basketball team and current basketball analyst for Sportsnet. He was in town to cover the Raptors game, and he asked if we had tickets. Sadly we were leaving that day and had to pass. Such a nice person. Their surprise meeting crystalized for me the gift that Linda had given to him and many others decades earlier.

The culmination of all the energy, passion, and time that Linda dedicated to her students for the first ten years of her teaching career was the receipt of a teacher-of-the-year award from the Peel district school board. During the year that proved to be her last as a full-time teacher, her multi-year contribution was recognized by her peers and management. She still plays down the incredible award, but I don't.

As we celebrated our first year together, we started to discover our families' unique cultures. I was impressed with the Polish and Newfoundlander aspects of language and food. Linda liked the red wine, cheese, and pure maple syrup. Since my extended family was mainly French, Linda made an incredible effort to learn a new language and impressed all of us with her progress during those first years. Bilingualism proved important as we relocated to Hawkesbury to start our life together. Linda made the first of countless sacrifices by taking a leave from teaching to join me in a community of under ten thousand people, which was located five hours from her mom, friends, and family. The saving grace was that Linda could drive to Montréal in less than one hour, and we had my family and some of our friends in striking distance for weekend social activities. We lived a simple, happy life in our small semi-detached home. Even though it was a rental, we still painted the entire place, put up wallpaper, took care of the yard, and created a comfortable home. We had agreed to make the move with the knowledge that it would likely be under three years, followed by a move back to either Ottawa, Toronto, or Montréal. But by the time winter arrived and Linda witnessed more snow than she had ever seen, I decided it was time to start our future and not wait any longer. I proposed to her on Christmas Eve just before midnight at the cemetery next to her dad's tombstone. Knowing how much she loved her dad and how proud he would have been to have his eldest daughter engaged, I chose the location with the hope that my intuition was correct. It was.

Things moved quickly as we started 1998. We wasted no time having the wedding, and Linda went into supercharged project management mode to execute the event. We selected the Isaiah Tubbs Resort between Montréal and

Toronto as the location and decided to make a weekend of it for our guests in the last days of May.

Summer weather arrived early on the shore of West Lake in Prince Edward County on Saturday the thirtieth as we awoke to bright sunshine and a blue sky. Everyone enjoyed the beautiful resort property, pool, and surrounding area. It was different for me, as I was nervously hiding out in the chalet with my parents, so I would not run into Linda. Our friends and family were incredibly positive, sharing our joy, and they created an amazing atmosphere for the entire three-day weekend. When we gathered in the wedding hall at mid-afternoon on Saturday, there was a peaceful, happy atmosphere as I made my way to the front with mom and dad and joined Steve and my other groomsmen for the ceremony. When the processional music started, I turned to face Linda as she made her way to me in her beautiful dress. Apart from my left leg shaking for a few seconds in nervousness, I stayed calm and could not take my eyes off her. After walking out to cheers, I was elated with happiness, knowing that we would be together forever. Linda was classy and beautiful.

Our escape to Paris on Sunday night after the wedding day for our honeymoon was a dream. I had never been to Europe, and after a few days of walking the streets and visiting the landmarks, I had a better understanding of our history and diversity. As my youngest daughter, Emilie, so poignantly said recently during her first visit to London as an adult: "I get it."

One gains a richness of mind, personal growth, and appreciation for the vast complexity of our world when one travels to other countries. As smart as people can be about their field of expertise, true knowledge and sound judgment is only gained by witnessing different environments with an open spirit. As Linda and I walked everywhere and visited the most notable museums and structures known to humankind, we fell into a trance of love and beauty. I would get coffee and croissants early in the morning, which we ate outside in the hotel courtyard. We never went to any fancy restaurants and instead focused on local foods at brasseries and bistros. The weather was very pleasant, the early June air cool enough to keep our walking energy at top level. Apart from taking a taxi to and from the airport, we never used transportation. We got lost a few times, but my little map and tour book always helped get us back on track. The discovery of different streets, parks, old churches, and cafés supplemented the "must see" tourist destinations like Notre-Dame Cathedral, the Arc de Triomphe, the Louvre, the Eiffel Tower, the Champs-Élysées, and the Seine. Since that trip to Paris, I've had the chance to visit many other world-class cities, and I don't really have a favourite. Each has its own story and alchemy that resonates with people in different ways. When we visit different places, we always try to melt into the local culture, pace, and values. My experience in Paris sparked a desire to discover other places. Luckily, Linda also has the need for adventure and movement.

Our wedding summer was capped off by another trip, this time to Whistler, British Columbia, to join Linda's sister and brother for their national ball tournament. Linda was a spare player on the mixed team, so we tagged along with the rest of the crew and shared a large condo during a week that was marked by an uncharacteristic heat wave. Being mostly a winter destination, the rooms didn't have air conditioning, and the windows were small. Suffice to say that Linda and I did not spend much of the night cuddling!

The weather was warm and sunny, so we took time away from the ball diamond to play golf, go to the top of the mountain, swim in the lakes, and visit the village. I had been to Banff, Alberta fifteen years before during March break with my family, but this was my first time in BC experiencing the beauty of Vancouver and the drive on the Sea-to-Sky Highway. We had so much fun with the ball players. Although they did not win Nationals, the trip ended up being more important than the actual games. Linda's sister, Laura, has continued to play ball competitively and has had the fortunate annual routine of playing ball in many other Canadian cities each summer.

***

I opened the door to our Hawkesbury home after work one day, and Linda greeted me with her usual smile, but this time she followed me as I made my way upstairs to change out of my banker's suit. As I entered our bedroom, she called me over from the bathroom and asked me to look at something. I was thinking we had some plumbing issue, but her flushed face quickly indicated that this was not at all a request for a repair job. She extended her arm and presented a positive test to me. "I'm pregnant!"

Another dream had come true.

After our wedding, we had discussed that starting our family should not be delayed and that we should let nature take care of timing. Fortunately, the chemistry was a perfect mix, and we now found ourselves in September starting to plan for what would come next spring. Being in Hawkesbury and not close to any family or friends did not bother Linda during the first year, but as the second year continued, she hinted strongly that staying much longer in the small rural town would not be ideal. Once the pregnancy arrived, we started planning our exit, regardless of what my employer could do for me to relocate. We continued our regular weekends to the Laurentians and visits to Linda's mom in Mississauga, but we also started to look at neighbourhoods in the eastern part of Ottawa. This was not the time to start a new job at another company and have the uncertainty that comes with a career change in the midst of starting our family. Simply put, we were making it payday-to-payday anyway, so we did not have the luxury to be selective. It was at that time that I started using the phrase "Got to fill the fridge," five words I continue to use with my girls.

I waited until before Christmas to inform my boss that we were expecting our first child and that Hawkesbury was not in the cards for many more months. An agreement was reached that even if they could not relocate me in the next few months, I could move to the Ottawa area and make the daily drive and continue my mandate in Hawkesbury. With that settled, I was thrilled to make Linda happy and did not care that the possible daily drive would be horrible. It was my turn to make sacrifices.

Linda was glorious during her entire pregnancy. She loved every moment of it and glowed with happiness and pride. There were the bad days and pains that came as part of the journey, but it never took away her positive approach and excitement about the future. In addition to planning for a new home, we started to purchase small baby items and think about names. We decided not to identify the sex, so it would be a surprise, which we also did for our second. Our realtor sent us listings regularly, but since this was before the days of online shopping, we were reliant on paper copies and actual visits. Once we settled on the east end, it became easier, and we finally found a good home just north of the Place d'Orleans Shopping Centre, close to an express bus terminal (in case I ever got a job downtown and needed transit).

We got possession after the holidays and went into hyper-renovation mode for a few weeks with the help of friends and family to refresh the home and prepare it for the little one. We painted every inch of that house! Most of the rooms were empty for months after our move given that we did not have furniture and needed to save before adding to our inventory. Once the essentials were done, we focused on the baby room and spent days planning, painting, and decorating it. Linda took great care to have everything in the right place with all the little supplies on hand for the first several weeks. Of all the painting and cleaning I did in that house, I remember most taking my time with the baby room and enjoying every second of it.

During those nine months, I learned a lot about love and dedication. Linda and I met as grown adults with individual goals and careers that were taking us down successful paths. We had the opportunity to spend our twenties thinking about ourselves and doing the things that we wanted to do without the limits of time or a serious relationship. Everyone should have that time in their life, and we were lucky enough to enjoy it. Conversely, those years also made me realize that there is a finite level of happiness that can be gained from focusing on myself and that self-actualization is not attainable on that narrow path. The planning of activities, sharing time with friends and family, travelling, and building a solid career provide good fulfillment, but there is more. During both of her pregnancies, Linda exuded a contagious sentiment that I had not felt before. It was a higher level of purpose and vision. It was during this time that we both understood that having children and giving unconditional love and generosity had created a wider path. By the time May arrived with all of its fresh scents and greenery, we were ready.

CHAPTER 12
VOS SOURIRES FONT LE BONHEUR

Afternoon nap with Julia and Emilie following a birthday party.
May 14, 2005, Montréal, QC.

The warm water flowed into the tub as I adjusted the hot and cold faucets to create the ideal temperature for the nightly ritual. Since Julia's birth on a beautiful day in early May 1999, I had adopted the responsibility of ensuring that our girls always went to bed clean. It was also my way of ensuring that Linda had some time to herself after dinner to relax and do what she wanted after over twelve hours of constant time with the little ones. I never missed a night unless I was travelling for work. At first when Julia was days old, I was learning, adjusting, and with Linda's help, finding the right approach. But by the time Julia was a few weeks old, I got free rein and took full responsibility with pleasure. I was lucky that Linda had a completely open and modern approach to being a mother, which allowed me to get involved and do things my way without criticism (I was a good listener and accepted all feedback). It was during that first summer in our Ottawa home that I started to select a music album and play it on the stereo while I spent precious time with Julia. Since it was summer, Linda often went outside after dinner to enjoy the nice weather, so the music did not interfere, and it allowed me to combine two things I love: music and being with Julia and then Emilie. At first the selections were quieter types like Bruce Cockburn, Richard Séguin, and Don Henley, but as new rock albums were released by some of my favourites, I ventured into heavier stuff that resulted in a higher volume—a much higher volume. Julia did not seem to mind, and Linda never said a word, so I continued with my music selections before the start of bath time each night.

Then one night late in August the next summer, something magical happened. Julia had finished her bath, and after putting on her pyjamas and combing her hair, we made our way down the stairs as the last song from Don Henley's *Inside Job* album was playing. Before I knew it, she was bouncing around to the music with her arms in the air. She had been listening all along! *That* was when Linda and I renamed the nightly activity "Rock 'n' Roll Bain," and it lasted for years. Once Emilie was born the music never stopped, although I admit to turning down the volume a little for her first few months. By the time we moved to Montréal and both of them were very active girls, their dancing became a regular affair whenever music was played in the house. As young girls, they expanded their repertoire beyond my music selections, and I was glad to partake and try to learn the lyrics of their music in order to share their love of other artists. As I write this on a cold and windy November morning, both girls are waking up at Emilie's apartment in Ottawa after attending a Luke Combs concert at the large arena in Ottawa. The pictures and videos they sent late last night make me happy knowing that they have the magical power of music in their lives.

***

Julia Victoria Demers was born at 3:42 p.m. on May 12, 1999 at Riverside Hospital in Ottawa. She was exactly eight pounds. Emilie Martine Demers arrived almost exactly two years later at 7:33 a.m. on May 21, 2001, at Ottawa General Hospital on another beautiful spring day. She was just under eight pounds. For both pregnancies, we did not know the sex of the baby until delivery, as all we wanted was to have a healthy child without complications for Linda. There was also a certain excitement about not knowing the sex and having to quickly select a name from our list once each child arrived into the world. Linda was also very adamant that if she was lucky enough to not have complications, she would deliver naturally without the help of any drugs or painkillers. Even with Julia's arrival being long and painful, Linda never relented even though I suffered emotional distress while witnessing the agony Linda was enduring. We had done all of the preparation classes and learned the techniques that came into use during the contractions for her first delivery.

Emilie was a different story, as she came into the world quickly, and her birth did not inflict the same level of pain on her mother. Linda tells the story of not being certain that it was time for Emilie when she woke up at 3:00 a.m. on the morning of the twenty-first. Her contractions were mild, but since we were staying at the family cottage in the Laurentians, two hours away from Ottawa, Linda woke me, and we drove to the hospital. Emilie was born a few hours after we checked in and minutes after Dr. Fleming arrived in the room.

The pleasure of having two daughters was overwhelming for me. I did not have sisters and was mainly surrounded by boys all my life, so to have two girls was the best gift. Once Emilie was born, Linda asked me if I was disappointed that I did not have a son. I quickly replied that it did not matter and that I could not be more fortunate. It would be up to my nephew, Philippe Demers, to represent. He accepts that responsibility with honour and is always looking out for his cousins and sisters. With Emilie's arrival, the game changed in our life. It became all about the girls all the time, and we adored it.

Our daughters are the third and fifth born of the next generation for the Demers family and the first and second for the Szargas. Steve's daughter, Camille, is the oldest, with Philippe coming a few years later and his third, Elise, born six months before Emilie. Linda's brother, Mike, and his wife, Jennifer, had Ryan in 2004, and he is the only other blood cousin on that side of the family. Ryan's older siblings, Stephen and Taylor, are from Jennifer's first marriage.

Being a twin brother and becoming an uncle to your twin's children is a different experience. First of all, when the kids start to recognize faces and say words, they ask questions and make funny comments about why someone else also looks like dad. Amazingly though, the kids never mixed us up, unlike uncles and some friends who continue to struggle—to my disbelief.

When Camille was born (before I met Linda), I did everything possible to visit Steve and Josée weekly either in Montréal or at the cottage to spend time with her. I was the first family member to see her at the hospital when she was born after Steve called me, and I am blessed to be her godfather. Now that she is to become a mother for the first time later this year, I'm engulfed with pleasure knowing that she will be an incredible parent. Our bond as twins has made me equally close to Steve and Josée's three children, whom I love immensely. Linda and I have always felt like all of our nieces and nephews are like our kids, although we respect and recognize the role and unmatched love of their parents. Linda has always been there for each of them and provided guidance, advice, car rides, treats, and anything else they need. Unlike many families, we are together for all of the important moments, share notes and snaps every day, and see each other frequently. But like all families, we don't always agree on some smaller things, and we work continuously to respect the choices and behaviours of different members. This bond developed years ago when the kids were babies and has evolved over the last twenty-five years. Being together made that happen.

When Julia and Emilie were little, they always had a good group of friends and playmates outside of the family. Linda was deliberate about including the girls in playgroups and preschool programs, so they could have fun with others their age but more importantly learn how to be social and adaptive. In the early years, the girls were not always happy with being away from home. Tears flowed (accompanied by little fits) when they were dropped off and Linda walked out. Both Emilie and Julia had their own moments and prolonged periods of shyness or apprehension about being left alone without a family member. They never had any issues staying with grandparents, uncles, aunts, or even our adult friends, but leaving them in a room without that security proved to be challenging at the start. To Linda's credit, she never quit, and she handled all the tears with great patience. I had to jump in a few times and skip work when Linda was done with it and told me that it was my turn to experience the tension. It only made me love and appreciate my wife more for her relentless drive to do the right thing and teach the girls important life lessons. The building of confidence with friends outside the family developed eventually and continued throughout their childhood. But nothing is more important to them (and us) than the hours and weekends that they spent with their six cousins in the last twenty years. Not being a very large family surely helps focus the energy.

As I watched our girls grow in the first five years, it was striking how different they were. Julia was very shy, reserved, and a great listener, while Emilie tended to scoff at requests from me or Linda and get frustrated quickly when things did not go her way. As the older sister, Julia took advantage of this and used every opportunity when the parents were out of sight to tease her sister, only to act innocent moments later. Because they were together all the time, their individual personalities were fascinating to us as parents. How could they be so different when we did everything the same for them both? We never let things get out of hand, but we rarely had to discipline them and intervene in their affairs. Linda and I both believed that freedom was important and that free time would be good for their creative side.

During their preschool years, Linda took a balanced approach to their development by introducing structured home activities each day like painting, reading, art, and playing games. And she allowed lots of hours for just being kids. Thank you, Linda!

The other funny difference between our girls is their sleeping patterns. While Julia was quick to cut out her afternoon nap, Emilie slept for hours each afternoon, with us having to wake her up sometimes for dinner. To this day Emilie needs her "beauty sleep," and Julia can stay up into the early morning without any effort.

The seven years from the time Julia was born to Emilie going to school full-time was a great period for our family. All we wanted to do was be with them and spend time with family or weekends with our friends, who were also busy with raising their children. We did some classic road trips to New

Brunswick, gathered at family cottages seasonally, went on some annual vacations together, and drove for hours on weekends to see our friends, so we could get some adult time. We still joke about how the kids outnumbered the adults during all those years of adventures. The culmination of our unrelenting willingness to travel with ten kids was the Disney trip in the summer of 2010. We found the perfect balance between the kids having fun and parents finding great moments to enjoy life—and have a little fun!

By the time we relocated to Quebec City, it was time for Emilie to start grade one. We moved into our home in the middle of August and had only a few weeks to settle in and prepare the girls for their first day at school. The school year starts a week earlier in Quebec than in Ontario, so the first day is in August, not after the Labour Day long weekend.

I was already in the thick of my new job by the time the family joined me full-time, so my time as a dad outside of the evenings and weekends was pretty much nil. I was travelling all over the province, visiting branches in my territory or attending meetings in Montréal and Toronto. I tried to sleep at home as much as possible, but Linda still reminds me today that those first four months in Quebec City were the worst in my entire career. Again, it was up to Linda to manage our family and the new school for the girls.

Julia's start at the new school went pretty well, and in her quiet way she adapted, followed the school routine, and made friends quickly. Emilie was another matter altogether. While we still don't know why, she was not having it with being at school for a full day without her mom. For the first few days, we thought it was just normal adjustment fears, but as the temper flares continued into September, we were both worried. Linda even used *The Kissing Hand* book as a tactic. (Emilie shares that having mommy kiss her hand each morning did get her through.) Fortunately, her teacher, Mr. Simons (a saint in our opinion), found a way to embrace the challenge and started making progress with Emilie each morning. He used his piano and other tactics from over thirty years of teaching small kids to make her feel more secure, eventually getting her to at least start the day without constant tears. Mr. Simons would also give Linda a quick email update most days at lunchtime on how Emilie was doing to relieve Linda's anxiety (although we're pretty sure he only shared the good updates). Once October arrived with falling leaves and morning frost, Emilie was good to go. We are still friends with Mr. Simons and are forever grateful.

The girls had different friend groups and started to spend a lot of after-school and weekend time with the three kids who lived next door. They were about the same age. Luckily, there was a boy who took part in all the games and performances. The routine was simple: when the kids arrived home after school, the moms left them outside to play until dark. It did not matter if it was a warm June afternoon or during the depths of the freezing winter in January. The activity intensified during the summer holidays with outside plays and Cirque du Soleil-type shows being rehearsed on our front lawn with late-afternoon performances for the parents. This is where having a boy in the group was important to ensure all of the roles and characters could be filled. The imagination those five kids displayed was unbelievable. We even filmed some of their shows, with their cousins Elise and Camille sometimes taking part as special guests when they visited from Montréal. Although the first weeks were difficult for the girls, they adapted and enjoyed their new "French" life. Like my parents did for me, we gave the girls challenges and stretched their ability to adapt to change and appreciate diversity.

***

The snowdrifts gathered around the house and wrapped our home in thick white powder, and Julia and Emilie climbed them with vigour. The crisp cold air, well into the negative double digits for consecutive days, did not reduce their energy or voices as the blue sky retained its vibrant colour until disappearing well before dinner time. There was a sense of defiance in the lifestyle of enjoying the outdoors from November to March in that historical city. We were located only a few kilometres from the house of my ancestor, Jean Demers, who lived many winters with similar winter conditions. While our current standards allow for unlimited comfort within our modern homes regardless of the outside conditions, families in the 1600s focused mainly on survival. There was complete hibernation with fires burning constantly to retain a reasonable interior temperature and cook food. Darkness consumed more than half of the days for three consecutive months with small family gatherings, school, and church being the only social activities.

As we walked the small streets of Old Quebec on many occasions during our two winters there, I always thought about the strength and positive thinking that must have been required to keep a family happy. It felt like I was completing the circle and returning to where my ancestors started their life in North America. It gave me an appreciation for their sacrifices and a passion to preserve the positive light. As I watched my girls slide down the snowdrifts with laughter and excitement, I could only hope that Jean's children also had such moments.

***

The minivan pulled into our long driveway. The large moving truck that had departed from our home filled with all of our belongings was already in the distance, bound for Toronto. Linda and I wandered inside our empty home and then walked the property that we adored for the last time. We felt sad and more emotional than we would have ever imagined when we decided to leave the Toronto area almost exactly two years earlier. Linda loved the lifestyle and freedom that she had in Quebec City. To this day I think that if we would have stayed another year, we would still be living there.

On that day of moving boxes, the girls had decided to stay away and spend time with the Hurley kids. Over the last school year, our friendship with the Hurley family had become closer, with their three girls and our daughters spending countless hours together. As a result, Linda became very close with their mom, Josée, and I became close with their dad, Patrick. When we had shared the news of our return to Toronto, all the kids seemed to understand and continued their daily routine for weeks as we planned and organized the move. But when Josée stopped the minivan in the driveway and opened the doors to drop off the girls for the last time, the weight of the departure took full hold. A flood of sadness and tears overwhelmed all five girls, especially Emilie and Sarah. You never really know how important someone is to you until they are gone or you are unable to be with them as often as you wish. I recall feeling somewhat helpless as the moms tried to console the girls who eventually had to leave while they were still in tears. Our friendship with the Hurleys has continued over the years. We still visit Josée and Patrick, and they visit us regularly. We would have never had those amazing emotions without the willingness to take a chance and try the journey to Quebec City.

The two years taught me that no matter the uncertainty and the unknown, you should always seek out new adventures and not be held back by your current level of satisfaction and comfort.

***

Julia's tenth birthday signalled the start of an active decade for our family as we returned to the GTA with a move to the suburban city of Oakville. There would be no relocation for at least the next ten years, so the girls would have stability during their teenage years. This allowed Linda and the girls the freedom to make long-term plans, develop new friendships, and take part in multiple community activities. We found a nice raised bungalow with a pool and large trees for shade on the hot, humid summer days. The neighbourhood had excellent public schools and countless sport and social activities available nearby. As a nature and tree lover, I was delighted to be able to jog on quiet trails along Joshua Creek, which led to the vast Lake Ontario. After having completed my first half-marathon in Quebec City in 2008, I was now an avid runner and loved the freedom of discovering all the streets and trails within ten kilometres of our home. I never get tired of taking the paths on the shores of the lake and looking out on clear days toward downtown Toronto or the edges of Niagara and Hamilton. Contrary to Quebec, Southern Ontario offers much warmer temperatures and longer summers with lovely spring and fall seasons. I love the longer days, increased sunshine, and the proximity to the Szarga cottage, which we started to visit almost every weekend during the summers after our return. Even as a busy family unit, we made time for escapes and adventures on a regular basis.

The search for the name of the only island on Lake Eugenia had taken hold of me since the first time I circled it in 1996 on a bright August day with the powerboat. The dense forest and natural shore all around the two kilometre circumference creates a natural environment for plants, trees, and animals. There are no structures on the island, with only a few trails and clearings created by visitors. I was amazed during my first few years of enjoying the lake that none of the family members or fellow cottagers knew the name of the island that we all faced. Some, including my wife and family members, told me it was just called "the island."

"Impossible!" I would reply. "How can an island have no name given that it's been there for a hundred years?"

Others shared that it was called "Hydro Island" since the lake had been created to generate electricity and the island had survived the flooding.

"A poor excuse for a name," I replied.

To end the mystery and ease my mind, my research having produced nothing, I took matters into my own hands and named it what I thought was most appropriate for the kids and me: "Adventure Island."

A small opening between the branches that extended over the water was just big enough for the boat to enter and allowed me to jump onto shore and wrap the anchor rope around a tree. It was located on the east side of the island and was protected from wind, waves, and onlookers. It was also next to my favourite fishing spot where Emilie caught her biggest largemouth bass, which we named "Taco." Since my first time on the island with the girls when they were only a few years old, I have used the same location to launch countless adventures over the last twenty years. Although the entry point is the same, each adventure is different with a unique goal, destination, and outcome. On one of the adventures before the girls were ten years old, we decided that our goal was to penetrate the deeper woods of the island's slim south leg. The area was filled with red pines and carpeted with fallen needles. There was only light brush, so we found ourselves walking gently for most of the first half of the adventure. It was a warm day, so the mixture of shade and sun suited us fine as I educated the girls on all the different trees and plants we were seeing. Each adventure also included stories about my days as a Boy Scout and all of the interesting things I had learned about survival in the wilderness. As we looked around and searched for anything abnormal or beautiful, Emilie let out a screech as she pointed to the ground. "What is that?"

I moved closer to discover large animal bones that had obviously been there for some time. As I cleared away the pine needles, it was clear that they were the bones of a deer or a black bear. Upon further analysis of the longer jawbone, I concluded that we had found the skeletal remains of a small deer. The girls were fascinated and wanted to take the bones with us to show the family. Unfortunately, I never took my phone on these adventures for reasons of purity, so there would be no pictures, and our words would have to do. I also instilled in my girls an important rule of nature that if you find something that belongs to the environment, you leave it there. Suffice it to say that the bones adventure is legendary, and the story has been told many times. We even revisited the area a few more times to show the bones to nieces and nephews in later summers. There is nothing I enjoyed more than declaring in the morning to the kids that there would be an adventure after lunch! In addition to Adventure Island, we have discovered many other spots around the lake, including Old Balby, the Beaver River, the secret frog pond, and many more. The more popular Hoggs Falls is a short drive into the Beaver Valley and became our favourite camping spot. We'd go once a summer for an overnight stay when my niece, Elise, visited. We would set up our small tent in the afternoon, walk in the river leading to the falls, swim in the falls, then return to a small fire, where we would cook a simple dinner. The girls did not like the natural outside bathroom (essentially a hole in the ground next to a tree), but they endured and drank minimally. One night we were awakened with the sounds of what I knew were raccoons. They were very close to the tent and the girls were a little rattled.

"I think the little sounds are from doves," I said. "It will be dawn soon. Nothing to worry about."

Too sleepy to refute me, they relaxed and put their heads back inside their sleeping bags. I stayed on alert for the rest of the night since I feared the girls might have brought food into the tent. We used the crown land at Hoggs Falls with respect and always cleaned the entire area of debris and garbage before leaving. Linda did not care much for sleeping in a tent, so she would leave with the car after we put out the fire and return for the pickup at 8 a.m. the next morning. We would return to the cottage with excitement, as we knew Linda always prepared a great breakfast with lots of bacon.

***

As much as the girls loved their time in Quebec City, they adapted quickly to their new home and were young enough not to dwell on the past. Linda also got heavily involved with the schools and began to tutor kids in mathematics. She went on to help hundreds of high school students and still does today. There was never a dull day in the house, with friends coming in and out and multiple events on the calendar. The girls started to do horse riding every weekend, played sports, had multiple sleepovers and birthday parties, participated in school clubs, and spent countless hours in the pool and at the lake during summers. The teachers recognized their balanced approach to academics and diverse social skills, which was rewarded with more attention and recognition. This only increased their confidence and fuelled their dedication to their classes and to increasing their marks. They will share that they were far from perfect and experienced some tough moments, along with doing some silly things, but their discipline for homework each day (encouraged by their mom) and preparation for class paid dividends. Also interesting was their choice of friends and social circles. They always had an open mind (likely influenced by the relocations) about friendships and did not focus on only a few friends or one gang. Somewhat like Linda and me when we were kids, they stayed in the middle and enjoyed what different individuals and diverse groups had to offer. We witnessed this as new faces would come to the house, and old faces would return after some time off.

A light fog hovered on a cool Saturday morning as we pulled into the long gravel driveway leading to the barns where dozens of horses awaited the arrival of children. Julia and Emilie exited the car and gathered their gear from the trunk for the day ahead. I handed over the cash from the car window to one of the trainers and followed the other cars around the circle leading back to Dundas Street on the edges of northwest Oakville. As I departed, the girls were excitingly making their way to the main barn to begin their complete escape for the next eight hours. They had made a deal with the owners to pay for the lessons in the morning, but also to stay for free during the afternoon to help with various chores. Both of my daughters just wanted to be around the horses and would do anything to make that happen. Once their day was complete, I returned in the afternoon to pick them up and endured (sometimes enjoyed) the strong smell of the farm that filled the car. They were exhausted, and after a good shower, followed by dinner, they crashed hard, full of happiness.

Their older cousin, Camille, was the first to start riding. She was also completely taken by the sport and even owned a horse for years. Once the girls experienced it, they were hooked and quickly found a location nearby to start their equestrian journey. Unlike many families who spent their winter weekends in the rink or at the ski hill, we were barn rats. These were the years before high school, so rugby had not yet monopolized our time, and we enjoyed the routine and attended all of the show jumping competitions. The girls also did some summer camps during their involvement in the sport, which lasted more than five years. While other sports captured their interests later on, they both talk about how much they love riding and how they hope to get back to it later. Emilie's dream is to have a hobby farm close to the city with horses and all the natural escapes that such a lifestyle provides.

When Julia made the jump to high school, she took some time to adjust and learned to navigate the large population of over one thousand students. With the public schools being good in the area, we registered Julia at Oakville Trafalgar High School (OT) where most of her friends were also going to attend, apart from a few who selected the private system. The school was very safe and had excellent teachers. With a long history and a solid reputation, there were some routines and traditions that the freshmen needed to learn apart from the academic content. Most important were the rules of engagement or "law" for the infamous central atrium inside the building. Once Julia figured out the ground rules, she focused on building a successful first year. Unknown to her as she completed her first semester and enjoyed the Christmas holiday season was how a sport was about to change her life—and our family focus.

A casual comment from a friend to Julia about how rugby was fun and that the junior team was about to hold its annual tryouts caught her attention. Her friend even said that it was going to be pretty much a "walk on" to make the team. At one dinner in mid-January, I recall Julia talking about this new possibility and that she would like to give it a try even though she knew nothing at all about the sport. As per our usual approach, Linda and I asked a few questions and did not deter her determination to discover something new. The benefit of making friends and enhancing her social inclusiveness at her new high school seemed to eclipse the physical risks. The funny thing is, once Julia attended the first practice, she knew within minutes that this would be anything but a "walk on." Instead, it was a gruelling effort to learn the game quickly and impress the head coach, who seemed intent on putting together a contending team. Every night for days we learned about the game and the rules as Julia shared her observations and initial passion for this new sport—and how she liked crushing players! The road to making the team was not easy and was full of emotions. When the day came for the coach to post the names of the girls who had made the team, Julia's name was not on the list. She called from school and sobbed to Linda about being a failure and how embarrassing it was for her friends to look at her while they themselves had made it.

That evening when I came home, it was not a happy situation, and dinner time was very emotional. That was when Linda turned on her master skills as a mom. She listened and suggested to Julia that if it was that important to her, she should talk to the coach the next day and ask how she could improve for next year. She said this would also demonstrate her drive and passion to be on the team. The next morning Julia got the courage to approach the coach between classes and had a good discussion, although she noticed he looked a little puzzled. An hour after their meeting, Julia was sitting in class when the coach asked to speak to Julia in the hallway. To her elation, he said that a mistake had been made, and her name was erroneously excluded from the list posted the day prior. She had made the team after all! We will never know if there was really an error or if Julia's mature and passionate meeting with the coach turned the tide, but regardless, a new path had opened.

Julia went on to play for all four years of high school, and Emilie joined for her full high school term two years later. The coach was one of the best in the country for rugby and led the team to multiple OFSAA gold medal championships during his tenure at OT (he now coaches at the university level and has elevated his successes). More importantly, the coach was an incredibly positive influence on my girls and created an environment where they both enhanced their self-confidence and work ethic. As a result of their leadership skills and contributions to their teams, both girls received the coveted athlete of the year award while in grade ten. When their coach presented the awards, his remarks at the two different occasions made Linda and I very emotional and proud. Both girls were humble and kept working just as hard for the rest of their time in the program. Linda was completely immersed in all of their sports, but rugby brought things to an entirely new level. She never missed a game (she even attended practices), became their main photographer, and acted as their number one cheerleader no matter the weather. Food was always brought, and if something needed to be done or a special task was required by the coaches, she was the first to volunteer.

When the girls also started playing in the summer and on other rugby teams outside of school, we were there. Rugby brought us to all parts of the GTA during the week and on cold autumn weekends to other fields we never knew existed, sometimes over an hour away. I loved watching the girls and seeing them in action. Their passion and ability to excel at a sport they only started in grade nine impressed me. Their teammates were amazing, with some of them making the Canadian team at junior and senior levels, including international tournaments and the Olympics. We still follow some of their old teammates from high school when they play in important tournaments. Rugby bonds are for life. To think that our daughters once played with these international athletes is amazing.

Sly, our great teacher friend who coached high school basketball for decades, helped put this in the right perspective when he told us that winning only one OFSAA championship would be a significant accomplishment for any player or coach, let alone winning multiple championships in only four years. "Lightning in a bottle," as he put it.

In an extraordinary way, the girls were never the same after their rugby careers ended. They had both matured, gained an elevated sense of personal confidence, and perfected their determination to succeed. Julia and Emilie never played again after high school, but the experience of being part of those teams was more than anything we could teach or show them. They continue to stay in touch with the coaches, help their old teams when they can, and hope to possibly coach when they get older. Having truly exceptional coaches helped them understand the impact one person can have on others. It was truly life changing. For her part, Linda spent six years as a dedicated rugby mom and had a great time. She comments today with a tear in her eye that it was probably the best years of her life as a mother so far.

***

We never pushed our daughters to select a certain career path or professional designation while they were in high school. Like our parents did with us, we wanted our girls to make their own choices and hopefully gravitate to an industry they found interesting. The only preference we communicated was going to university, no matter the program. I kept repeating to them that to have the benefit of different job choices for years to come, an undergraduate degree was foundational. We were thrilled, therefore, when Julia elected to go to McGill and Emilie to the University of Ottawa two years later. They were both very excited to live away from home, enjoy residence life for the first year, and make new friends. Montréal and Ottawa offer so much outside of school for students to keep their social lives busy, with the added benefit of having friends and extended family nearby. It was also easy for them to make those cities their second home since they had lived there at a younger age. For Linda and me, it also made the adjustment easier knowing they were in locations we knew well and that someone could be there quickly if they needed urgent help, which happened for both girls on a few occasions!

With Julia leaving home first, Emilie found it more difficult since she was two years behind and had to see her older sister gain freedom while she stayed home and became the de facto central focus of her parents (not always to her liking). However, before she knew it, Emilie was also looking at university choices and planning her future away from the Oakville bubble. Despite the distance, social media kept the frequency of our interactions as a family unit constant and full of conversations. Supplemented with many drives on Highway 401, the close family bond we had built over eighteen years continued to prosper and mature. Surprisingly, Linda and I never felt lost or sad as short-term empty nesters. We increased some social activities, played more golf, continued our weekly pub night, and used the opportunity to undertake more frequent adventures to different destinations. As most parents who have had children away for post-secondary school will share, "Never clear out the kids' rooms, as they will most likely come back!"

Julia graduated with honours from McGill in June 2022. By that time, Emilie had finished her third year and was well on her way to academic success as well. It was during this period that I started joking (actually not) with my girls that we needed them to keep us up to date and share their knowledge, so we would not become stale parents. Over the years I have taken the time to read some of their papers and projects with admiration as they comprehend complex subject matters and tackle important issues. I want our daughters to be influential and challenge past thinking to improve our society and evolve it further toward the values that we hold dear. I want them to inform Linda and me about current affairs capturing the minds of young people and share their views, so we can have a better understanding of new factors impacting our communities. And I want them and their friends to have discussions and debate strategic themes for our country and political landscape. I'm interested and dedicated to listening to them while providing feedback using my good judgment (which is one thing I think older people have and continues to improve with age). Looking back at our generation, I think we lived somewhat in the shadow of the baby boomers and never impacted our surroundings like we could have. Maybe being too passive, Generation X was "along for the ride" and enjoyed the fruits of their parents and grandparents' labour. I see an entirely different tempo for Gen Z, which makes me excited about witnessing and participating in the next decades.

Postscript

Julia has decided to obtain a master's degree in international relations, specializing in peace and conflict resolution, and has been accepted at the University of Queensland in Brisbane, Australia. The two-year program started in February 2023. She has joined her boyfriend, José, who has entered his second year at the Queensland Faculty of Medicine. Their international experience will give them solid career opportunities for years to come.

Emilie graduated with honours from U Ottawa in June 2023. She has decided to continue her studies and attend the Faculty of Education at York University to obtain a bachelor of education. Her goal is to become a high school teacher. I can only hope that she will positively influence hundreds of kids like others before her.

Regardless of the choices they make, I wish them success and to be surrounded by positive people.

***

Be it in Quebec City, Brisbane, London, San Francisco, Toronto, Quito, or any other place that my children and their descendants choose to live, I wish them happiness. The world is already so much more open than it was when I was a kid. Diversity and different beliefs easily cross borders and have become mainly global, for all to enjoy and critique. As I write these words, my daughter is studying in Brisbane, but we don't feel like she is fifteen thousand kilometres away on the other side of the world. We text constantly, and at least once a day she connects with us for a video chat. Like my grandparents were happy when I learned a new language, I'm fine if my grandkids don't speak French (or English for that matter). I've learned that allowing the future to bring you new opportunities and challenges only enriches your life; it doesn't diminish it. I'm very open to learning another language if it means I can communicate with family and friends. And Linda and I are also open to visiting new places to discover and spend time with people we adore. Values are demonstrated and reinforced in the actions you take, not the words you speak.

I've always felt like I've had an unlimited reservoir of positivity in my soul. I know I was not born this way; it came from the actions of people around me. The virtuous circle of love and joy provides an endless supply if you choose to be a multiplier and repel hatred and bigotry. I've been lucky to avoid any unthinkable tragedy or the infliction of an incurable illness on a loved one. I get it! I'm well aware of my fortunate path thus far, and I know that the future will present unexpected turns and deep holes. I'm not sure how I will respond. However, I have faith that the experiences and resiliency of my ancestors will guide me.

I believe in the power of reinforcement and encouraging people to use their strengths, spending little time on weaknesses. Unleashing one's full potential to reach a pinnacle of self-actualization requires skill, knowledge, dedication, and most importantly, people who encourage you. Without a circle of friends, family, or colleagues, the well will run dry, and purpose will be lost. We belong to a grand macrocosm that has demonstrated time and time again that we are all linked. Everyone has a role to play and a responsibility in their broader community to advance into the future with a light that shines brightly.

BOOK 3

ESCAPOLOGISTS AT WORK

"PLAN NOT EVERY ESCAPE. IF YOU DO IT COULD ELIMINATE
THE VERY INTENT OF THE ADVENTURE."

Steve Demers

PROLOGUE 3

The *Canadian Oxford Dictionary* defines *escape* as to "break free or free oneself by fleeing or struggling." Conversely, *The Merriam-Webster Dictionary* defines the words *stay* and *remain* as antonyms. The word *escape* is made up of the Latin prefix *ex*, which means "out of," and the Latin word *cappa*, which means "head covering" or "cloak." In modern times most people use the word to define breaking free from something undesirable with no intent to return. Movies such as *Escape from Alcatraz* with Clint Eastwood have helped create a singular bias around the use of the word. I like to focus on the emotional definition and impact of escaping. The American Psychology Association defines *escapism* as "the tendency to escape from the real world to the delight or security of a fantasy world." This can include listening to music, reading, dreaming, gaming, or dancing. It can also involve travelling, adventuring, and discovering. Like a prisoner's elation and complete sense of freedom when breaking out of prison, similar emotions can be experienced by those who simply "get away." The distinct difference is that for those temporarily getting away, it does not assume the return will be negative or undesired. For me, the magic of escape is gaining great pleasure and new knowledge from the adventure, all the while understanding that I will return to my fulfilled and happy routine life. I can't have one without the other.

My first escapes occurred as a young teenager and included trips with the Boy Scouts, immersion in music, and adventures on foot or in a canoe. Before then I struggled with being away from my parents for any length of time, and they had to have grandparents stay with us if they travelled for more than one day. I'm sure there is some psychological analysis that could uncover why this was the case, but it would be futile now that I'm more than happy to escape anywhere at almost any time. I acquired great confidence during those years of camping in the depths of nature hundreds of miles from home. They proved to be my first experiences of shedding daily routines and the comfort of home for the benefit of discovering new places. I felt liberated learning all about the natural environment, such as which wild plants we could eat and how animals interacted with one another within their unspoiled territory. There was even greater mystery in the evening hours when only a fire or flashlights guided our movement through the quiet darkness, interrupted by sounds and imaginary shadows (and raccoons trying to break into our food supply!). The sense of escapism was most powerful when we stared into the orange fire for hours, singing songs and telling stories. The celestial night sky appeared amazingly once we put out the fire and walked to our tents.

Polished marketing and structured vacations to well-known travel destinations are now the dominant preference for those looking to get away from the stress of their daily routine, work, or even family. With travel to anywhere in the world available to anyone who can afford it, making a selection can be overwhelming. Notwithstanding some of the complexity and challenges the world of travel has created, the magical aspect of the experience continues to be present. No matter the scale of luxury one selects, the pleasure and the feeling of discovery motivates millions each month to leave the comfort of their homes. This has not changed in thousands of years for human beings. Our ancestors travelled first by land and then by sea to discover new species, peoples, and cultures and to expand the world as they knew it. Some of their travels were for purely scientific pursuits, some for cartography, some with the goal to be the first discoverer, and some simply to adventure. It has been at the core of humankind to seek out new things, be curious, and move.

CHAPTER 13
THE SEARCH FOR AURORA BOREALIS

The Demers boys: nephew Philippe, Steve, and me.
Old Quebec, September 24, 2020.

The sunshine began to light the blue winter sky over the trees to the east as I awoke at 6:53 a.m. on February 22, 2020. There were no other cars ahead or behind us as I started to focus my eyes after a short sleep of less than ninety minutes in the passenger seat. Steve looked over at me and smiled. "Sleep well, man?"

"For sure," I replied. Then I asked him where we were and how the north-bound road had been since entering the Vérendrye Wildlife Reserve. We had started our adventure in the middle of the night from Montréal, so we could reach our destination on the edge of James Bay before sundown. That part of the journey did not require daylight for sightseeing as we had been on that road before in the past. We were also trying to avoid any traffic on that most dangerous stretch of winding highway. While we chatted and planned our next stop to switch drivers, both young discoverers, Phil and Simon, were sound asleep in the back and showed no sign of life. They had shared the night before that they were not at all interested in driving and were happy to leave the responsibility to my brother and me, which suited us fine. There had been a dusting of snow overnight, but the temperature was relatively mild for that time of the year, leaving the roads safe and the visibility excellent.

As we reached the north end of the reserve and exited the natural sanctu-ary, I reminded Steve that I knew the Abitibi region well since it was part of my territory when I was working in Quebec City, and I had travelled to the mining towns of Val-d'Or, Malartic, and Rouyn-Noranda on multiple occa-sions. As I was to find out during the next few days, the beauty of the "Grand Nord" is truly beyond the fiftieth parallel.

It was my nephew, Philippe, who was the catalyst for this inaugural north-ern discovery adventure when he said he wanted to see the northern lights. Not being an expert on when or where would be the best location to witness this phenomenon, he turned to his dad, who recommended heading north "to the end of the line," the remote town of Radisson. Steve had been there by plane a few years earlier to visit the Hydro Quebec (HQ) facilities as part of his role with them. So, after some discussion during the holidays they asked me to join them. Also joining would be Phil's good friend and all-around fantastic guy, Simon. A few days before our departure, I did some research on where we were going and realized we were about to reach the northeast coast of James Bay just south of the opening into the world-famous Hudson Bay. Now I was excited!

Once we stopped in Amos for brunch and entered the town of Mattagami just after noon to fill up with gas, the trip took on a different purpose. As we read the large road sign stating "Route de la Baie-James, Km 0," we were all in full exploration mode. The well-paved road with minimal traffic was clear of snow and mainly dry from the heat of the bright warm sun. There was snow everywhere else with a diminishing volume of trees as we drove north for six hours. Every few hundred kilometres, we crossed a river or rapids that flowed with a thunderous sound. The contrast of the deep blue sky, pure white snow, and dark green trees created a calm mood. We crossed large sections of the forest that had either been clear-cut or destroyed by recent summer wildfires, with nothing left but a few sporadic tree trunks still standing. The most incredible thing to observe was how short the trees were versus what is found in the warmer climate of southern Quebec and Ontario. I had been told that the shorter days of sunshine and colder weather impacted the growth and the type of trees in northern Canada, but I was surprised at the magnitude. Without any cell service and with non-existent roadside services, I enjoyed the peace and could not stop thinking about all the open space we have in Canada. As we travelled through the area, we recognized and acknowledged that we had entered the Eeyou Istchee territory, offering our respect to that land and the people who resided there and to those who for centuries had lived with nature.

On the final stretch before arriving at the southern edge of the Grand River Airport area, I saw a pickup truck in the distance. Realizing that the truck was stopped on the side of the road, I slowed as I approached to ask if they needed help.

"Wow, look at that!" Simon shouted from the backseat. "He's shooting a shotgun in the air!"

As I stopped only metres behind the truck, we realized he was hunting on the side of the road. I rolled down my window to smile and show him that we were friendly, though I was mainly curious to observe what he was doing. He looked at us for a few seconds and then lifted his arm in our direction to wave while holding a dead white partridge in his hand. Then he walked in front of our car and over to his wife, who was standing outside their truck, and handed her the prize. Seconds later she began to pluck the feathers with precision and speed. Simon and Phil could not believe their eyes, as they had never experienced the handling of a gun and hunting like that before, let alone seeing the routines of local Indigenous people on their land. As the man walked back in front of us, he placed his rifle in the back of his truck and replaced it with a pair of large snowshoes to tackle the deep snow and retrieve his other prizes in the thin forest. Later, we investigated the exact location of that incredible encounter and confirmed that it was near the main road leading to the Cree Nation of Wemindji on the shores of James Bay.

Our arrival in Radisson around dinner time was well deserved. We had travelled over sixteen hours in good weather, and our reward was to have a nice meal with drinks at the only hotel in town. We ventured outside after dinner to see if the northern lights were present, but there was nothing but cold temperature and a black moonless sky. This was followed by a long night of sleep before starting two days of discovery.

The bright sunshine and crisp -20°C air welcomed us for our first day of discovery. Steve was very excited to show us the incredible HQ Robert-Bourassa hydroelectric power complex near Radisson, but the boys and I had one destination in mind for our first day in the north: James Bay. Only few ever make the journey to visit one of the most important areas in Canada's history, and we were determined to drive westbound from Radisson on the James Bay Road until it ended on the rocky shores of the frozen water.

The search for a sea route through or around America escalated as Columbus's successors confirmed the size of the land and the rich value of having access to the Pacific. Now known widely as the search for the Northwest Passage, it began in the late sixteenth century even before Samuel de Champlain arrived to explore North America in 1603. During the time de Champlain was busy charting America's Atlantic coast from 1604 to 1607 and founding Quebec City in 1608, others were looking for the ultimate prize of a priceless passage. Different countries invested large sums to fund the voyages, and some of the best captains were recruited to command the risky adventures. Martin Frobisher led the first legitimate voyage in 1576 and followed from 1577 to 1578 with the added purpose of finding mineral ore. (Unfortunately, what he brought back to England was determined to be fool's gold.) During the next few decades, other explorers tackled the difficult conditions and made voyages without ever finding an open strait. Much of the area is now named after them: Frobisher Bay, Davis Strait, Baffin Island and Baffin Bay, Hudson Strait and Hudson Bay, and Foxe Basin.

Henry Hudson was the first to travel the waters of what is now known as James Bay, but it was Thomas James who made it famous in 1631. Instead of exiting for the winter and returning to England, James decided to winter in the bay, which was the southernmost extension of Hudson Bay. We can only speculate that the warmer temperature and shallow, calm waters influenced his decision. However, it was a brutal decision for him and his crew as they suffered for months, with some dying during the ordeal. Interestingly, while they fought for their lives, the shores of the Hudson Bay and James Bay were home to many Indigenous communities who thrived year-round. We can only speculate, but past hostilities with Europeans or the pride of the explorers most likely discouraged efforts of cooperation. Returning to England in 1632, James was in a miserable state and had minimal successes to share but for the details of his horrific winter season, which he captured in his account called *The Strange and Dangerous Voyage of Capt. Thomas James*. It became a classic story of survival, later called upon a hundred and fifty years later by Samuel Taylor Coleridge in his longest poem, "The Rime of the Ancient Mariner." The return of James and his crew marked the end of the decades-long search for the Northwest Passage. They discouraged all potential explorers with their stories of famine, scurvy, towering icebergs, violent tides, and bone-chilling cold.

It was with a real appreciation for the history and significance of the land and water that we travelled westbound from Radisson toward the massive bay. But before racing to our destination, we realized there was another landmark worthy of our attention: the Cree Nation of Chisasibi and Fort George. Mainly a summer gathering place for the nomadic Cree centuries ago, what is now known as Fort George Island is located on the eastern edge of James Bay and became a permanent trading post for the Hudson's Bay Company in the early 1800s. In 1852, expansion continued with an Anglican mission being established, followed in 1907 by an Anglican school and Catholic mission in 1927. As the Cree shed their nomadic way of life, they settled on the island full-time in the twentieth century. It was not until the 1970s during the development of the massive hydroelectric stations on La Grande River that relocation from Fort George to the mainland occurred with the creation of the present-day Chisasibi Cree village. As part of intense negotiations with HQ, a deal was reached to relocate the community from the erosion- and flood-risk area to higher ground south of La Grande. As we drove through the modern neighbourhood and witnessed the beautiful buildings, homes, and services, I was struck by how it contrasted with what millions think of when they imagine an Indigenous community. There is a clear purpose and pride. We would have liked to complete our discovery with a visit to Port George, but we were informed that the island is mainly used to host summer gatherings each year in July. It is a week when family and friends return to simpler times to enjoy games, dances, and feasting.

After ninety minutes of driving from Radisson, we only had ten minutes before we reached the end of the line. Surprisingly, we came across a few locals driving on the dead-end snow-covered road before we arrived at an empty parking area with a few empty buildings and a vacant observation tower. White snow was everywhere, with the bright sun providing some heat to counter the cold wind. Simon and Philippe were so excited, they jumped out of the car to reach the frozen shore and take pictures. Steve and I followed in a more pensive state as we kept reminding ourselves how lucky we were to have made the trip to this Canadian landmark. As I took time to share a bit more history with the boys, I was fascinated with the number of fishing boats and canoes that were frozen in place on the beach for the winter. Like we had witnessed with the hunter on the northern route, fishing was still very much a part of their culture. Also interesting is that all the islands on the bay are part of Nunavut, not Quebec or Ontario.

After walking around for some time and taking lots of pictures, I approached Simon and heard him talking, but no one was around him. When I reached him, he was on FaceTime with his mom! The Cree Nation of Chisasibi have invested to provide cell service in their village and most of their community, like the beach where they spend countless hours during the summer. It is good to respect and appreciate the past while always moving forward.

Our second night did not produce northern lights.

***

When Steve recommended Radisson to Philippe as a possible destination to see the northern lights, he had another motivation: to show the boys one of the wonders of the modern world. The town of Radisson never existed before HQ initiated the Robert-Bourassa hydroelectric development in the early 1970s. In fact, nothing was there but wilderness. For safety, the town was built seven kilometres west of the dam on elevated land. Along with the mining town of Schefferville, it is the only non-Native town north of the fifty-third parallel in Quebec. It was named after the fur trader and explorer who helped create the Hudson's Bay Company. At the peak of construction in the late 1970s, thousands of workers lived there either on a temporary or permanent basis to sustain the multi-year project. Now less than five hundred permanent residents support a seasonal workforce from HQ, and they're mainly present during the summer months to conduct maintenance. Incredibly, less than a hundred workers are required at any given time to manage the world's largest underground hydroelectric power station. The dam is as tall as a fifty-three-storey building, holding back a reservoir with an area of 2,835 square kilometres and 4,550 kilometres of shoreline. The heart of the operation is one hundred and forty metres underground with the capacity to produce the largest energy supply in North America. It was not only the metropolis of Montréal that was building gigantic infrastructure projects in the late 1960s and 1970s (Expo 67, the 1976 Olympics); the province of Quebec also had momentum on many fronts.

On our second (and last) day of discovery, we woke early after a good night's sleep, following dinner at a small local restaurant the night before. It was Monday, so more places were open, which made our day easier. It was dedicated to viewing hydro stations and visiting the nearby area around Radisson. We had also secured a tour of the Robert-Bourassa power station that afternoon.

Before lunch we drove around every public road in the town and ventured to the large dam reservoir and the Giant's Staircase to view the immensity of the project. Since everything is underground for the generators, the entire landscape was pure and silent. Apart from the spillway, it looked like a massive lake with some buildings and roads on its western edge. I could tell that there were significant man-made structures and impact on the environment, but it was much less intrusive than the normal above-ground hydroelectric plants. While reading all the signs and researching the methods used to build the huge complex, I gained a strong appreciation for the level of planning and engineering expertise that was utilized. Some of the country's smartest minds had worked on the project for years—and without computers!

When we entered the complex that afternoon, we were in awe. Our tour guide was a member of the Chisasibi Cree Nation who had also worked inside the power station before assuming her current role. Her ability to link the technical aspects of the project with how it impacted the Indigenous community in the past and present was enriching. She was incredible, and we could not thank her enough for giving us a better understanding and appreciation of her people. Since it was the dead of winter, there was only one other person with us (an airline pilot living there on contract for the month), which allowed us to ask all types of questions. Our tour guide was great and provided us with more information than we had expected. The sheer size of the turbines and the vast cavernous underground space was something none of us had ever seen before. To our surprise, not all turbines were active given the demands on the grid for that week. Our tour guide explained that it was the hot summer days that required more supply from the entire HQ system. This reminded us that while Quebecers have the benefit of their own power at a very low cost, huge amounts are distributed to our American neighbours south of the border and other provinces for higher prices.

By 5:00 p.m. we had returned to the hotel for a visit with El Dorado and stayed in the building for a final dinner at the adjoining restaurant. One last time we looked for the northern lights, without success. Seeing as we had witnessed a beautiful evening sky with few clouds and minimal wind, we were not disappointed that we did not witness the aurora borealis. Actually, the unplanned aspects of our adventure were the most rewarding. And we sure learned a few things!

Bedtime was early in preparation for our 4:30 a.m. departure the next morning.

Unfortunately (and very different from our voyage northbound three days earlier), the first six hours of the drive were cold with constant snow flurries. The excitement of discovery had faded, and the boys slept most of the way in the backseat. Steve and I exchanged driving duties and chatted most of the time to keep each other company. By 4:00 p.m., we had exited the southern border of the Vérendrye Reserve, with three hours to go. Steve dropped me off at the airport in Montréal to board my flight home, and I was in my own bed before midnight.

The next day, Wednesday, February 26th, I returned to work with an empty feeling after completing an incredible adventure. I sensed a change was coming.

CHAPTER 14
THE GHOST OF ALGONQUIN PARK

Me on the northern shores of Canoe Lake,
Algonquin Park, November 2, 2020.

Thick wet snow flurries began to fill the early November sky as we travelled on Highway 60 heading northeast. Patches of snow in the forest and next to the road from a light overnight snowfall brightened the entire area from the dark brown colour of the fall. Winter comes early here compared to the largest city in Canada, only two hundred and fifty kilometres directly south. When we departed late in the morning from my home in Oakville, it was 5°C, and my adventure partners, Steve and Phil, were wearing light coats. The northern winds and high elevation presented a climate that was more severe and full of surprises beyond the fringes of the great lakes.

After stopping on the edge of Huntsville for a quick break and food, Philippe turned to me. "So, where are we really going, Dan-Dan?"

My nephew had agreed to join us once again for another discovery adventure but was not too informed as he knew very little about anything north of Toronto.

"We're heading to the greatest park in the country," I replied. "Algonquin!"

"Okay, sounds good!"

His positive response was accompanied by a shrug as he took another bite of his sandwich in the car's backseat.

Back on the road, as I provided more context and history for our destination, I recognized a certain inquisitive surprise in their voices. The west-gate entry on Highway 60 was empty with no personnel to greet us or anyone present to provide guidance and advice. Since I had been there years ago for a wonderful canoe trip with my friend, Soko, and had read extensively in the past ten years about the park, I knew my way around. I was also glad that it was free of guides and staff since I wanted the experience to be full of undisturbed discovery. We passed by Whisky Rapids Trail and drove next to Tea Lake where Camp Tamakwa is located, co-founded by Omer Stringer, whose family had a significant presence in the park. Omer was a legendary canoeist who loved Algonquin and created the popular Beaver Canoe brand with the help of Roots.

As we drove on the small bridge over Smoke Creek that leads to the large lake of the same name, I informed my partners that we would soon be turning north and heading to the Portage Store and tourist base on the southernmost edge of Canoe Lake.

"This is the lake where one of the greatest Canadian painters, Tom Thomson, mysteriously died," I said as we parked the car in the empty lot.

Algonquin Provincial Park was created in 1893 by the Ontario government as per the recommendation of the Royal Commission on Forest Reservation and National Parks. Essentially, the intent was to protect some of the ungranted crown land from the timber industry. Regrettably, the same lands that are now part of the park were cleared of all big red and white pine trees in the early nineteenth century to meet European demand and supply the shipbuilding industry, among other things. And disappointingly, dozens of sawmills continued to operate well into the twentieth century after it was designated as a reserve. Today, most visitors don't even realize that the landscape was even richer and more beautiful two hundred years ago when a forest as high as some of the monster trees on the west coast towered over the dark virgin lakes. We can be thankful to Chairman Alexander Kirkwood and his fellow Commission members for their bold recommendation, which allows thousands of people each year to visit the 1.8 million acres of magical wilderness. It has become a camping and canoeing playground for many who live in southern Ontario and a home away from home in the summer for the thousands of kids who attend the numerous long-standing summer camps. My daughters have experienced Algonquin Park a few times by attending summer camp or staying with friends who have cabins on leased land near the quiet lakes. Unlike the busy, noisy lakes in Muskoka just south of the park, a peace and respect for the environment takes hold when entering the park. Without having to travel hundreds of miles farther north or to the end of unmarked roads to escape, Algonquin offers an experience unlike any other for nature lovers within reasonable distance from urban centres.

The highway we used to enter Algonquin and begin our discovery was created by timber companies. The same is true for almost all of the roads, trails, and old train tracks in the park. The small towns on the edges and inside the park were first developed to house the workers who descended on the area for the cutting seasons. Like so many other remote places in Canada, profit was the catalyst for discovery. For example, the small village of Mowat on the northwest side of Canoe Lake grew to house over five hundred residents just before the start of the twentieth century. The railroad tracks leading into the park were well developed at that time, so in addition to men travelling to make money, tourists and professionals began enjoying the area in the summer. The start of the mandate for the park's second superintendent,

George W. Bartlett, in 1898 marked the start of a proper strategy to make the park more self-sufficient. Land leases were made available for camps, lodges, and cottages to generate revenue. By 1912 there were new lodges, camps, and many cottages present in the area, which increased the awareness of the beautiful lakes and pure air for the privileged living in Toronto who were looking for a place to escape the hot, humid metropolis. This proved to be a period of new purpose for the southern half of the park as the timber companies migrated north for new supply and left their infrastructure behind for the tourists. What the superintendents and the province of Ontario did correctly during the first decades of the park was to limit the construction of buildings and the number of leases. Instead of the park allowing for the development of large structures and possibly villages for commercial purposes, it stuck to its raison d'être of ensuring the preservation of a primeval forest. It is evident to any who visit today that the superintendents succeeded.

Walking on the edges of Canoe Lake at 2:00 p.m. during that cloudy afternoon on November 2, 2020 made me very happy. It was my first official day of retirement from my banking career, and I was starting a short northern adventure that would bring us to some places I knew and some I would be discovering for the first time. It was a last-minute change for me to bring the boys to Algonquin after I realized our planned drive to North Bay on day one would bring us to the edges of the legendary park. Given that I had read thousands of words on the park and its history, I felt it was time to revisit it and show it for the first time to Steve and Phil. The cool, cloudy day with snow and a strong wind was less welcoming than I had hoped, but the boys became much more interested once they read the large boards that are displayed outside the Portage Store.

To my surprise Steve and Philippe did not know about Tom Thomson or his story. When I mentioned his name a few moments before, they acknowledged it, but it was not until they took the time to read the boards and listen to my additional details that they got excited. Phil is a filmmaker, so the dramatic story captured his curiosity. I had always wanted to go deeper into the surrounding area of the lake and discover the locations where Tom spent many months from 1912 to 1917. But that is impossible to do with ease during the busy summer months when the park is full and numerous staff and park rangers monitor the area. The moment I suggested we take some extra time and try finding the landmarks, my mates were filled with jubilation and hurried back to the car.

As we drove out of the parking area, I did my best to recall the details of the excellent book *Northern Light* by Roy MacGregor, which I have read twice. It provides the most researched, beautifully written, and accurate account of Tom Thomson's few years in Algonquin Park and his mysterious death.

Our first goal was to reach the north end of the lake, so we turned east on Highway 60 and then took the first road heading north. As we slowly advanced down the snow-covered gravel road, the guys were not very confident we were going the right way. We saw some nice streams and evidence of wildlife, but it was not until we passed the sign for the Taylor Statten Camps that I knew we were on the correct path. The renowned summer camp is a century old and located on the shore of Canoe Lake (well-known individuals like Prime Minister Justin Trudeau frequented the camp in their youth). The road continued for a few minutes until we arrived at a crossing that was the old train tracks, now turned into a gravel road. My memory of the old maps of the area I had studied became clear in my mind, and as we drove west and across the small Joe Lake bridge at the north end of the lake, I told my discovery partners that we were entering the land where the village of Mowat and adjoining train station stood more than one hundred years earlier. To my amazement, there was nothing left of it, not even an old building or signs to indicate where the lodge, school, post office, cemetery, and other staples of the vibrant community once stood. It was like the superintendents and the Ontario government made a point of not wanting the area to be remembered at all. A ghost town.

I knew the next turn had to be soon on our left to make our way closer to where the Mowat Lodge would have been located and where Tom Thomson spent his last days in 1917. Again, stunned by the lack of signage, I had to stop the car at one point to walk on the road and near the lake to reorient myself. It was at that moment that I realized we were standing exactly where the centre of the village would have been on the edge of the lake (which was at a lower level during those years). I told Steve and Phil how Tom had chosen that year to paint one sketch per day of different places in the park, how he did some guiding for tourists to earn a little money, how he fished on the lake regularly, how he loved to escape in the bush for days instead of staying at the lodge, and how he had a secret girlfriend who lived a few cottages down from the lodge. Her name was Winnie Trainor. She was from Huntsville and spent time during the summers on the lake at the family cottage, starting in 1912. She first met Tom in 1913 when she was twenty-eight and he was thirty-six. For many people (including family members), their relationship was unknown, but for locals around the lake, it was very obvious that the two had a romance. They also knew that Tom kept some of his paintings in the Trainor cabin and that she retained many that he gifted to her after his death. After 1917, Winnie also frequently visited the graveyard up on the hill behind her cottage where many believe Tom Thomson still rests today. As I relayed this to Steve and Phil, they were entranced as we continued travelling south toward more modern seasonal cottages. By then my partners were completely taken by the mystery and lost all track of time. They asked numerous questions and had somehow found themselves discovering a person and a world they had never known existed just two hours before. For them it was unplanned, enriching their understanding of Canada, and allowing for the most satisfying sentiment of escape.

At that point we had not seen anyone at all, and my curiosity took hold as I decided that we had to find the Trainor cottage. I knew from Roy's book that it still existed in 2010 and that it was close to where we were driving on the laneway.

"I hope it's still there," I said as I slowed the car to a crawl in the gathering snow.

Then my instincts took over, and in a burst of adventurous energy, we exited the car (I even forgot to turn off the engine) and walked in the bush toward the lake. I just kept moving, hoping to see some type of white structure. The falling snow made the experience completely silent. After a few minutes of my mates (who were not really dressed for a hike in the snow) asking whether various buildings were the cottage, I shared that it was a very old white cabin. "If it's still standing today," I said, "you will know immediately as there is no other."

I sensed that Phil and Steve had started to resign themselves that the great discovery would not occur, but then a small patch of thicker bush appeared. The other properties and newer lakeside cabins all had reduced tree cover and some open spaces. Could this thicker environment be introducing us to where the legendary white structure was located?

"Here it is," I said. "We found it!" I was elated.

"That's amazing, Dan-Dan."

There is nothing to indicate the building's historical significance, no signs or family name on a tree or post nearby to state who owns it. Without a fence or clear property markers, it stands alone and boarded up but with the same wraparound porch where Tom and Winnie spent their romantic summer evenings. He likely also used the covered space to dry his sketches and paintings, which he gave to his love and to other friends. As I thought about the routines of that place one hundred years before, I wondered if one of Tom's sketches could still be in there.

The only thing I couldn't find that day was the Mowat cemetery. I've since researched different videos and articles on how to reach the landmark, but I don't intend to try finding it. It seems to be located in the middle of the bush with no easy trail or signage, somehow wanting to remain a mystery. In July 1917 when Tom disappeared for days and only his canoe was located, I don't think he was meant to be found. Whatever you believe happened to him (drowning or murder) doesn't matter anymore. It also doesn't matter if you believe his work would have been less revered had he not died a dramatic death. The Group of Seven who were influential years later always praised Tom's talent and leadership in bringing Canadian landscapes to life. His iconic paintings, *The West Wind* and *The Jack Pine*, are at the pinnacle of Canadian art and will remain treasures of our country forever. His work lives on for us to enjoy while the place he loved the most has returned to its natural habitat. Busy during summer months, it is vacant from fall to spring each year, except for the constant presence of the painter's ghost.

***

Our arrival in North Bay was much later than planned as a result of our extended visit inside Algonquin Park. Also contributing to our late arrival was the snowstorm that engulfed us during our ninety-minute drive from Algonquin into the empty streets of North Bay. I've been to the largest city on Lake Nipissing many times and have never found it very interesting. Apart from being known as the area where the Dionne quintuplets were born back in 1934, it is a typical moderate-size northern town with the benefit of college and university campuses. To us the snowy city was only a sleeping stop, as we were heading to much more remote destinations.

After a good burger and beer at the only restaurant that seemed to be open, we had a solid sleep. The next morning, Steve and I had a nice jog around the snow-covered town, had our first coffee in the room, and then jumped into the car for the first stop to fuel up on McDonald's coffee and breakfast sandwiches (Phil's favourite) before taking Highway 63 into Quebec.

Instead of driving the direct route (boring!) to Cochrane, which was our destination for day two, Steve wanted to visit the Frappier family cottage in Temiscaming, where we had spent some summer days during our university years. Along with Boy Scouts escaping into wilderness as a youth, the time we spent in Temiscaming as late teens was magnificent. Without powerboats, telephones, television, radio signals, or nearby stores, we embraced paddling for hours on the lake and staring into a warm fire late into the evenings. The area is known mostly because of the pulp and paper industry that has been present there for over one hundred years. Driving through the dense forest was familiar, as it resembled so much of the travel I had done in central Ontario over the past thirty-five years. I enjoy the multiple lakes and rivers that wrap around the mountains and never seem to end.

As we approached the Frappier cottage, we entered a less desirable flat landscape that has been ravaged by clear-cutting. Our best friend's family has had the cottage for decades, so it was great to see it unchanged and share the special meaning of the place with Philippe. We had hoped to walk around and peek through the windows, but to our surprise, someone was there on that cold snowy morning. Steve was concerned that it was squatters (the cottages around the lake are usually vacant in the winter), but a quick text to our friend, Frapps, confirmed it was his aunt.

With some time to spare, we decided to embrace the theme of escape and took some dead-end back roads that brought us to the most beautiful small lakes. Phil was impressed with the unspoiled natural environment and thought it would be a brilliant base for his filmmaking and editing. Surprisingly, the lakes are located where chainsaws had not been used, so larger trees were present and towered over the water. If it were not so far from our home, I think Steve and I would own some land there.

After rejoining Highway 11, we made another detour to see the town of Kirkland Lake. When we had sent a few pictures of our adventure to our friends the night before, Harry had said, "Make sure you go see the lake behind the mall. I used to swim there as a kid. It's beautiful."

As per Harry's recommendation, we decided to visit his hometown on our way to Cochrane. I had been there once twenty years before for work and had not found it particularly special, but Harry's enthusiasm convinced my partners that it was worth it.

Kirkland Lake was built on gold. Without the mines there would be nothing there since the landscape is underwhelming. We entered the town and drove the entire length eastbound on Highway 66 to witness a sad situation for the local economy. On our way back heading westbound, we followed Harry's advice and drove behind the mall looking for the lake. The laneway ended abruptly at a high fence without an opening for regular cars. At that point we exchanged some texts with our local expert for clarification.

"Well, it has been some time since I've been there!" he replied.

With much laughter, we sent a few pictures to Harry as proof that the lake was not really a "thing" anymore. After more fun banter and some friendly teasing, we left town and turned north to discover places new to the three of us. A subarctic feeling penetrated us as we passed the westbound road to Timmins and instead continued north on Highway 11. We were now on the only and most northern route in Ontario, which loops around to link the remote towns. No one drives there unless they need to.

Our 5:00 p.m. arrival was early by our standards, but the sun had already been gone for a while. I can only imagine how early in the afternoon it gets dark in those northern towns during the dead of winter. Cochrane is located one hundred kilometres north of Timmins and for years was treated like an extension of it. With a population of just over five thousand, it stands proudly in the vast lands with a strong heritage of bilingualism. It is located in the Indigenous territory of Abitibiwinni Aki, which extends east into the province of Quebec and borders the Eeyou Istchee territory that we had visited earlier in 2020. We learned that the community had been present there for centuries and that the area was used for summer camps.

The first thing we noticed when we arrived was how wide the streets were in the downtown core and residential areas. Because there is so much snow and most people drive large trucks (and snowmobiles), the wide streets provide extra room for movement when the snowbanks take over. The other thing I noticed was how cold it was. In a moment of courage before dinner, Steve and I decided that we should take a short walk downtown (we needed it since it was US election night, and the next few hours would be interesting, not to say worrisome). What awaited us was a vicious wind with temperatures at -20°C, which I captured on SnapChat and proudly shared in real time with friends and family. We were also the only people out in the entire small town, so we headed back inside for more El Dorado rum.

In the warm comfort of our simple hotel room, we had a fun evening. A combination of things kept the laughter coming.

1. The only place in town that could get us food after 7:00 p.m. was a convenience store that had a pizza oven. After much discussion with the most pleasant gentlemen, I devised a plan that would get us two pizzas, delivered by the only taxi driver available, for a hefty fee.
2. The El Dorado with Coke and ice was flowing.
3. Steve predicted a quick election result with a solid Democrat win—not.
4. The pizza arrived with no plates, utensils, napkins, nothing. Get the toilet paper out!
5. The pizza was very good, and we finished it all.
6. The rum was still flowing.
7. Steve stuck to his election prediction and declared, "It will be all done by ten o'clock."
8. Phil gave up on us and went to sleep.
9. I declared that we were pretty much out of El Dorado.
10. Steve questioned why they were no longer covering the Florida state results.
11. Steve joined his son and went to sleep.
12. I made sure the rum was finished, then turned off the TV, realizing there would be no convincing political outcome that night.

Up early the next morning and after a nice jog with Steve around Cochrane, we completed our usual morning "fuel" stop and then headed westbound to find Route 634. Running along the Abitibi River, it would take us to the northernmost stretch of official roadway in northeastern Ontario. Like we had discovered the winter before, those roads would not exist if not for the hydroelectric power stations and the logging industry. What many don't know is that Ontario Power Generation (OPG) has three large stations on the Abitibi River and another four only a few dozen miles west on the Mattagami River. Both are linked to James Bay and provide a strong, steady water supply to generate the power used throughout Ontario. The largest of the seven has a capacity of 345 megawatts compared to the little station located next to our family cottage, which has a capacity of just six megawatts. Without the powerful currents of large rivers or the force of immense waterfalls, our electricity demands in Canada would be supplied by very different means.

Turning at Smooth Rock Falls, we observed a large sign announcing the location of the boarding station for the Polar Bear Express excursion train.

"This is the train to take us to Santa," Phil joked.

Interestingly enough, it was the only train and only method of transportation to reach the town of Moosonee located on the shores of James Bay. Apart from that, the northernmost route was the one we were about to travel. We stopped at all three dams during the two-hour drive to reach the end of the line at Otter Rapids. The large facility was completed in 1961 as the final project for the area. Once it passes above the dam and reaches the site of the small train stop, the road simply ends at the OPG operations building. That's it!

At the time of construction, there was a town for the workers, which reached a population of several hundred. Today, the only remaining infrastructure is linked to the power station. The volume of water flowing through the bypasses and spillovers is impressive and generates a massive sound. Contrary to what many would assume, the rivers in the far north flow northbound toward James Bay and don't feed the great lakes. Since the Indigenous communities use the roads for regular travel, it is possible to drive on the dams and witness the power of the systems up close. There is also no security or anyone present to monitor the area, only a few OPG trucks that employees use to get around. I asked Steve about the security risk given his experience at HQ, and he mentioned that it was never really discussed. I guess not many curious adventurers like us are willing to make the drive!

The afternoon without any cell service ended when we returned to Smooth Rock Falls. It is rare these days to have no connection for hours, but

I appreciate it. My mind tends to focus on the moment, making me more aware of my surroundings and encourages conversation. The three of us also listened to a lot of music, which Phil would thoughtfully select before our daily departures. I'm always impressed with his diverse musical taste, which I appreciate as a music lover.

There was one picture I had taken when we were on the road between Abitibi Canyon and Otter Rapids that I wanted to investigate. It was an old sign on the side of the road in the middle of nowhere that simply stated "New Post." Once we arrived in Timmins for the night, I discovered that the sign indicated the location of the trail to New Post Falls. Based on the pictures, the falls are stunning and completely in the wild. If we had known the falls were there, we might have tried to venture to see them, which would have ended up being a mistake given some feedback from hikers that the trail is quite difficult (especially with snow on the ground). The Indigenous community has stated that the falls were a very different size before the man-made diversions of the local rivers took place for the development of the power stations. Interestingly, the falls are near where a Hudson's Bay Company fur trading post was located centuries before.

**

The hometown of country and pop megastar Shania Twain welcomed us with a bright morning sunshine on our last day of travel. Steve and Phil had never been there, but I had visited Timmins a few times for work over the last two decades, in the summer and winter. Although I have a few friends who have either lived in or are from Timmins, it is plainly an industrial town that exists for the extraction of natural resources. On prior visits my curiosity had driven me to investigate the city and the surrounding area, although I concluded there was not much to see. Appreciating my honesty, the boys agreed, and after less than an hour of driving around some of the streets, we grabbed our usual morning "fuel" and then headed south toward Sudbury.

The drive was beautiful, with sunshine and warmer weather as we drove on Highway 144, passing through Mattagami and Gogama, and next to some provincial parks. We were joined by many transport trucks, who used the road to deliver raw materials to the south. By lunchtime we reached the outskirts of the "capital of the north" and had a classic lunch at the long-standing Deluxe Hamburgers restaurant, which looked the same as it had thirty years earlier.

Phil had never been to our university town, so we took him around all the important locations, including the places where we had lived. He was interested but somewhat underwhelmed. Steve observed that there were more trees than he remembered, which was good news for the city's regreening program. The stagnation of northern Ontario is evident when travelling long distances and visiting multiple places. Apart from the retail superstore centres, there are few new buildings, and most others have not been renovated, except for necessary upkeep. Not unlike the larger city centres to the south, the older neighbourhoods are worn down, but because there is less new construction in northern towns, the rundown areas represent a larger share and are much more evident. With most of the growth occurring over the last fifty to seventy years, it will be interesting to see how the towns renew (or replace) the buildings and homes as they reach a state of decay.

***

The observations we shared in the car during this trip and the economic implications we discussed while travelling the vast geography of our country is why escape and discovery are so important. It makes a person appreciate different perspectives by seeing a multitude of lifestyles and socio-economic realities. Travelling to places with a long and diverse history helps us appreciate the importance of time and how proper long-term planning for our society is critical for prosperity. One moves away from thoughts of today and immediate needs to thoughts of what it will take to ensure that fifty years from now our cities and core infrastructure will be renewed while respecting the environmental implications we now better understand. Fortunately, well-balanced approaches are underway in different sectors and countries, and I read about new projects and technology every day that should help us grow with pride. Conversely, I sense that many people (political leaders included) have surrendered their decision-making and responsibilities on the matter. Many fear the debate and resist taking action due to possible political setbacks. Similarly, many entities, large organizations, and even individuals in the private sector avoid anything that could impact the value of their brand. In the history of the world, incredible things have happened when someone (or a group or an entity) has tackled a project with an unrelenting conviction without fear of reprisal. I believe that with all the intelligence and technology we have today, changes can be achieved with positive outcomes for all stakeholders.

***

While heading down Highway 400 to Oakville, Phil started to ask about Tom Thomson. "What did he paint? How much are his paintings worth? Was the reason for his death ever legally determined?" And most importantly "How come I didn't know about him before?"

I answered his questions with much more detail than he was seeking, but I got stuck on the last one. Do Canadians do a poor job of celebrating our legends, or is the country still too young for us to care? Why did Phil know so much about the legendary characters in the history of England and the US but not Canada? We debated the topic without a clear answer, although Phil did say that it would be cool to make a proper modern film about Tom Thomson's life. I told him that Canada needed its own version of the great American historical documentary filmmaker Ken Burns, and that Phil would be superb!

Nation of Chisasibi Fishing Canoe on the shores of James Bay,
February 23, 2020.

The Giant's Staircase. Two football fields can fit into each of the ten steps of the Robert-Bourassa development dam spillway. It is two kilometres long. February 24, 2020.

Mascot Chimo welcoming us to Cochrane,
November 3, 2020.

Trying my luck in the small rapids to Lac Rending, September 17, 2021.

Reaching the end of the road. The Otter Rapids Hydroelectric Station.
Impressive infrastructure in the wilderness, November 5, 2020.

Soko and Pascal getting ready to launch for the day. June 16, 2023.
Pontiac Region, Quebec

CHAPTER 15
LE GOÛT DE L'EAU

Ruisseau Lamarck near Chapais, Quebec, June 19, 2022.

nestled at the front of the boat as we departed from the dock next to our cabin on a cold rainy September 12th morning. I was looking at Pascal, who was sitting in the middle, and Danny Soko, who was positioned at the back next to the engine wearing more layers than I had in all my luggage. He had his hand on the throttle of the twenty-five-horse-power Mercury outboard and told me to secure my fishing gear as he accelerated to maximum speed. It took only a few seconds for me to realize why he had given me that warning. Sitting at the front of a fishing boat when there were waves provided quite the rock 'n' roll ride. As I bounced around, the other two guys laughed.

"How do you like it so far?" Pascal asked me with a big grin.

After fifteen minutes of boating, we arrived at our first fishing spot, and the rain receded as I prepared to cast for the first time in my bright yellow "beginner's" rain suit (which the guys joked about all week long). I didn't pretend I knew what I was doing and humbly asked Pascal for advice on what to use and for any other tips he might have. The larger boat with Gil, Eric, and Steven had also stopped nearby. Not having a lot of expectations given my lack of fishing experience, I simply casted to the left and started to turn the reel, so I didn't snag on the bottom. I was told the depth was a little more than ten feet and that the fish we wanted were usually in the colder water at the bottom of the lake. Then my line tightened, surprising me with the power of the tension.

"I think I have something!" I yelled.

"Fish on!" Pascal replied.

The other two guys immediately reeled in their fishing lines, and then Pascal coached me through what I felt was a pretty good catch. I was a good student, I did as I was told, and I brought the fish closer to the boat as Pascal scooped it in the net. I was excited to have caught something on my first try, and once we pulled it out of the net, I told the guys that it was probably the biggest fish I had ever caught. They both giggled, generally unimpressed.

"That's crap," Soko declared. "Put it back into the water."

That was when I remembered we were there to catch "doré" (walleye) and not the lower status pike, which was what I had just caught. Regardless, I was very happy, and I have a picture of me dressed in my bright yellow rain gear with my twenty-four-inch prize as proof that I was the first to pull something out of the water within thirty minutes of leaving the dock!

Chef Soko was the leader of the annual fishing trip to the mid-north of Quebec. He had never missed it in over thirty years, and he inherited the job of organizing everything since his father and uncles could no longer attend due to health reasons. Gil was the next longest-tenured attendee with over thirty years of experience in the deep wilderness and had adopted the second-in-command role. They had talked about their escape to the rich waters of the Chapais area for decades and knew that I wanted to go whenever my schedule allowed for more free time. So it was at the start of 2021 that I was approached as their top choice to join the group and replace some of the other long-standing attendees who could no longer include the eight days away in their busy calendars. Although fishing is a pastime for me, I had never done it seriously, and I had never embarked on a multi-day adventure filled with eight-plus hours per day in the fishing boat without touching ground. At first I was a little hesitant to accept, but Linda gave me the nudge. "You'll love it," she said.

I followed her advice. The other change for the group was that we were going in early September instead of their usual June date, so there was concern about the quality of the fishing, but there would be no bugs! Our destination, the small town of Chapais, is located essentially in the middle of the province of Quebec. Again, mining and logging were the two industries that provided the economic motivation to develop the roads, electrical lines, and small communities. Mining activity has diminished in the last few decades, with logging and the service industry taking the lead as the driving force of employment. For us, the only thing that mattered was the sustainment of the environment and a prosperous fish habitat. Fortunately, the low population and difficult access to most lakes had resulted in little change and a low risk of overfishing the lakes. There is a large annual walleye fishing competition in late June that sees hundreds of avid fishing enthusiasts descend on Opémiska Lake, but it is well managed and monitored to respect limits. This is why the guys have continued to make the seven hundred kilometre trek to the north versus staying closer to home and being disappointed with the size and quality of the fish. More importantly to me, the remote location was a true escape on lands and lakes that only a few had a chance to discover. Paradise.

We were completely self-sufficient for the entire week once we arrived at the cabin on September 11, 2021. We had all the food, gas, drinks, fishing

223

gear, and clothing to enjoy all types of weather. We even brought a special lamp, folding chairs, and some kitchen accessories to be comfortable and ensure that our chef could perform at a high standard. The north-facing two-bedroom cabin was on the south shore of Opémiska Lake near the camping site that hosted dozens of families during the summer months. Nearby are other cottages and a few permanent residences scattered on the only gravel roads on the entire lake. The cabin was used by the owner's family throughout the summer, apart from the week he rented it to us. It had not been renovated in many years but was kept very clean and had all the modern amenities. The basement was used for storage and had extra beds and a small bathroom. As a rookie I set up on the lower level. Outside, the large property was mostly clear of trees with plenty of space to park the trucks and boats. The edge of the lake was only about twenty feet from the front of the cabin, protected by a steep fifteen-foot drop-off full of small bushes and trees. The lack of dense forest on the property was a good thing as it reduced the bugs in the spring and early summer, which I experienced on my second trip there. Best of all, a large deck wrapped around the cabin and provided a great view of the lake and the surrounding area.

Opémiska Lake is large with over one hundred and fifty kilometres of shoreline. The water's depth varies from a few feet to dozens of feet. The fish population is diverse, with pike enjoying the shallower weedy waters and walleye staying mostly in the deep areas for their nocturnal feeding. Without a good knowledge of the lake or a proper topographical map, you will surely hit bottom. The boreal forest landscape is flat all around the lake with dark, dense evergreens reaching the waterline almost everywhere. The only real mountain is at the north end of the lake. The guys have nicknamed it Mount Mummy since it resembles a large horizontal Egyptian mummy. Located next to this landmark is the newly built Indigenous village of the Oujè-Bougoumou Cree Nation. As traditional inhabitants for centuries of the Eeyou Istchee territory, their story is a difficult one, with several challenges. The economic development of the area and inadequate respect for their lands during the last one hundred years is a troubled story. The people were forced to relocate several times during the last century as a result of aggressive mining and forestry development. The destruction of villages led to a dispersed community at the end of the twentieth century, with inadequate shelter and services. Only after difficult negotiations with the federal and provincial governments in the 1980s did they reach an agreement to establish and restore a proper community on the shore of Lake Opémiska. With respect for their history, customs, and traditions, we are fortunate to share this beautiful, peaceful area with the over eight hundred people who live in the village.

Day one of fishing was unusually short for us on the water versus the regular routine, with six hours of relatively good fishing success, although I sensed from the veterans that they were concerned that September may not yield the return they were accustomed to when they were almost the first anglers on the water in June.

The daily post-fishing routine included securing the boats, gathering the gear, charging batteries, cleaning the fish, and fixing anything that needed repair. It was done immediately after arriving at the cabin each day. There was almost a military approach to these tasks, with each of us having a role to play. As the new guy, I assumed the responsibilities of garbage duty and cleaning the fish in addition to anything else Soko asked of me. Of course, that was when the fishing stories and the debate about which boat was the most successful and who got the best fish escalated to a jovial level. It was also when I first observed Soko transform from fisherman and boat captain to grand chef. Gil had told me dozens of times why the evening dinner routine was almost better than the fishing, and I was about to experience it.

Our chef took great pride in his culinary abilities, and from the moment he cleaned up after fishing, he started his daily pleasure of preparing a masterpiece. Gil ensured that Soko had a proper drink and then hovered around the kitchen, ready to tackle any task while the others cleaned fish and prepared the dining room. Best of all, Soko took his time, prepared appetizers, joked about the day, and created a wonderful environment. He was completely in his element and adored every aspect of the week. Nothing was work to him; it was all pleasure.

As I sat for my first official end-of-the-fishing-day meal, I enjoyed a perfectly prepared selection of food, accompanied by excellent wine. I was delighted and could not thank Soko enough for his effort, which he repeated every night of our trip.

After dinner I led the duties of cleaning and doing dishes while the others made our lunches for the next day. Our evening ended with a raucous poker game and too much rum.

Day two was disappointing on the fishing front. After almost eight hours on the water, the ice boxes only had a few small walleye and a couple of pikes that we kept for dinner. The talk was all about how we need to change strategies, which meant a new lake and the loading of the boats onto the trailers, so we could take them to Lamarck.

"It will be better on Lamarck," the guys kept saying, followed by, "You'll see, Dan; there are big walleyes there."

We departed early on day three with the two smaller boats secured behind the SUVs to make the forty-five-minute drive to the mysterious lake that the guys had been talking about constantly. We only drove one-third of the way on the main highway heading westbound away from Chapais before turning onto a hidden gravel road.

"Get ready, Dan-Dan," Gil warned. "It will be slow and bouncy."

I soon understood what he meant as we were surrounded by trees on both sides while driving on a sandy road full of potholes and stones. I love deep forest trails, so it was great for me. The bugs were non-existent, so I opened the window, inhaled the fresh air, and kept an eye out for any wildlife.

After some time, we passed a small cabin without electricity or any services that was halfway to the lake and belonged to a local Indigenous family. In years past, the boys had used the route to the lake when the owner was there and had some conversations about their different fishing habits and how the locals still used nets (strictly prohibited for us).

Once the cabin was out of sight, we turned right for the final stretch and finally arrived at an opening no wider than a few car lengths and about one hundred feet long, which provided access to the water. We were the only ones present, and we quickly prepared the boats and gear for the day. As we unloaded the boats into the calm water using a small natural ramp made of sand at the water's edge, Gil told me that it was the only place to launch boats in the entire Lamarck Lake system. Complete seclusion. I was excited!

The cool, cloudy day was good for fishing. Walleye like dark, cooler water and are known for their special tapetum lucidum eyes, which allow for excellent vision at significant depths. This was one reason why the boys wanted to move away from the shallower waters of Opémiska and attempt a day on Lamarck, whose official name is Lac des Deux Orignaux with the Ruisseau Lamarck, Lac Grey Goose (awesome name), and Lac Kapunapotagen linked to it.

The moment Gil and I jumped in the boat and started the engine, we had a feeling it would be a great day. I adored the quiet water and uninhabited shoreline that have never had permanent residents. Before we passed through the beautiful stream leading to the wider parts of the lake, we cast a couple of lines and caught a few nice pike to warm up for the day.

Once we arrived at the spot that Gil wanted to try next to a smaller island on the east end of the lake, the other boat was out of sight, trying their luck on the western shore. Minutes later, we caught some nice walleyes. Gil was thrilled as he trolled up and down the western side of the island, catching fish on every pass.

"Now this is what I told you about!" he declared.

Gil ensured we kept only the ones within the size limits, and we only kept the walleye, as they tasted better than pike.

As our success continued throughout the day, I named the location "Gil Island" and declared it to be my best fishing day thus far. Interestingly, the name stuck, as we used Gil Island later that week and the next year to identify our location on the lake and our favourite fishing spot. Most surprising was how quickly eight hours went by on a small fishing boat when we were busy catching fish. We supplemented our experience with some music and a break for lunch, but my apprehension of spending so many hours each day on a small boat was completely unnecessary. After the third day, I was hooked!

We spent the next day at Lamarck, again with great success. We went back to the main lake on Thursday, a beautiful warm day without clouds and with calm winds. During our return that afternoon, we decided to finish our week at Lamarck, as it was by far the better location in September. That evening Soko suggested we make a big fire outside and enjoy some drinks after dinner without the trouble of fighting off the bugs (something they could never do in June).

Our final day was gorgeous with a bright sun and a breeze from the south. We had been lucky to avoid rain except on our first day, with this final day being the best. We rotated fishing partners and boats every day, and on our last day I was with Gil and Pascal as we tackled Gil Island once again (with less success). We also floated in the middle of the lake to try something different, which yielded Gil the biggest catch of the week, a nice pike of over ten pounds.

After lunch we made our way to the end of the lake where some small rapids flowed into a stream leading to little Lac Rending. There was no way to get the boats across to the other side of the rapids, but the guys mentioned that they had had success close to the rapids years ago. Once we approached, they were surprised to see how calm it was compared to June with the higher water levels. As we cast into the ripples from a distance in the anchored boat, I had the idea to jump out of the boat and get closer. Gil said they had never done that, but he was happy to navigate the boat to the shore and have me jump out.

Minutes later I found myself standing on rocks in the midst of the flowing water and enjoying the full natural experience. After breaking a few fishing lines and losing the lures I had brought with me, it was time to wrap up and return to the boat. It was late in the afternoon as we made our way back through islands and streams to the little opening at the south end of the lake where the boats were loaded onto trailers for our return home the next day. My first real fishing trip had been extraordinary with incredible food, friends, and escapes to empty lakes.

***

I had already told the boys at the last dinner of my first fishing adventure in September 2021 that I would like to join them every year from then on. Therefore, I was delighted when Soko sent the invitation email just a few months before Christmas for the next trip, in June 2022. This time the guys had decided to return to their normal time of year with the hope that the walleye would be excellent on the big lake when the water was cold. It is also aligned better with normal vacation schedules, and with more hours of sunshine and heat! For me, anything worked as long as I got to spend time on the water and enjoy the beautiful, quiet natural environment, although I was aware that thousands of new little biting friends would be present in the early summer months and that I would have to adjust accordingly. Linda reminded me of my extensive camping days as a kid, which I had survived without trouble, and to get some strong bug repellent.

Our arrival in Chapais was on Friday, June 17th, the week prior to the big Quebec national holiday, St-Jean-Baptiste Day. It was also one week prior to the kick off of the large "Festival du Doré," which was hosted at Camping

Opémiska just down the road from our cabin. Our timing was superb since we would fish before the professionals arrived, hopefully catch big fish, and depart before the crowds arrived.

This time Soko's cousin, Steven (who is a great fisherman and a super guy), had to pass on the trip, and we swapped Eric, who could not take the time off, with Danny L., who was returning after a few years off. The fleet of boats were about the same as the last year with Gil's smaller Lund for Lamarck, Soko and Pascal's Princecraft for both lakes, and Danny's large Princecraft for the big lake.

I travelled with Gil from Ottawa as we followed the others on a beautiful, clear sunny morning. What I quickly learned is that the June heat of Oakville is not guaranteed in the near north. We arrived in the rain with a cool wind and no sunshine. I was thinking that maybe it would not be so summer-like after all. Following a few hours of unpacking and preparations at the cabin, we ate an excellent steak dinner with asparagus and baked potatoes before closing the night with rum and cards.

After a first day on the big lake with strong, steady winds (but no bugs) and a lot of good-size walleyes, we decided to load the boats for an escape to Lamarck on the second day. It was cool in the morning but truly incredible without a cloud in the deep blue sky and with no wind. I started the day with a great catch while we weaved in the calm waters of the stream, and the good weather continued throughout the morning and afternoon. We also let ourselves have fun and catch a few pikes. As I had experienced the year before, the sense of being completely alone in such a large space without another boat or person around was like paradise for me. Like the time when I visited James Bay and Radisson, the effect of not having cell service and knowing we would not have it for hours put a spell on me. That day with Soko and Pascal was one of my favourites of the entire week, with close to eight hours on the water.

I loved the food that Soko prepared each night and the excellent healthy lunches that the guys made with care each evening. It reminded me that life's pleasures are not about fancy places with high-priced items but instead good experiences with great friends and excellent food. The vacation reflected how Linda and I had been evolving our travelling over the last few years with more thought about the location and friends joining us and less about the star rating of the hotel, the restaurant menu, or luxury services.

Our week continued with a rotation of lakes for each fishing day. Day three was another beautiful one on the big lake with everything nature could provide except for fish in the morning. Luckily, we had heat and no wind, which made it very comfortable. Then out of nowhere, just as we were getting ready to leave for the day at 3:30 p.m., Gil radioed to our boat: "Got a big one, boys."

Pascal and Danny jumped up (I stood all day long in the boat each and every day) and started looking around to see where the other boat was located. Once they spotted it, Danny started the engine and we approached. Minutes later I was pulling in one of the largest walleyes of the week and my biggest catch ever. Then only fifteen minutes later, a second bigger one was being photographed in my hand. It was then at 4:45 p.m. on June 20, 2022 that the boys told me I was finally a legit fisherman.

The adventurer in each of us came out in full force on our fourth day of fishing. Instead of staying close, we decided to drive over an hour and visit another large body of water in the area, La Trêve Lake. The gravel road to reach the boat launch passed under massive power lines connected to the large Robert-Bourassa Power Station in Radisson, which I had visited in 2020. I could hear a loud buzzing from the electrical transmission lines perched dozens of metres above the ground and held up by massive metal structures that wove their way hundreds of miles to give the Montréal area power. I joked with the guys that there was no way fish would be around that area given the high-voltage lines. It was no longer a joke when our small boat engine quit when we passed under the lines to access our fishing spot. It took Gil about thirty minutes of herculean effort to get us going again, but only after the other boat towed us away from the buzzing structures. Coincidence? I think not!

There was an unwritten rule that no matter the weather, we would fish every day. As we made our way through the narrow stream to the bigger part of the lake, that rule was put to the test. First, the rain was unrelenting and driven hard by a strong, cool wind with no sign of stopping. Second, I was beginning to feel water penetrating my rain gear. Third, our cushioned seats were retaining water, and it was only a matter of time before our bottoms were soaked. Fourth, the fish weren't biting at all. Fifth, the waves were huge for our small boat once we reached the open water. A choice had to be made, and we elected to listen to music! I brought my little Bose speaker on every trip and had tucked it away deep in my bag that morning to keep it dry. Following a quick (and soggy) lunch in the rain, I turned on Sting's masterpiece album, *Nothing Like the Sun*. By then Gil had decided to get us some cover and head back to the stream to try our luck there. The moment the first song kicked off, we stood and started dancing (badly), fishing rods in hand. Sting must have a special power on walleye because throughout the fifty-five-minute playlist, we caught enough fish for Soko to make us the best fish cakes ever that same night. Without Gil, that day would have probably turned somewhat negative for me. Instead, it was a celebration of our friendship.

Summer weather arrived for our last two days. We were in T-shirts by noon each day and had the luxury of minimal bugs on the lake, which was a good respite from their vicious attacks on land. I spent a wonderful Wednesday with Soko on the large "home" lake with good tunes but no fish. Given the poor results, the guys decided we would take all the boats out that night and return to Lamarck with the two smaller boats for our last day. During dinner we assigned boats. Once Soko realized he was with Danny and me, he declared, "We're going pike fishing tomorrow, boys."

"Really? Wow!" Danny said. "Yes, sir!"

Soko had been listening to Danny's stories all week about the large sport fishing he did regularly with his son closer to Ottawa. We had also noticed that he had multiple toys in his oversized tackle box to catch the "big one." I was happy to try something different, but I was most excited when Soko said we would be going to a shallow, secluded stream at the end of Lac des Deux Orignaux for the adventure.

By 10:00 a.m. we reached the nicest fishing spot and started having fun. I guess the pike were happy to see activity, as we caught one after another. Soon the pleasure turned to competition as we challenged each other for the biggest catch of the week. I kept catching really fun ones that were about twenty-four inches long and gave a good fight every time. The landscape was immaculate with minimal wind, a clear blue sky, and a dense green forest. It was a completely private oasis. We followed the stream until we reached Lac Grey Goose to do a few more casts before making our way back.

Just as we were about to have lunch, Soko's face lit up with excitement. "Fish on! Oh, it's big!" He never says that.

Danny and I stored our rods and prepared the net and the camera to assist and witness what could be the prize of the week. Until he passed by the boat, we guessed it was a good-size pike, but after the first pass, we changed our estimate to "very big." Soko is an experienced fisherman, and without his years of knowledge, that fish would have never reached the net. It measured thirty-eight inches and was over eighteen pounds, by far the biggest I have ever had the pleasure to see caught live. Suffice it to say that Soko has a big smile in the picture.

We completed the day on the water with a slow return to shore, a sober drive to the cabin, and a tasty meal, our last of the trip.

I did not want that day to end. On my phone I have a thirty-second video from that afternoon of June 23, which I filmed at 1:58 p.m. while standing in the boat. It is not of us or any fish. Rather, it is a 270-degree non-stop pan of the mirror-like lake without a ripple, bordered by dark green tree-lined shores and covered with a cloudless blue sky. Thus far in my lifetime I have experienced hundreds of days when I am completely at peace in a natural environment. It is a blessing for me to be able to gain this satisfaction and share it with friends, family, Linda, and my girls. Sometimes it is in a quiet, secluded place like Chapais, and sometimes it is in a little busier place like Sugar Beach, tucked away between the Pitons in St. Lucia. The location does not matter; it is the state of mind that is important. Those who are lucky enough to capture such a spirit of contentment know that it only comes when you take the effort to go see something new.

EPILOGUE

We crossed the Pont de Quebec just before the sun started to descend on the northwestern edge of the mighty St. Lawrence. The one-hundred-year-old black steel bridge took us from the south shore of the Quebec City area into the heart of Sainte-Foy and the road that would lead us to our destination inside the old city. We drove near the home where we had lived for two years. Then in the distance we saw the legendary Château Frontenac and Price Building as we entered the walled city through the St. Louis gate. The car immediately began to make a rumbling sound as the tires rolled on the narrow cobblestone street. Slowing down, we recalled the names of the many restaurants and shops that we had the pleasure of visiting in the past. Samuel de Champlain waved to us as we circled past the château and began to descend the four-hundred-year-old Cote de la Montagne toward Basse-Ville. Suddenly, I noticed the address of our destination on a little door between the tourist retail stores that lined the sidewalk. The old building was perfect and captured the charm of that romantic and historical city. Linda and I walked up the numerous stairs to reach the third level and opened the door to a comfortable condo. The original brick-and-stone walls were exposed in a refreshed living area and modern kitchen. We were impressed with the view of the seaway through the authentic windows, which were encased in the thick stone walls. We soon learned that the walls and double windows were an excellent sound barrier on windy days and busy tourist weekends. As we settled into our new home for the next month, Linda smiled at me. "This is my happy place," she said.

The view from the front bedroom windows extended all the way to my favourite ski hill, Mont-Sainte-Anne, and the mountains that border the north of the St. Lawrence, overlooking the massive l'île d'Orléans. It is no wonder that the Indigenous people enjoyed this land for countless centuries. It was through these waters that Jacques Cartier and de Champlain first set eyes on present-day Quebec City. These days the waters are used by large cargo ships bringing goods into Canada and taking raw materials and products to other countries. Smaller pleasure crafts and sailboats (some of which travel from other countries or provinces) also cruise the river during the pleasant summer months.

As we looked out the windows early in the morning, the sun lit up the Montmorency Park national historic site, located directly across the street. Luckily, the view from the back living area windows was also marvellous, with a mixture of beautiful large trees, the water, and the rooftops of the unforgettable Rue du Petit-Champlain. The small balcony linked to the master bedroom allowed for a quiet appreciation of the enchanting area, along with wonderful odours when the small restaurants began cooking. It also provided the perfect setting for morning coffee and pre-dinner cocktails. I was impressed with the care that the owners had taken to ensure that the old buildings retained their character and charm while also providing modern comfort and conveniences. There were decades in the twentieth century when Basse-Ville was less desirable, with structures not maintained and the economy in a slump. Without the city planners' vision and courage from local politicians, the story would have been very different. Today, the care, investment, and planning by multiple Quebec commissions and acts, in collaboration with UNESCO, ensures the area's long-term vitality.

Having lived there for two years, I thought I knew the old city well, but after a few days of walking around, I realized that my knowledge was limited, with new things catching my attention every day. Since we were there when the girls were younger, and my work was so busy, we did not have the time to relax, escape, and discover (apart from the obvious landmarks when family and friends visited). This time, just in the first week, we learned that the Morrin Centre building was used as a large jail hundreds of years ago and that the Literary and Historical Society of Quebec, which manages it now (along with the stunning library) was founded in 1824 and is the oldest learned society in Canada. I also discovered that the Cathedral of the Holy Trinity was the first Anglican cathedral built outside the British Isles and that its bells date from 1830 and are the oldest change-ringing bells in Canada. I also recaptured my love of the smaller St. Andrew's Presbyterian Church, which looks lovely in the evening with the Price Building in the background. We also visited the only archaeological crypt in North America, located below Dufferin Terrace at the base of the château. The impressive site was the official residence of the French and British governors from 1620 to 1834. And finally, I couldn't get enough of sitting quietly in Place Royale enjoying a warm Smith Café while facing the seventeenth-century Notre-Dame-des-Victoires Catholic Church.

During our extended stay in 2020, we were joined by friends and family on weekends and then enjoyed our time alone during the weekdays. We walked the empty streets every evening and were enchanted with the lights and completely different vibe of the old city at night. I actually liked it better after daylight. We frequented local bars and restaurants and enjoyed talking to locals, who sometimes were the only ones in the establishment. I loved the pride and optimistic approach each and every one had about their place and their contribution to the community. From time to time we took the car for road trips to places like Charlevoix, Cap Santé, Jacques-Cartier National Park (for a morning hike with our good friends, Josée and Patrick), Lac Beauport, l'Île d'Orléans, Cap Rouge, and Lévis. We also made time for regular golf games at different courses and stayed healthy by doing epic walks. One day Linda essentially circled the entire city, including its steep hills. Most enjoyable was the discovery of little streets, stores, historical places, and art. We enjoyed it so much that we have returned since then for a few winter escapes to enjoy the best ski slopes in Eastern Canada. Spending hours outside in the thick snow and cold is so refreshing. Few people choose to embrace the frigid weather, but the reward is magnificent. Julia, Emilie, and friends and family joined us at different times to tackle the mountains and finish the days with heart-warming food, drinks, and laughter. I can only hope for more such moments in the years to come, wherever that might be.

ADDitioNAL RESOURCES AND INFORMATioN

Reviews are an author's best friend. I thank you in advance for taking the time to share your feedback on the book.

Website: www.danieljdemers.ca

For more on the Demers family history, including additional images, please visit my website.

To read my latest short stories of selected escapes, please visit my website.

ACKNOWLEDGEMENTS

This book could not have been written without the vision and care that my grandfather, J. Raymond Demers, took in creating his family coat of arms in 1957. He valued certain traditions, loved his family, and was very proud of what he and his ancestors had accomplished since reaching the shores of New France. My father's dedication as the current caretaker of this volume is why it survives today as a family treasure. It was when my father brought me the coat of arms during a visit to Quebec City that I began to pull together the facts, names, and dates and wrote the first paragraphs of this book.

Embarking on a writing adventure for the first time requires strong support and encouragement from loved ones. My wife, Linda, was the first to show an interest while not questioning the extended time I spent quietly writing. She was the first to read my initial scribblings, and to my delight, she declared, "I like this. It's good," which was quickly followed by the most valuable of words: "Keep going!" The subsequent readings by my daughters, Julia and Emilie, solidified my commitment to complete the adventure.

I want to thank my brother, Steve, for being the first pivotal critic and a most important partner in shaping the content of the book. He spent dozens of hours reading the first draft and provided priceless feedback and guidance—very direct and honest! I'm thankful for his unconditional support of the project and his attention to detail. I am grateful and lucky to be able to share my story with him, an exceptional twin brother.

Thanks to my mother and father for their unlimited wealth of information and the rich stories that evolved and helped fill many chapters. Providing context, sharing the emotional state of family members at certain times, divulging secrets, confirming facts, and giving me their own personal thoughts added to the depth of the content. I did not refrain from including what I discovered, good or bad.

Linda's cousin, Jerry George, provided me with the Bishop ancestry research and report of Linda's genealogy. The details and interesting facts captured in the documents enabled me to form a clear picture of the family's history in Newfoundland. Jerry is the keeper of so many facts and details about the Bishop and Dawe families, and I'm so thankful for his help.

Thanks to the oldest man in the family, Jean Hinse, for his unlimited inventory of stories and his passion in telling them. To this day he continues to share tales of his life and the people around him with great accuracy and detail. The pages of this book would not be nearly as full without his relentless drive to make sure his children and grandchildren remember the past, its people, and the things that shaped their lives. He is also dead set on telling it like it was and not rounding corners. I'm glad to have captured his thoughts and tales for posterity.

Thanks also to my inseparable brothers, friends, family members, teachers, colleagues, and other persons mentioned in this book for being part of the story and for enriching my life. My intent was to include the facts, reflect on our relationships, and celebrate the short or long routes we have travelled together or crossed. Hopefully I got it all correct, but if mistakes or misinformation is included, I apologize and will be happy to correct errors in future editions.

Thank you all. It would have been a boring story without you!

Special mention to Scott Donovan, my publishing consultant at FriesenPress, for being the first to call me and kickstart the journey. You have been informative, pleasant, encouraging, professional, and most importantly, patient with all my questions. I value your counsel and the style in which you helped me understand that I could do this and that it would be my project, 100 percent.

Thanks to the entire team at FriesenPress. Special mention to the dedicated group who supported me throughout the journey, including Leah, Drew, and Teresita.

I am grateful for my editor Kevin Miller who provided valuable feedback and did exceptional work to bring my writing to a higher standard. His advice, ideas, and counsel were welcomed and improved the entire project.

SELECTED BIBLIOGRAPHY

This is not a complete record of the various photo albums, books, websites, articles, and archival materials I consulted over the years. Most importantly, it does not capture all the shared stories and memories from family members and friends during the last few decades. It is a list of the publications I found most informative and useful and for which I am very thankful.

Bown, Stephen R. *The Company: The Rise and Fall of the Hudson's Bay Empire*. Penguin Random House Canada, 2020.

Demers, J. Raymond. *Family Coat of Arms*. Victoriaville: 1957.

George, Jerry. *Ancestry Report: Linda Susan Szarga*. Toronto, 2022.

Hanbury-Tenison, Robin, ed. *The Great Journeys in History*. London: Thames & Hudson Ltd., 2020.

MacGregor, Roy. *Northern Light: The Enduring Mystery of Tom Thomson and the Woman Who Loved Him*. Toronto: Random House Canada, 2010.

MacGregor, Roy. *Escape: In Search of the Natural Soul of Canada*. Toronto: McClelland & Stewart, 2002.

McCullough, David. *John Adams*. New York: Simon & Schuster, 2001.

Peart, Neil. *Traveling Music: The Soundtrack to My Life and Times*. Toronto: ECW Press, 2004.

ABOUT THE AUTHOR

Daniel J. Demers was inspired to delve deeper into his family's history after reading a book about his family's coat of arms that contained a lot of facts but no real story. Hoping to bring that tale to life, he dove into the research, eventually producing several short chapters on his family's heritage. Having built up so much momentum, by the time he reached the story of his own life, he found he was unable to stop, extending the narrative all the way into the present. He hopes these stories of ordinary people doing incredible things amidst their everyday lives will inspire others to seek positivity and goodness and remind them of the importance of family. Daniel lives in Oakville, Ontario, with his wife, Linda. This is his first book.

Daniel J. Demers